# PARTICIPATORY
# ACTION
# RESEARCH

# OTHER RECENT VOLUMES IN THE
# SAGE FOCUS EDITIONS

# PARTICIPATORY ACTION RESEARCH

**William Foote Whyte**
**editor**

**SAGE** PUBLICATIONS
*The International Professional Publishers*
Newbury Park   London   New Delhi

*For information address:*

SAGE Publications, Inc.
2455 Teller Road
Newbury Park, California 91320

SAGE Publications Ltd.
6 Bonhill Street
London EC2A 4PU
United Kingdom

SAGE Publications India Pvt. Ltd.
M-32 Market
Greater Kailash I
New Delhi 110 048 India

Printed in the United States of America

**Library of Congress Cataloging-in-Publication Data**

Participatory action research / William Foote Whyte, editor.
    p.    cm.— (Sage focus edition;  vol.  123)
    Includes bibliographical references.
    ISBN 0-8039-3742-3. — ISBN 0-8039-3743-1   (pbk.)
    1. Social sciences—Research. 2.  Action research. 3.  Social participation. 4. Decision making, Group. 5. Management—Employee participation.   I. Whyte, William Foote, 1914-   .
H62.P295  1990
300' .72—dc20                                      90-8859
                                                       CIP

92  93  94  15  14  13  12  11  10  9  8  7  6  5  4

Sage Production Editor:  Susan McElroy

# Contents

*ch. 1-7*
*11, 12, 15*

## 1

# *Introduction*

## WILLIAM FOOTE WHYTE

This book aims to make a case for participatory action research (PAR) as a powerful strategy to advance both science and practice. PAR involves practitioners in the research process from the initial design of the project through data gathering and analysis to final conclusions and actions arising out of the research.

In reflecting upon the Xerox and FAGOR cases earlier reported and reprinted here (see Chapter 2), we proposed the label of *participatory action research,* but that does not mean that we invented the methodology. Before and after these projects, others were working along the same lines but using different labels. We do not claim that *participatory action research* is the best possible label to represent the sociotechnical processes involved, but it is confusing to readers to find that highly similar research processes are given different labels by different authors. It may, therefore, be useful to begin with a ground-clearing operation, exploring the lines of development leading to PAR and also placing PAR in the context of other action research strategies.

It seems to me that PAR evolved out of three streams of intellectual development and action:

(1) social research methodology,

(2) participation in decision making by low-ranking people in organizations and communities, and

(3) sociotechnical systems thinking regarding organizational behavior.

## *Social Research Methodology*

One stream of development has its source in the continuing tension between pure and applied science in social research. In the mainstream view, the social researcher should aim at discovering basic scientific facts or relationships and not get directly involved in linking social research to action. That this is the mainstream view at least in sociology is indicated by the fact that two books published decades apart (Faris, 1964; Smelser, 1988), which undertook to present an overview of advances in sociology, are entirely devoid of any chapters dealing with applied sociology.

Although no mainstream behavioral scientist would argue that research in his or her field is entirely devoid of any practical significance, the prevailing view—supported by common practice—is to assume that it is up to the behavioral scientist to discover the basic facts and relationships, and it is up to others to somehow make use of what social researchers discover. Recognizing that the link between such social research and action is seldom established, the mainstream researcher nevertheless assumes that good science must eventually lead to improved practice. Here the important word is *eventually.* How long must we wait before what mainstream researchers discover eventually gets implemented in practice?

The alternative view, espoused by many authors in this book, is that it is important, both for the advancement of science and for the improvement of human welfare, to devise strategies in which research and action are closely linked. Those espousing this view necessarily have the responsible of demonstrating how the linkage can be established and also of demonstrating that their research advances science as well as producing practical results. We address this book particularly to a minority—but, we hope, a growing minority—of our colleagues who want their research to lead to social progress and yet do not want to give up claims to scientific legitimacy.

We do not claim that we have discovered the *one best way* to do applied social research. Different problems and different situations call for different strategies. We are simply arguing that, for some problems and for some situations, PAR is a more powerful strategy than other types of applied social research. We can also show how PAR emerged out of a concern with the limitations of other approaches to applied social research.

Probably the most common type of applied social research is what we call the professional expert model. In this type, the professional researcher is called in by a client organization—or talks his or her way in—to study a situation and a set of problems. to determine what the facts are, and to recommend a course of action. In this type, the professional researcher is completely in control of the research progress except to the extent that the client organization limits some of the research options. This type of research is perfectly appropriate where the objectives of both the researchers and the decision makers are simply to get the facts and examine action implications.

Those aiming to help organizations carry through major processes of socio-technical change have come to recognize the limitations of the professional expert model. In such situations, we need to develop a process of change, resulting in organizational learning, over a considerable period of time. To be useful in stimulating and guiding this process, the researcher cannot simply stand aside and just report research findings to the decision makers.

For major organizational change processes, we need a hands-on set of relationships with the social researcher. But that does not tell us how such a relationship should be structured.

To what extent do some in the organizations we study get involved in the research process? I can cite at least three cases in which members of the organizations studied became actively involved in my research. This began with my first research project (Whyte, 1943), in which I involved several members of the community in gathering and interpreting data. I jointly wrote articles with practitioners (Whyte and Braun, 1968; Whyte and Garfield, 1950-1951). In those cases, my practitioner partners probably had some expectations that our collaboration would do some good for some people at some time, but we had no action objectives. To distinguish it from PAR, I prefer to call such a project "participatory research."

Long before the term became popular, social anthropologists and sociologists were carrying out projects that fit under the label of *participatory research*. Anyone who serves as a participant observer in an organization or community for an extended period of time discovers that not all informants provide information and ideas of equal value. We always encounter one or more individuals who are especially knowledge-able, insightful, and perceptive regarding the dynamics of their organiza-tion or community. We do not simply give such key informants standard interviews. It is useful to the researcher and more enjoyable to the key informant if we expand the social process to discuss with these individuals what we are trying to find out and also consult them about how to interpret what we study. Key informants thus become active participants in the research.

## Participation in Decision Making by
## Low-Ranking Organizational Members

Influenced by our own democratic values and our concern with the human costs of autocratic management, many social researchers have been studying worker participation in decision making. In the decades of the 1940s to the 1960s, we rarely encountered a factory that had any element of worker participation, but at least we could document the technical and economic blunders management people made when they did not seek input regarding the work by those who understood it best: the workers themselves. In the 1970s, there was a growing management interest in worker participation in a framework called quality of work life (QWL). This type of program focused on the human aspects of work, without direct attention to productivity and costs. Management people, who supported such programs, assumed that a higher quality of work life would lead to lower absenteeism and turnover and more loyalty to the company and, therefore, indirectly, increased efficiency, but this efficiency interest remained in the background until the 1980s. In the decade of the 1980s, American management people became alarmed with the loss of international competitiveness, particularly to the Japanese. This led them to shift the emphasis from QWL toward worker participation in solving problems in productivity and costs, as exemplified in the Xerox case reported here (see Chapter 2).

If worker participation in decision making seems suddenly to be regarded as a good thing, this naturally led us to wonder whether more active participation by practitioners—both management and labor—in the research process might also be a good thing.

In agriculture, until very recently, the technology transfer model of research and development prevailed throughout the Third World. This meant that it was the responsibility of the professionals to determine what worked best for farmers, on farms large and small, and then to persuade the farmers to accept the information and ideas of the professionals. In other words, this was strictly a top-down model, which had no place in it for utilizing the information and ideas gathered by small farmers in helping them to better their lot. The dominance of this model was strongly reinforced by the spectacular successes of plant scientists in developing high-yielding varieties of the basic grains such as wheat and rice. As the new high-yielding varieties were put into the field in large farms around the world, enormous increases in grain production were achieved. At first, it was generally assumed that these scientific advances were scale neutral, but several years of experience indicated that the great grains in yields were secured predominantly by large farmers with irrigated fields, and only those small farmers who happened to have access to irrigation stood to gain the same advantages.

This recognition on the part of both biological scientists and social scientists led to a shift in the focus of thinking toward studies of what could be done for small farmers and especially for those farming in rain-fed areas. This also led to a new interest in learning more about the agricultural practices of small farmers in such areas and then to the notion that perhaps they had learned things about operating under disadvantageous conditions that might even be useful for agricultural professionals.

Although the interest in farmer participation in the research and development process arose later in agriculture than in industry, in general, the spread of participatory approaches in small farm agriculture has been extraordinarily rapid. To illustrate this point, consider the recent publication of the Agricultural Administration (Research and Extension) Network of the Overseas Development Institute in London. In June 1989, ODI published *340 Abstracts on Farmer Participatory Research*. My rough count of those abstracts indicates that only thirteen appeared as reports before 1980—and seven of those bear the date of 1979. This indicates an explosive growth of interest in participatory strategies. Many of the cases can be interpreted also as reports on what we call PAR rather than simple participatory research, but it is impossible to discriminate between the two categories on the basis of such abstracts.

## The Sociotechnical Framework

The third line of intellectual development can be traced to the sociotechnical systems framework, which first appeared in the literature in the 1950s (see Trist, 1981, for a review of the development and application of the underlying ideas for sociotechnical systems in industry).

When I began field research in industry in the early 1940s, I accepted the dictum by social anthropologist Burleigh G. Gardner that "the factory is a social system." I found this a useful corrective against the technocratic approach of Frederick W. Taylor in scientific management. Of course, we all recognized the importance of technology, but we relegated it to the background, as something that required some description but somehow did not enter into the analysis.

The sociotechnical systems framework presents one simple but important idea: that the workplace is not simply a social system; understanding behavior at work depends on integration of social and technological factors.

How do we gain enough knowledge regarding technological factors to fit them into our theoretical framework? In general, we have simply gone into the field to learn from engineers and administrators in industry to acquire at least a superficial knowledge of the technologies in place at the research sites. The integration of the technical with the social then depended upon the behavioral scientist.

Is there a better way to acquire and then integrate technological knowledge into our social research? Because we try to learn something about the technology from those who create it and those who implement it, it is just one further step—but an important one—to move from treating the practitioners of the technologies as passive informants to involving them in the research as active participants. If we need to learn some of what they already know through their professional studies and practice, would we not be better off if we invited them to participate with us in the research process?

If this principle is valid in industry, it should be equally valid in agriculture, where the behavioral scientists need to learn from plant, animal, and social scientists and from agricultural engineers. In the rest of this volume, we will explore the development and implementation of participatory ideas and practices in both industry and agriculture.

### On the Structure of This Book

The writing of this book began in response to the initiative of Sage Executive Editor, Mitchell Allen. Noting the announcement of a session on participatory action research in the 1988 meeting of the Eastern Sociological Society, he called me to express interest in what seemed to be a novel theme and asked two questions: Would this be a good focus for an issue of *American Behavioral Scientist*? If so, would I be willing to organize and edit such a project? I answered yes to both questions, and the project reached publication in the May/June 1989 issue of *ABS*.

In that project, the focus was limited to the use of PAR in industry. For several years, I had also been pursuing research on small farmer participation in agricultural research and development in the Third World, and I was noting the emergence of PAR projects there also—though under different labels. This parallel struck me as potentially important, both for science and for practice. The idea moved me then to plan a book, adding several new contributions to the industrial studies, and balancing industry with a series of chapters on participatory action research in agricultural research and development.

Following my Introduction, Part I, on PAR in industry, opens with a chapter in which Davydd Greenwood, Peter Lazes, and I make our case for the scientific as well as practical value of PAR. We support our argument with two projects developed in very different industrial scenes: Xerox Corporation with the Amalgamated Clothing and Textile Workers Union (ACTWU) in New York State and the FAGOR group of worker cooperatives in the Basque country of Spain. Chapters 3 to 5 present interpretations of those cases by our key participant collaborators: Larry Pace and Dominick Argona for Xerox, Anthony Costanza for ACTWU, and José González for FAGOR.

Chapter 6 presents a critique of PAR, as we interpret it in the Xerox case, by Chris Argyris and Donald Schön, who see their own model of "action science" as aiming toward the same objectives as PAR but with somewhat different methodology. Chapter 7 (not included in the *ABS* issue) presents my own comparison of PAR and action science, as an effort to advance this friendly discussion toward further clarification and sharpening of ideas.

Chapters 8 to 10 reflect what we might call the "Scandinavian connection." Because so much of American thinking and writing on participation has been influenced by research and practice in Norway and Sweden, it seemed important for this book to examine that Scandinavian connection more fully than was possible in our *ABS* article by Richard Walton and Michael Gaffney. Their Chapter 8 here is a fitting introduction to that connection because it focuses primarily upon Einar Thorsrud's pioneering PAR project to reorganize the sociotechnical systems of the Norwegian merchant marine and goes on to show how what was learned in Norway has stimulated action along similar lines in the United States.

Chapters 9 and 10, by Max Elden and Morten Levin and by Jan Karlsen, focus on the distinctive Norwegian features of research and action involving worker participation and industrial democracy. In contrast to the United States, where worker participation is increasingly seen as important for regaining international competitive strength in manufacturing, Norwegians moved earlier toward worker participation out of a strong value commitment to industrial democracy.

Part I concludes with Robert Cole's interpretation of his own role as a participant observer-activist in studying the diffusion of quality circle programs in the United States, as one phase of his research comparing the spread of worker participation in Japan, Sweden, and the United States.

Part II begins with my chapter tracing my own learning process on small farmer participation through observing how practitioners were learning. Here I am following Latin America, where trends are developing along similar lines as in Asia and Africa. I focus particularly on Guatemala, which early on developed an impressive participatory program in agricultural research but then had difficulty in integrating this program with a traditionally organized extension service.

In Chapter 13, plant scientist Ramiro Ortiz discusses how Guatemala has been overcoming this deficiency through a new program in which researchers and extension agents are working together throughout the R & D process.

In Chapter 14, Richard Maclure and Michael Bassey report on a PAR project to improve maize storage systems in Togo, Africa. Maclure writes (personal communication) that Canada's International Development Research Centre recently reoriented its policies to foster participatory action research throughout its programs in rural and agricultural development. The Togo case reflects this orientation.

As in industry, PAR projects in agriculture necessarily require interdisciplinary collaboration. Furthermore, the involved behavioral scientists are likely to be more committed to participatory methods than their more technically oriented colleagues. This suggests that they should play leading roles in PAR projects, and yet they have been latecomers into fields dominated by tech-nical specialists.

Chapters 15 and 16 deal with the problems and potentials of behavioral science roles in these technical fields. Reflecting on his formal education in anthropology and sociology and years of experience in interdisciplinary programs beginning in Guatemala, Sergio Ruano discusses the barriers to behavioral science participation in agricultural research and indicates how they can be overcome.

Chapter 16 pursues this theme in a review of the experience of the International Potato Center. CIP (its initials in Spanish) seems to me to have moved earlier and advanced further in integrating social scientists into its research programs than any other international agricultural research center. Author Douglas Horton joined CIP as head of its economics unit and in time converted it to a broadly based social sciences unit, with a strong involvement of anthropologists and sociologists. In his chapter, he describes how this broadening was accomplished and goes on to show how participatory strategies have been reshaping the internal administration of CIP and its relations to the umbrella sponsoring organization, CGIAR (Consultative Group on International Agricultural Research).

In a concluding chapter, I undertake to set forth some of the implications of PAR in industry and agriculture for both research and practice.

# References

Agricultural Administration Network (1989). 340 Abstracts on Farmer Participatory Research. London: Overseas Development Institute.

FARIS, R. E. L. (1964) Handbook of Modern Sociology. Chicago: Rand McNally.

SMELSER, N. (1988) Handbook of Sociology. Newbury Park, CA: Sage.

TRIST, E. (1981) The Evolution of Socio-Technical Systems. Toronto: Ontario Ministry of Labour.

WHYTE, W. F. (1943) Street Corner Society. Chicago: University of Chicago Press.

WHYTE, W. F. and R. R. BRAUN (1968) "On language and culture," pp. 119-138 in H. Becker et al. (eds.) Institutions and the Person. Chicago: Aldine.

WHYTE, W. F. and S. GARFIELD (1950-1951) "The collective bargaining process." Human Organization (Winter-Spring).

# PART I

# PAR in Industry

## 2

# Participatory Action Research

## Through Practice to Science in Social Research

WILLIAM FOOTE WHYTE
DAVYDD J. GREENWOOD
PETER LAZES

The research models currently dominating the field of organizational behavior, though increasingly refined, are the culmination of a development that identifies scientific progress with survey research and quantitative modeling. While valid and valuable, these research strategies are only a small portion of those currently deployable. The hegemony of one research style deprives social scientists of a variety of other research strategies that have equal, and possibly superior, claims to the mantle of "science."

No scientific logic demands unilateral commitment to one kind of social research model or method. Increasing reliance on such a narrow theoretical and methodological base deprives the field of the scientific vitality of other research approaches that can be at once scientifically challenging and practically useful. The complexity of the world around us demands the deployment of a variety of techniques and strong intellectual and methodological discipline, not a commitment to the hegemony of a single research modality.

In this chapter, we argue for the scientific and practical value of participatory action research (PAR) and advocate its incorporation into the tool kit of the social sciences. Our chapter follows this sequence: We begin by defining participatory action research and placing it in the context of more widely practiced research methods. We then illustrate the PAR process with two case studies: one with

Xerox Corporation in New York State, the other with the Mondragón cooperative complex in the Basque country of Spain.

The two cases differ not only in physical location and organizational form but also in the nature of the objectives of the PAR process. For Xerox, PAR was focused upon very specific cost-reduction and job preservation objectives. For Mondragón, PAR was used to explore a range of problems, to rethink those problems, and to devise new organizational strategies. This contrast illustrates the potential flexibility of the PAR process.

Our case descriptions should demonstrate the practical value of PAR. We also claim that PAR can yield significant advances in social theory. Whereas researchers on one of the most frequently studied problem areas had hitherto been unable to demonstrate any consistent relations between worker participation and productivity. In the Xerox case, we show how a particular form of worker participation yielded cost reductions and improvements in what we call "total factor productivity" of from 25% to 40%. These striking results have led us to reconceptualize both variables—participation and productivity—thus opening up a new and promising line of research and theory. In the Mondragón case, results have not lent themselves to quantitative measurement, yet we will show how they led to fruitful shifts in conceptualization of organizational processes of participation and decision making.

**Defining Participatory Action Research**

In participatory action research (PAR), some of the people in the organization or community under study participate actively with the professional researcher throughout the research process from the initial design to the final presentation of results and discussion of their action implications. PAR thus contrasts sharply with the conventional model of pure research, in which members of organizations and communities are treated as passive subjects, with some of them participating only to the extent of authorizing the project, being its subjects, and receiving the results. PAR is *applied* research, but it also contrasts sharply with the most common type of applied research, in which researchers serve as professional experts, designing the project, gathering the data, interpreting the findings, and recommending action to the client organization. Like the conventional model of pure research, this also is an elitist model of research relationships. In PAR, some of the members of the organization we study are actively engaged in the quest for information and ideas to guide their future actions.

Participatory action research can be organized in a variety of forms that are just being explored. It is clear, however, that the scientific demands and possibilities of PAR are considerable, an argument we will make in the abstract and then support with reference to the PAR case studies.

Science is not achieved by distancing oneself from the world; as generations of scientists know, the greatest conceptual and methodological challenges come from engagement with the world. The scientific standards that must be met to conduct a successful PAR project are daunting. And yet, as the cases will show, it is possible to pursue both the truth and solutions to concrete problems simultaneously. Indeed, we are led to wonder about the mystification that permits some of our colleagues to believe that research and action are incompatible.

We do not claim to have invented participatory action research. In organizational behavior, we have been influenced particularly by the development of sociotechnical analysis (see particularly Trist, 1981) and by work democracy research in Norway (Thorsrud, 1977; Elden, 1979). While PAR can come in a variety of forms, we do claim that the forms represented in our cases have important strengths that are worth reporting. We see these strengths for both practice and theory building.

### Case Studies

#### Case 1:  Saving Jobs in Industry—
#### The Xerox Corporation

The first project to be discussed arose out of the declining international competitiveness of the Xerox Corporation. In copy machines, Xerox had enjoyed a monopoly for many years. As the original patents were expiring, the company found itself confronting ever-increasing competition. From 1970 to 1979, the Xerox share of the world market for copy machines had dropped from 94% to 44%. This drastic change in competitive position caused grave concern to top management and prompted a thoroughgoing reassessment of management structures, policies, and programs.

Xerox was still strong financially, so it was possible to take some months to put into place policies and programs designed to restore its manufacturing competitiveness. Nevertheless, it was clear that Xerox would eventually be forced out of producing the machines it had invented unless major changes could be made.

When David Kearns moved from IBM to become chief executive officer of Xerox, he contracted with McKinsey and Company to make a major study of management and business administration to recommend changes from the top down. At the same time, management called on the union at its main copier production facilities in Webster, New York, for help in improving quality of working life (QWL), lowering manufacturing costs, and increasing productivity.

This initiative grew out of years of reasonably cooperative relations between Xerox and the Amalgamated Clothing and Textile Workers Union. At the time, there was nothing novel in American industry about the idea of management and a union jointly developing a worker participation or employee involvement program. Although this was not common practice in American industry, a number of major companies had mounted such programs before Xerox. On the other hand, few companies had begun such programs on the basis of such mutual respect between management and union leaders or with such a strong commitment by leading figures in personnel and human resources to develop worker participation to the greatest practical extent. Furthermore, the personnel people took pains to familiarize themselves with the research literature and the experience of other companies so as to be able to work with the consultants who were called in to organize and guide the participation program.

Sidney Rubenstein was the first consultant, and he brought in Peter Lazes. Rubenstein worked with labor and management for a year, and Lazes continued for the following period under discussion, serving as consultant, trainer, and process facilitator. For training purposes, he brought a group of management and union people to Cornell University for two weeks of off-site discussion, instruction, and planning. (This led to the establishment of relations between Lazes and Donald Kane, director of management programs for the Extension Division of the New York State School of Industrial and Labor Relations—and later to the institutionalization of the process developed at Xerox within the ILR program.)

QWL at Xerox began under the conventional limitations: Workers and managers focused attention on shop-level problems and excluded from discussion problems affecting the labor contract or involving managerial prerogatives and policies. As the number of studies have shown (Lawler, 1986), if the parties adhere to these limitations, the programs tend to deteriorate. Labor and management people lose interest after exhausting the limited range of problems that can be resolved on the shop floor. The basic problem is that, in many companies, direct labor costs (wages and fringe benefits of production and maintenance workers) amount to only 15% to 20% of the company's total costs, so that even a 20% improvement in shop floor productivity will yield only a 3% to 4% improvement in the bottom line—far short of what Xerox needed to cope with the intensified competition of the 1980s.

This means that a rational cost-reduction and productivity improvement program cannot be limited to the shop floor. Planners and organizational leaders must visualize their organization as a sociotechnical and economic system made up of mutually dependent parts, with the organizational performance depending in large measure upon the effective integration of shop floor into the total production organization and the integration of the production organization with higher management, marketing, purchasing, research and development, and various staff services.

Conceptually and practically, therefore, the question is this: How do you get from the conventional shop floor focus to the much broader sociotechnical economic focus? And is it possible to do this without alarming leaders of labor and management that this radical shift will open Pandora's box, releasing unprecedented problems with which they are not prepared to cope?

At Xerox, the breakthrough occurred when management confronted the union with a crisis. Management studies had demonstrated that the company could save $3.2 million annually by closing the wire harness department, laying off workers, and buying what they produced from vendors. The report was not presented as a study of the problem but rather as a solution to the problem. The solution, which has become known as "outsourcing," was already widely practiced by American companies, and at the time management people assumed there was no other solution to the wire harness problem. In accord with the labor contract and the spirit of cooperation with the union, management announced its intentions well in advance of the proposed change. The expectation was that the parties could then begin discussing how to minimize the human costs and the damage to labor relations.

While the union leaders were considering their response, Lazes suggested that they propose the creation of what we are calling a cost study team (CST). (This social invention was first named a "study-action team" by Xerox and later was called a "commodity study team." We prefer the title of "cost study team" because it indicates more clearly than "study-action" the focus of the task, and because the process has been used elsewhere to study cost problems not linked to a particular commodity.) The objective of the CST would be study the possibilities of making changes internally that would save the $3.2 million and retain the 180 jobs. Shortly thereafter, Lazes made the same proposal to management.

Such a radical shift in the participation program could not be decided upon at the time it was presented; neither did Lazes press for a quick response. He was proposing a radical shift in the organization of worker participation. Such a plunge into the unknown involved serious risks for both union and management. It was obvious from the outset that such a plan would involve abandoning the rules that declared certain topics of study or discussion out of bounds. Major improvements in shop floor productivity would probably require rule changes. It was also obvious that wage and benefit concessions from the workers were not the answer. Achieving a $3.2 million saving in labor costs through such concessions would have meant a sacrifice of $17,777 per year for each of the 180 workers—a figure too absurd even to warrant discussion. For management, the proposal called for opening up for study all of the costs the plant management charged to the wire harness department—including, among other items, overhead, which has traditionally been considered an inalienable management right to determine.

Between the initial proposal and its final acceptance, there was a period of about a month of discussion and reflection. By this time, Lazes had spent two years (about 10 days a month) working with labor and management. This had provided him an intimate familiarity with the organizational structures and cultures of both union and management. With key people in both parties, he had developed the kind of trusting relationship that enabled him to talk with them informally and freely about their hopes and fears. He followed up the initial presentations of the idea with detailed discussions and interviews with key people to be sure he understood their reservations and anxieties.

On the union side, the chief risk was that the CST might propose changes that could be implemented only through changing contract clauses applying to the wire harness department, and such changes might constitute precedents to reopen the contract for other departments, with unforeseeable consequences. Of course, there was also a high risk of failure, in which case management would have the right to proceed with closing the department. Although failure would have a cost in frustrated hopes and expectations, the union leaders recognized that basically it would only take them back to the point at which management had announced its outsourcing plan. The parties could then fall back to discussing how the layoffs should be managed, as would have happened without the Lazes proposal. Considering the possibility of saving jobs and pressing further with the participation program, the union leaders decided the risks were worth taking.

For management, the risks were also substantial, and yet managers' satisfaction with the progress of participation so far fostered a spirit of risk taking. Management had already gone far beyond its contractual obligations in providing union leaders with information on its strategic business plans and in inviting discussion of those plans. Xerox had established a regular pattern of meetings for this purpose, bringing together CEO David Kearns and other top management people with top union people, including President Murray Finlay and Secretary-Treasurer Jack Sheinkman. The meetings were first held quarterly and then, as the participants gained increased confidence in each other, became semiannual events.

Nevertheless, key decision makers had to work through their worries about the potential risks involved in implementing the proposal. In the first place, management was asked to provide members of the cost study team and the joint steering committee far more detailed financial information than had hitherto been discussed with the union. Managers were naturally worried that such proprietary information might be leaked to competitors. In addition, it was hard to predict the consequences of inviting union members and leaders to share responsibility with management for key business decisions that previously had been considered the exclusive prerogatives of management. Also, accepting the proposal imposed a substantial cost in time and money upon management. No one in management believed it would be possible for a CST to reach the target of $3.2 million cost savings. In that case, the process would delay by months the change that management believed inevitable while costing Xerox the full-time wages and salaries of CST members along with substantial additional costs to support the process. (Xerox later estimated the direct cost of the wire harness CST as approximately $250,000.)

Lazes helped key management people to think through and talk through the potential advantages and disadvantages of accepting the proposal. On the positive side, the evolving relationship between union and management had strengthened management's respect for the quality of the information and ideas coming to the company through shop floor participation as well as from top-level discussions. If the wire harness project were successful, this would further strengthen the relationship with the union. Of course, refusal to undertake the experiment involved a potential cost of weakening this relationship already highly valued by management.

Underlying these discussions within management was an intellectual challenge and also a fallback position in case the project did not succeed. The challenge arose out of management's growing experience with worker participation. For example, the corporate directors of engineering and finance said to Lazes that the current shop floor participation activities had increased their appreciation of the *intellectual* contributions workers could make. They were intrigued by an experiment to see to what extent such contributions could be extended into the heart of business administration. At the same time, if the CST failed to reach its target, management retained the right to revert to its original plan of shutting down the department and laying off the workers. Furthermore, the failure of the project could help to persuade workers and union officials that management had done everything possible to preserve the jobs.

not much
to lose

As a result of informal discussion with Lazes and among leaders of union and management, by the time the Joint Steering Committee met to act on the proposal, in effect the decision to support the project had already been made. The meeting served simply to formalize the agreement and to work out the means for its implementation. Having made the decision, management went to extraordinary lengths to make sure that the project would have every opportunity to succeed. In addition to their genuine interest in the project, managers wanted to avoid the possibility that Xerox could be blamed for providing only half-hearted support, if the CST did in fact fail to reach its target.

In conventional quality circle or QWL programs, workers on committees meet once a week or once every two weeks for an hour of discussion. In the wire harness case, an eight-person team was to work full-time for six months.

Following interviewing of volunteers from the department—and most members of the department volunteered—the union leaders selected six workers to represent different levels of skill, experience, and functions to work with the department supervisor and an engineer selected by management. Before this CST was formed, leaders of the two parties compared their selections to assure that the team would not be handicapped by preestablished interpersonal hostilities. Management offered the team access to all financial information they might require and authorized them to call on anyone within the company for consultation. Furthermore, management designated two internal technical consultants, one on operations research and one on cost accounting, to be available to the CST. Management also financed trips of team members to the factories of vendors to gather ideas that might be applied at Xerox.

The CST analyzed engineering aspects (machines and work flow), business administration aspects (allocation of costs including charges for space and divisional overhead), and organizational aspects (rethinking jobs and work rules and increasing worker responsibilities). Furthermore, the team could consider any and all possible changes without limitations. This did not mean that proposals for changing work rules or other contractual matters or for changing management policies would automatically be accepted by management and the union. It did mean that such major changes could seriously be considered by the leaders of both labor and management.

The CST project represented an intensification of the Xerox organizational learning process. Let us assume that a standard-shaped box represents the customary ground rules determining what types of information and ideas can be legitimately gathered and analyzed to determine what shall be done to solve a problem. Information and ideas that don't fit into that box are thereby automatically excluded from analysis. If those studying the problem remain within the confines of that standard box, they are doomed to seek conventional solutions that are not powerful enough to cope with radically changed conditions. The CST process made it possible to change the shape of the box to provide space for the introduction of new ideas and information.

As a consultant/facilitator, Lazes operated with a disposition to identify the problems in such organizations as caused primarily by blockages, the development of adversarial positions, turf issues, immobilization, and a general loss of the sense of control and ownership of the organization's activities. In a word, behavior had become largely reactive. To address this, he emphasized "changing the shape of the box"—throwing out a broad array of options and tactics that temporarily disorganized the blocked system and might eventually lead to a sense of joint responsibility, openness, and control and ownership, if properly handled. In other words, he attempted to facilitate a transition to a more reflective and active mode of organizational behavior.

The CST research was not limited to discovering previously unknown facts. In some cases, the CST was learning how to use previously known facts that had been excluded from the standard box. The cost of labor turnover is a case in point. Turnover in the wire harness department arose primarily out of the labor contract clauses allowing workers, according to their seniority, to "bump" into and out of that department. The standard box that had previously applied to shop floor participation activities determined that changes in these costs could be considered, if at all, only at contract renegotiation time, every three years. Long before the start of the CST, management had experience-based cost estimates: the cost of training each new worker plus the cost of lost production until the new worker reached the production level of experienced people, times the number of transfers into the department each year. The figures remained idle in management files because they did not fit into the standard box. Changing the shape of the box brought these figures out of management files, and the CST was then able to project annual savings of $743,000 through stabilizing wire harness personnel—provided that the parties would then negotiate contractual changes to make this possible (Lazes and Costanza, 1984).

Similarly, management people knew the figures not only for total divisional overhead but also for the various categories of staff services to the wire harness department. Union people previously had not had such detailed information. If they had had access to it, they would not have been able to do anything with it because it did not fit into the standard box shaping their thinking and action. Reshaping the box enabled the CST to call upon management to explain and justify all staff services.

The team found that the divisional overhead charges were based in large measure upon services that were not actually being delivered or upon services that team members believed could be performed more efficiently within their department. This incursion into traditional management prerogatives and policies enabled the CST to propose a reduction of $582,000 in overhead charges.

These and other substantial changes detailed elsewhere (Lazes and Costanza, 1984) made it possible for the CST to complete its six-month study with a report justifying "anticipated cost savings" totaling $3,642,000—almost half a million beyond the target figure.

There is, of course, a difference between projected savings and savings actually achieved. As might be expected in such a new project, the implementation of the accepted plan took longer than the CST had hoped, and the eventual calculated savings fell short of the projected figure. Nevertheless, the changes recommended were eventually put into place and management then calculated that the CST at least achieved the $3.2 million target.

Decision makers in top management of the Reprographic Division were so impressed with the results of the wire harness project that they moved quickly, in consultation with the union leaders, to establish CSTs in three other production units, which had similarly been noncompetitive with potential vendors. All of these CSTs reached the required savings targets or else came so close that management was happy to settle for the results—which came to savings of up to 40% of annual costs in the case of two of the teams. These experiences convinced leaders of both parties of the value of extending participatory management and union-management cooperation throughout the Reprographic Division.

The changes even involved the restructuring of research and development and the design for construction of new plants. In the conventional R & D program, the development engineers work out a basic design for the product and turn that over to the industrial engineers, who work out the details of how the product is to be produced and what labor with what qualifications will be needed at each point in production. Then they turn those more detailed plans over the foremen and plant superintendents, who are responsible for moving the project from the pilot stage and into production. When each specialized group does its own thing and then passes the project on to the next group, we often find that the company has to recycle the process several times. The plans developed at a previous stage often prove impractical at the next stage. Xerox now involves production and maintenance workers and production foremen into the design team at early stages so that the people who will be responsible for producing the product or responsible for supervising production will be involved early. This enables them to help the team to anticipate problems that might occur at later stages. Management estimates that this new design for R & D cuts about half of the time it takes the company to move a new project from the drawing board to actual production. In today's economy, the profit or loss on a new product or model often depends upon when it reaches the market. Thus the streamlining of the R & D process at Xerox involves an incalculable but enormous gain in future revenues.

Similarly, in designing a new plant, management departs from the conventional style of turning the project over to architects and engineers. For the toner plant, workers who were going to be responsible for production were involved in planning from the outset.

We can trace direct behavioral linkages between the CST projects and the inclusion of worker participation into the reshaping of the R & D process and the design of the toner plant. The head of the engineering and a plant manager, whose responsibilities included leading the design team for the new plant, were both members of the joint steering committee overseeing the CST projects. They recognized the importance of the organizational and intellectual breakthrough achieved through the CSTs, and this stimulated them to develop their own participatory innovations.

The success of the CSTs and these related developments made it possible for the union and management to work out a new labor contract providing employment security for workers in the bargaining unit. First, labor and management agreed that, in any future case where management found that a given department was falling seriously short of meeting competition, before laying off any workers, management would work with the union to establish a CST. Then management would only have the right to lay off workers if the CST was unable to meet the target. In the new three-year contract signed in April 1983, the parties went even further to guarantee employment security to all workers in the bargaining unit who had been employed more than 36 months—and the same clause was written into the 1986 contract. This did not guarantee workers the right to retain their current jobs—an impossible requirement in a highly competitive industry—but it did mean that, as jobs were eliminated, workers would move to other jobs newly being developed. The participatory program has thus made possible an extraordinary level of economic security for Xerox workers.

In the early stages of this reorganization process, management was not able to provide the same employment security to white-collar and managerial employees. In fact, the participation program in the Webster plants, combined with the changes instituted in top management in response to the McKinsey and Company study, led to a considerable shrinking of the managerial and white-collar ranks. The McKinsey consultants found that, during its monopoly years, the Xerox bureaucracy had far outgrown the needs of the production organization

(Jacobson and Hillkirk, 1986), while people at Webster were discovering that workers could solve problems that hitherto had been reserved exclusively to middle management and staff specialists.

From 1979 to 1985, Xerox reduced its overall employment in the Reprographic Division by half while doubling its total output, thus achieving a fourfold increase in productivity and beginning to regain at least a small fraction of the market share it had previously lost. According to Larry Pace, then Manager of Organizational Effectiveness at Webster, in 1979, Xerox had 2.1 indirect (nonproduction) employees to every 1 direct production worker. Today the ratio has dropped to .4 to 1. Pace explains the shift primarily in terms of the reduction of "$M^2P^2$: Men marking pieces of paper." This reflects a major shift of responsibility for the supervision and control of production down the ranks to the workers themselves and their immediate superiors.

Though Peter Lazes served as consultant to Xerox, he did not function in the conventional consultant role of making his own diagnosis and then presenting recommendations for management action. He conceived of himself as facilitator and participant in action research. He proposed a process leading to diagnosis and problem solution but he did not tell people what decisions to make. He provided training in group methods and in problem analysis. In the early stages, he sat in as an observer in meetings of the CSTs but never intervened except to help the parties to resolve an impasse. The labor and management members of the study teams did the research, digging out the facts and figures and organizing and writing the reports.

During the wire harness study period, Lazes devoted six of his ten days a month at Webster to that project. When the CST process was extended to the three other departments, his involvement was gradually phased out. Labor and management facilitators now took over the roles initially shaped by the outside consultant/facilitator.

At Xerox, participatory action research created and guided a powerful process of organizational learning—a process whereby leaders of labor and management learned from each other and from the consultant/facilitator, while he learned from them. Although the organizational learning process spread through the Webster plants, it should be noted that it did not spread to Xerox plants in other locations, where cost pressures were much less severe. It may take a combination of urgent economic needs and strong on-site program development to achieve wider diffusion of the organizational learning process.

The Xerox success, combined with growing interest in Albany in the work of some Cornellians on employee buyouts to save jobs, led to a 1985 decision

by New York State to provide the first solid financing of Programs for Employment and Workplace Systems (PEWS), which had been established a year earlier with Kane, Lazes, and Whyte serving initially as codirectors. (At this writing, Whyte is Research Director.) The creation of PEWS was designed to serve both practical and scientific objectives. The practical objective was to help leaders of labor and management, particularly in New York State, to save jobs through building more competitive organizations and, in the process, to institutionalize PAR within the Extension Division of the New York State School of Industrial and Labor Relations. The aim also was to test the scientific potential of participatory action research.

While we were inspired by the results achieved at Xerox, we recognized that the CST breakthrough there had been achieved under exceptionally favorable circumstances. Leaders in labor and management had built relations of mutual trust and respect over years of joint problem solving—albeit on problems and projects far less ambitious than the challenges they faced with the CST projects. Although Xerox faced serious problems, they had not reached a crisis stage that demanded quick and drastic rescue measures. By the time Lazes made the wire harness CST proposal, he had already worked with labor and management for two years on a shop floor participation program and had developed relations of mutual trust and respect with leaders of the two parties. Finally, although management people did not expect the wire harness CST to be successful, Xerox nevertheless provided exceptionally strong support financially and in the commitments of key management people.

If PAR could be successful in saving jobs only under exceptionally favorable conditions, then its scientific and practical values would be severely limited. PAR has been done under quite unfavorable conditions in Trico Products Corporation and achieved at least partial success and produced theoretically informative results (see Klingel and Martin, 1988).

## Case 2: The Mondragón-Cornell Project

The Mondragón-Cornell PAR project differed from the PEWS processes in the nature of PAR and also in location and in the nature of the organizations involved. The full account of this PAR project will appear elsewhere (Greenwood and González et al., forthcoming).

The Mondragón cooperative complex in the Basque country of Spain is increasingly recognized as an extraordinarily successful set of interrelated industrial worker cooperatives, a consumer-worker cooperative with outlets throughout the Basque provinces, a cooperative bank, a cooperative research and development organization, and other supporting and linked structures.

The development of the complex began in 1943 with the establishment of a small technical school that has now grown to provide an engineering education through the junior college level and somewhat beyond, with a business school founded later in 1960. The first industrial worker cooperative, Ulgor, was founded in 1956 by five of the first students to enter the technical school in 1943. From that small beginning, the Mondragón complex has grown to over 100 worker industrial production cooperatives and associated cooperatives, now employing well over 21,000 worker-members.

Bill and Kathleen Whyte first visited Mondragón for two weeks in the spring of 1975. Peruvian graduate student Ana Gutiérrez-Johnson joined the Whytes in Mondragón and stayed for five additional weeks beyond the Whyte visit to carry out fieldwork for a master's thesis. From that date up to 1979, Gutiérrez-Johnson made two additional trips to Mondragón for further fieldwork, leading to her doctoral thesis (Gutiérrez-Johnson, 1982).

In October 1983, the Whytes spent three weeks in Mondragón in connection with their plans to write a book on the cooperative complex. The 1975 visit was during a period when the cooperatives were still expanding. By 1983, Spain was deep in a recession much more severe than that affecting other industrialized countries, with unemployment nationally around 20% and the figures considerably higher for the Basque provinces. In 1983, many of the cooperatives were struggling with painful reorganizations. By 1986, the cooperative complex was once again expanding vigorously.

Almost from the outset in this collaboration, members of the complex encouraged and guided the research process. Toward the end of the 1983 visit, to provide a small degree of reciprocity for the collaboration given the Whytes during their fieldwork, Bill got together with some of those who had been helping the Whytes with information and ideas for a feedback session. In the discussion with a small group following his presentation, José Luis González, Personnel Director of FAGOR (the largest group of individual cooperatives), responded with enthusiasm and challenged Whyte with these words: "Will you present us with a research proposal and a budget?"

At age 69 and with other commitments, Whyte had no desire to direct a major research program. Nevertheless, he was so fascinated by the social and economic achievements of Mondragón that he could not refuse to respond. Davydd Greenwood provided a way out of the dilemma. A social anthropologist who had done research on a Basque town and surrounding countryside, on the impacts of tourism and industrialization on the local economy and on the history of ethnic conflict (Greenwood, 1972, 1976a, 1976b, 1977, 1985), he was Cornell's director of the Center for International Studies. Greenwood drew Whyte's attention to the Joint Spain-United States Committee on

Educational and Cultural Exchange. Using funds arising out of rent for naval and military bases in Spain, the committee supports educational exchanges involving collaboration between institutions and individuals in the two countries.

In consultation with José Luis González, Greenwood and Whyte proposed to explore possibilities of an interinstitutional relationship going beyond the personal relations the Whytes had developed with Mondragón. Grants from the committee supported first an exchange of visits between Cornellians and people from the cooperative complex and then, out of this exploration, a participatory action research project jointly directed by Greenwood and González. Whyte participated somewhat in the early stages of this project, but Greenwood provided the major Cornell involvement. (The grant also supported some technical assistance activities Cornell provided in management development, but these will not be described here.)

During the spring of 1985, Greenwood, accompanied by the Whytes, made an exploratory visit to Mondragón. At that time, González expressed an interest in a study of "industrial anthropology." While no one had a clear idea of what was meant by the term, we concluded that the FAGOR interest probably grew out of the current literature on "corporate cultures."

The first stage was devoted to orientation and exploration of the research and theoretical literature and seeking reactions to the issues posed there. It was also spent reviewing what had been written about the cooperatives by their members and by academic researchers. In other words, the PAR process began by presenting the team with conflicting views of the cooperatives and their success found in the existing literature. Nearly all the literature was found wanting by everyone. The cooperative members were critical of the utility of some social science concepts and genuinely disturbed by some of the incorrect and exaggerated views about the cooperatives. The academic researchers were under pressure to operationally define concepts such as "corporate culture" and to explain and justify methods in a way compelling to a group of practitioners who were intellectually well prepared but not inclined to spend time simply on abstract thinking. Thus the pressures of asking questions important to the FAGOR members and the formulation of specific research questions were intense.

One result of this combination of interests and expertise was the emergence of a clearly multidisciplinary focus. Expertise in anthropology, sociology, economics and finance, social psychology, organizational behavior and administration, and so forth were combined around the table until the reformulated project reflected a kind of breadth of expertise nearly impossible to achieve under any other circumstances.

As a consultant/facilitator, Greenwood's own view of the issues centered on an attempt to "create an organizational space" in which certain kinds of reflection and organizational change would become possible. His sense of the general dilemmas of organizations centered on their tendency to value uniformity over diversity. All democratic systems risk achieving equality by reducing themselves to the lowest common denominators or by having the organizational goals formulated in such an abstract and normative manner that they become meaningless in most everyday situations. If taken seriously, such uniform conceptions can lead to formula-driven approaches to organizational change and discipline and can undermine the very democracy they seek to create. As a result, he emphasized the diversity within the organization as a source of potential strength and the joint payoffs to be gained by making diversity into an organizational value. In this way, he hoped that the membership could initiate a process of taking more active ownership and control of the organizational culture.

Throughout the month of July 1985, a group of 15 cooperative members (mostly from FAGOR personnel departments) met with Greenwood daily, ultimately producing a 115-page monograph dealing with Ulgor, the founding and largest cooperative in Mondragón, with over 2,000 worker-members. A product of lectures on social science research methods, analysis of documents and secondary sources, teamwork on specific research projects, and substantive debates about the cooperatives themselves, the monograph had three sections. The first evaluated what had been written about the cooperatives by outsiders and insiders, including a review of about 20 draft chapters of the Whytes' book on Mondragón and of an interpretive article by Whyte on the cooperatives. The second section of the monograph reexamined the strike of 1974 (the only strike in Mondragón's history), and the third part dealt with Ulgor's responses to the worldwide recession of the early 1980s. Each of these sections took on major theoretical problems: theories of cooperatives within a capitalist economy, conflict management within a cooperative system, and the limits of adaptability of cooperatives to economic crisis situations. From this process emerged a view of the cooperatives as historically dynamic, flexible in structure, and responsive to changes that a priori would have seemed to constitute impossible challenges for a cooperative system. Thus theory and case study were linked.

The resulting monograph was passed on to the general manager of FAGOR and others for review and consultation on the next steps. Readers of the pilot monograph reacted positively and wished to see the project expanded to include the entire FAGOR group not because of any specific applicability but because they felt that the development of a new model of cooperative operation could be helpful to them in guiding future planning. They were also critical of some of the interpretations brought forward, providing convincing reformulations and complaints about biases. This kind of corrective discussion helped the model of the FAGOR group become considerably more sophisticated.

Following visits of some of the FAGOR group and other Mondragón people to Cornell, Greenwood returned to Mondragón in February 1986 to plan the next steps. The plan was to retain some of the materials of the first monograph but to supplement the documentary study with surveys and interviews and thereby teach these research techniques to the group.

By this time, the FAGOR personnel group had applied a survey instrument developed by González (containing a number of open-ended items) to approximately 50 members, and during Greenwood's February visit the group went over the responses and agreed that the documentation on the history of the FAGOR group should be strengthened with further interviews.

Many, occasionally heated, discussions were held on the subject of surveys and, more generally, on the appropriateness of particular social science methods to the PAR aims. The cooperative members felt strongly that results should be reliable, but they were not nearly as dependent on statistical concepts of reliability as many social researchers because they could ultimately judge the results for themselves by their own experiences and by their effectiveness in action. The debates about the value of statistical versus interpretative models of social behavior were as sophisticated as any held in a graduate seminar in the social sciences. The clients clearly had a stake in the "truth" and were at least as concerned as the external researcher about the methods and theories being deployed.

Greenwood served as a facilitator for the team in articulating an approach that would be systematic, falsificationist, and yet useful. He urged the group members to pursue a nonparametric conceptual framework, that is, to look particularly at variability rather than assuming that all phenomena would be arrayed in a normal distribution. The kinds of questions the members were asking about the cooperatives implied systematic contrasts of the experiences of those at different levels of the system. This meant encouraging the team to select the controversial issues and research them among people most likely to have been at odds over them. And this is precisely how the next step, interviewing, was constructed. In this regard, the contribution of the outside researcher was important because the nonparametric model of reality was not likely to have been applied otherwise. At the same time, the principle that

nonparametric conceptual framework

diversity is important was easy for the outside researcher to put forward, but knowing enough about the system to deploy it in a meaningful way required the store of knowledge of the FAGOR people.

The interviews were structured to confront those dilemmas regarding equality, equilibrium between social and economic concerns, participation, and so forth that cooperative members already felt to be the sources of both dynamism and conflict. Thus they were making explicit their theories about member behavior and its links to work situations and social background. Team members practiced interviewing through role-playing, went out to conduct interviews, and later held long sessions analyzing both the interviewing process and the diverse results.

The interviews were a turning point because they brought in a systematic body of information about conflicts, diversity of opinion, and problems in a form that fostered systematic reflection. Members of the team were surprised by the amount of new information gathered in this way. While much of this information was very sobering, because it portrayed the rough edges of conflicts that had been known about more indirectly before, it also showed that systematic social research produced important new knowledge. This enhanced FAGOR members' commitments to the formalization of research processes as part of the work of the cooperatives while also convincing them that the PAR team was producing a unique view of the cooperatives that had to be broadly communicated. Thus as practitioners they became persuaded that the link between theory and action was not only possible but necessary to their future success.

By the time Greenwood returned to Mondragón for the July 1986 intensive seminar, the personnel group was committed to producing a book on FAGOR both to clarify the lessons learned and to transmit them to the cooperative system in a form that could lead to positive future actions. Their motive was a commitment to the "truth" every bit as strong as that found in the academic research community, to disseminating within the cooperatives and outside what they felt to be a more "valid" view of the Mondragón experience. Thus, while the motive to write a book on social research was not professional in the narrow social scientific sense, it was simultaneously scientific and social.

The writing team was directed by Greenwood and González, with responsibility for analysis and writing of particular research areas apportioned to a core group of four FAGOR people: two from the central personnel department (Alex Goiricelaya and Isabel Legarreta) and the personnel directors of Ulgor and Copreci, the largest cooperatives of the group (Kepa Salaberria and Ino Galparsoro).

As the book project began to mature, it was clear to everyone that the interviewing strategy used, which focused explicitly on finding the most negative features of the system, needed to be balanced by other forms of data showing why, despite the problems, the cooperatives are so remarkably successful. At the same time, so much staff effort and time had been put into the project that the cooperative members and their colleagues and supervisors were becoming very impatient to see some practical results. This created a complex research dilemma in which the search for truth and the demand for action were intertwined, much as many academic social researchers fear. The results, however, show that these goals not only can be combined but can complement each other.

The strategy Greenwood developed for the July research was to use roundtable discussions with members of the cooperatives, led by members of the research team. Participants in each roundtable were selected to bring together people with a diversity of age and experience, formal position, and educational background. Six roundtables of eight persons each were held, with two each on the theme selected by the team. These themes had emerged from the previous documentary research, questionnaires, and interviews:

(1) the "value added" for being a member of a cooperative (What did it mean not just to have a job but to be a member of a cooperative?),

(2) evaluation of communication within the individual cooperatives and FAGOR, and

(3) problems of economic and organizational readjustment.

These roundtables served the research purposes while initiating an intervention phase. Setting up the roundtables involved discussions of the project and its aims with participants, enlisting their support and pointing out that the questions to be discussed had emerged as the most pressing in the cooperatives.

At this point, the cooperative members also began setting the research agenda for themselves. The idea of setting up these discussion groups was Greenwood's, and he and Whyte both presented ideas about the composition of groups and interesting topics, but the topics they decided upon were different from any that we had suggested. They appeared to welcome our suggestions and general guidance but were determined to do things in their own way—which indeed proved to be highly productive.

A member of the personnel team moderated each discussion group but refrained from expressing any personal opinions or entering into arguments.

The moderator's role was simply to facilitate the discussion and to tape-record the session for later analysis by the personnel group.

Each discussion group was scheduled for 90 minutes. After each such session, the study team convened to listen to the tape, then spending up to 90 minutes discussing the implications of what they had heard. The group discussions had a powerful impact on team members. They found the inter-change among line management people and workers a fruitful but painful experience. They became even more persuaded than before that the level of member participation in decision making in the cooperatives fell far short of the ideal. But the roundtables showed that members were far from apathetic. Although many of them had come to work in FAGOR simply to get a job, members made it clear that they had become committed to cooperative ideals and now were critical of the gulf between ideals and realities. They recognized that the formal structures and procedures reflected cooperative ideals but did not provide them sufficient opportunities to participate in decision making. In this way, the roundtables provided unexpected disconfirmation of an implicit apathy theory and suggested different lines of analysis and action.

The review of the roundtables had a strong impact upon members of the personnel group. Concerned with many of the negative lessons from the interviews, they heard similar, negative statements in the roundtable discussions. For every negative comment by a roundtable member, however, later in the discussion that person generally balanced it with positive statements providing evidence of the inherent strength or value of the cooperatives. In the roundtables, the positive group dynamics and will to solve problems became evident. Clearly, for most of those roundtable participants, being a member of a Mondragón cooperative meant far more than just having a job and a secure paycheck.

As members of the study team worked through the roundtable results, they gained an increased sense of member commitment and a somewhat different sense of direction. They were encouraged by the strong commitment of the members to cooperative ideals and resolved to continue participatory action research to find ways of resolving the discrepancies between ideals and operational realities.

Earlier, the plan had been to write a book on the nature of FAGOR, explaining the cooperative group to its members and to outsiders. Now the team was committed to writing a book on the problems and possibilities of participatory action research in FAGOR. Of course, to be intelligible to outsiders, such a book would have to present basic information about FAGOR, but the emphasis would be on PAR rather than on FAGOR itself. That is, the overall process in FAGOR did not pull the analysis away from its theoretical pole; conceptualization and application went hand in hand.

Beyond the individual and group learning process experienced by the personnel group members, the FAGOR PAR project has already had three other concrete effects. In 1986, José Luis González proposed that the budget of the personnel department for the next year and for the five years ahead should provide financial support by FAGOR of participatory action research. Up to this point, the money directly spent for PAR activities had come largely from grants by the Spain-U.S. Joint Committee on Educational and Cultural Exchange. Of course, FAGOR had contributed the salaries of the members for their time spent on the PAR project. Greenwood was hired by FAGOR as a consultant for 1987 to continue the development of the internal PAR capacity as well as to finish the book.

A second outcome from this PAR process involves personnel people beginning to work to develop in the individual cooperatives PAR projects designed to respond to problems and needs that came to light through the two years of exploratory research. The findings and methods are being deployed in new member orientation programs, in study groups working on the implementation of "total quality" programs, and in marketing of the corporate image and are gradually being incorporated into long-range planning.

A third outcome appeared in the November 1987 issue of *Trabajó y Unión,* the monthly publication of the Mondragón cooperative complex, reporting on an international conference, "Cooperatives and the Social Economy." At this conference in Bilbao in the Basque country, one of the main speakers was Alfonso Gorroñogoitia, one of the five founders of Ulgor and chairman of the Governing Councils of FAGOR and the Caja Laboral Popular, the cooperative bank. Following his summary of the history of the Mondragón cooperative complex and a description of its structures and basic policies, Gorroñogoitia devoted three pages to "La Experiencia de Mondragón Como Proceso" (The Experience of Mondragón as a Social Process), drawn entirely (with due credit) from the book manuscript for the FAGOR-Cornell project. Although this does not certify to the scientific validity of the interpretation, the fact that it could be accepted as a true reflection of Mondragón by one who may well be the most widely known and respected leaders of the complex indicates that its accuracy is acknowledged far beyond the small group that made the analysis.

*PAR as an Applied*
*Research Strategy*

These cases should indicate that participatory action research can have far greater impact than the conventional professional expert role of the consultant in stimulating and guiding major organizational change. The cases we have described suggest that the participatory research process not only can achieve results of current benefit to the organizations but can lead to a rethinking and restructuring of relations so that the impact of the process can carry far into the future. They also show that advances in thinking about how organizations work and learn are possible through PAR.

The process begins with the problems people who work in a firm are currently facing. Instead of beginning in the conventional fashion with a review of the literature, the specification of hypotheses, and the finding of a target organization to test out our design, we start by discovering the problems existing in the organization. Only as we work with members of the organization, diagnosing those problems, do we draw upon the research literature as well as our own past experience.

### Overcoming the Single-Discipline Limitation

In complex organizations, few problems arise in such form that they can be solved by the use of any single discipline. No student of organizational behavior can master all of the disciplines relevant for the problems we study, but we work in the field with those who have expertise in engineering, finance, accounting and cost control, and so on. As we participate with them, we learn enough about disciplines we have not studied academically to arrive at a far more useful and scientifically valid research strategy than would be possible if we simply tried to analyze a problem from the standpoint of sociology, psychology, or social anthropology.

In PAR, the consultant/facilitator acts less as a disciplinary expert and more as a coach in team building and in seeing to it that as much of the relevant expertise as possible from all over the organization is mobilized. The consultant/facilitator can also help bring in expertise from outside the organization.

### Testing Intervention Strategy Quasi-Experimentally

PAR enables us to study major changes that we helped to generate—changes that would not occur without our involvement. Of course, these are not true experiments, but very few genuine experiments are possible within the complexity of organizational phenomena. The greatly enhanced ability to study major changes far outweighs the potential problems of trying to compensate for the distortions in our thinking that may arise from our personal involvement in the process.

## Scientific Rigor

According to the conventional wisdom, no other research strategy can match the standard model for rigor. Whether this is true depends upon how we define *rigor*. In the standard model, the subjects of our studies have little or no opportunity to check facts or to offer alternative explanations. If we feed back our research reports and publications to members of the organization we studied, they often argue that we have made serious errors in facts and in interpretations. If the standard social science researcher hears such criticisms, he or she can shrug them off, telling colleagues that the subjects are just being defensive—defensiveness apparently being a characteristic of the subjects but not of social scientists themselves.

PAR forces researchers to go through a rigorous process of checking the facts with those with firsthand knowledge before any reports are written. In the Xerox case, the cost-saving figures developed by the CSTs were rigorously checked by higher management because decisions based on them involved millions of dollars.

In the case of the Whytes' book on Mondragón (Whyte and Whyte, 1988), the evolution of this writing project provided an impressive demonstration of the value of PAR in getting the facts straight and recognizing important alternative explanations. Following their 1983 visit to Mondragón, when the book project was still the exclusive personal property of the authors, Bill had his notes translated and sent to eight key informants with a request that they respond with suggestions and criticisms. That initiative yielded only one response—and that from a woman who had become a close personal friend. As draft chapters of the Mondragón book and an interpretive essay by Bill were incorporated into the PAR project directed by Greenwood and González, the relationship between researchers and informants radically changed. The Whytes' book now became a project jointly owned by some of the key informants in FAGOR and elsewhere in the Mondragón complex. Alex Goiricelaya, training director of FAGOR, read each draft chapter with great care and provided voluminous criticism and suggestions. Others responded with vital corrections and alternative interpretations on individual chapters. The active involvement of

Mondragón people in this cross-checking process has assured a far higher standard of factual accuracy than could have been achieved by standard social research methods.

## The Continuous Mutual Learning Strategy

In the standard model, the researcher operates his or her mental motor at full speed in designing the project. Then, as the researcher goes about implementing the research design, that mental motor is shifted to idle until he or she—or, more generally, his or her research assistants—have gathered the data. At that point, the mental motor is shifted into gear again, and the researcher tries to figure out what the data mean.

In PAR, the researcher is constantly challenged by events and by ideas, information, and arguments posed by the project participants. If the advance of science is a learning process, clearly continuous learning is more efficient than learning concentrated primarily at the initial and final stages of a project. We also argue that organizational learning is enhanced when members of the organization under study have active ownership in the project.

PAR also tends to extend the researchers' learning far beyond the termination of particular projects. Because PAR leads researchers into previously unfamiliar pathways, involvement in the process is likely to stimulate us to think in new ways about old and new theoretical problems, thus generating provocative new ideas. As we will discuss later, that has been our experience with two topics: the relationship between worker participation and productivity and the role of cost accounting in manufacturing organizations.

## Creating Organizational and Intellectual Space

Supporting these particular advantages just presented, there is a basic underlying principle: The way we think about problems is shaped to a considerable extent by the social setting in which we find ourselves. When we are at work, the organization provides that setting. We think and act within organizational structures and cultures that provide explicit or implicit ground rules determining what information and ideas are relevant for problem solving.

In situations of major social change, the prevailing ground rules are likely to block the path to creative solutions of serious new problems. Creative solutions will depend upon the ability of the organization to change the organizational and intellectual ground rules.

Though they used different metaphors, it is striking that key participants in our cases independently arrived at the same basic idea. Lazes visualized the wire harness breakthrough in terms of changing the shape of the intellectual box to encompass new information and ideas. Their experience with PAR led our Mondragón associates to see it as a means of creating new organizational space, within which new ideas could be acted upon effectively.

## PAR for Advancing Social Theory

For purposes of exposition, we have separated our discussion of methodology from our discussion of theory building. In research, such separation is neither practical nor scientific. Theory without links to empirical data is likely to be sterile, and, similarly, methodology without any guidance from theory is bound to be unproductive. Good methodology is required to build strong theory. Therefore, the preceding arguments on methodology have important theoretical implications.

Finally, let us venture beyond implications to stake our claim to the potential of PAR for building better theories. To claim theoretical contributions, we begin by placing our ideas in the context of the preexisting theoretical literature. We do so in terms of two topics: organizational culture and the relationship between participation and productivity.

An organization is more than a collection of people, structures, policies, and work activities. There are influences that link the elements together and shape the way members think, feel, and act. These influences are visualized as organizational culture. We agree with this general focus but question a common view visualizing culture as static and homogeneous across a given organization, like a mold into which the human elements are poured. This view tends to exaggerate consensus among members on important issues and to mask the existence of disagreements and conflicts, reflected in the differing ways members think about their organization and act in terms of contrasting conceptualizations. Our own work, particularly through the cases presented here, has led us to visualize organizational culture as dynamic, changing as members struggle to resolve conflicts and negotiate new understandings that tie together (sometimes loosely) heterogeneous elements.

The PAR process with the FAGOR group led the members to reshape the way they visualized the nature of their organizational culture and thereby the theoretical basis of their social change efforts. They entered the process theorizing that what they saw as an inadequate level of participation was due to member apathy. That diagnosis leads to theoretical and practical dead ends regarding the possibilities of inducing change within the organization. If those joining the organization are not predisposed toward active participation, leaders may try to stimulate participation through exhortation, but past research indicates that such efforts would enjoy no more than momentary successes. In contrast, the new theoretical orientation focusing on structures and social processes that provide inadequate opportunities for eliciting active participation offers FAGOR not only a sounder theoretical framework but also more practical guidance for efforts to enhance participation. In the relations between theory and practice, that is as it should be: Rethinking past practice leads to theoretical reformulation that in turn leads to improved practice. The processes of rethinking both theory and practice thus strengthen both theory and practice.

In the Xerox case, the history of union-management relations had built an organizational culture of trust and cooperation. Although this culture reduced the level of conflict, the worker participation program was initially limited to shop floor problems that could be resolved without changing the labor contract or infringing on managerial prerogatives. The cost study team proposal opened up new ways of thinking about problems and new social processes for resolving those problems. The successes of the CST projects then led to basic changes in structures and processes of participation—in effect, changes in organizational culture in the Xerox manufacturing plants.

This case, furthermore, led us to a theoretical reformulation of one of the most frequently studied problems in the organizational behavior literature. We began this analysis trying to make sense out of an apparent paradox: How can it be that the accumulated studies of several decades have found no consistent relationship between participation and productivity, whereas in just four cases in Xerox we could report participation leading to cost savings of 25% to 40%? To be sure, the dependent variables were different in the comparison cases, and yet costs and productivity appear to be just two sides of the same coin.

That paradox led us to rethink the participation/productivity literature, beginning with a comprehensive research review (Locke and Schweiger, 1979). This and other studies along the same line (Brett and Hammer, 1982; Hammer, 1983) all reach the same general conclusion: Job satisfaction does appear to be favorably affected by worker participation, but no consistent pattern for the relations between participation and productivity has been found.

Our analysis then led us to rethink the definitions and conceptualizations of the independent variable (participation) and the dependent variable (productivity). Could it be that the inconclusive results were produced by misguided conceptualizations—for all these years?

The participation variable is supposed to reflect some impact upon decision making in the organization through worker involvement in the decision-making process. The basic problem here is that researchers have tried to measure participation as if it were some monolithic phenomenon, not taking into account the wide range of settings in which participation occurred nor the wide varieties of forms of participation.

The research literature generally does not distinguish among various types of industrial situations that could affect worker involvement in the decision-making process. At one extreme, we find situations where workers have substantial control over the way they do their work and over how the job of one worker relates to that of another or one work group relates to another. At the other extreme, the nature of the work is almost entirely determined by the technology, as in the automotive assembly line or in the continuous process industries such as chemicals and petroleum. In the former type of situation, workers may have considerable latitude to change the way they work on their own initiative, or at least the changes they want to initiate can be agreed upon by a low level of management within that department or close to it. In the latter type of case, major changes in work methods, technology, and work flow can only be made with the cooperation of management, and the changes are of such a major nature as to require considerable rethinking of organizational strategies.

Then we also need to distinguish between participation in governance and participation in operational decisions. By *governance* we mean the structures and processes establishing the objectives and policies of the organization. By *operations* we mean the work activities carried out by workers and members of management. In the United States, worker or their representatives rarely participate in governance through being on boards of directors, but this form of participation history become fairly common in some European companies. In the United States, where a joint labor-management committee has been established, with a membership of top local union leaders and top local management people, this provides for some indirect worker representation in governance, but it does not necessarily assure that there will be worker participation in operations. We often find that leaders of labor and management have agreed to set up a joint committee but that agreement in governance has not led to active participation of workers in decision making on the way the work is actually carried out.

We also need to distinguish among a number of interpersonal forms within which participation takes place. One form involves individual consultation. There are no group discussion meetings, but the individual supervisor encourages workers to make criticisms and suggestions and is responsive to

worker initiatives. Then there are group discussion meetings in which workers get together—with or without their supervisor—to discuss problems and
propose solutions. There are also joint committees or task forces in which
labor and management people try to solve problems.

There are also differences in composition. Do all the members of a work
unit meet to discuss problems? Or does the process involve committees
representing workers and members of management? If so, how are members
selected for these committees?

Participation patterns differ in the topics accepted by management and
labor for discussions. In the most common U.S. pattern, discussions have
been strictly limited to shop floor problems. Any problem that might be
solved through changes in the labor contract is necessarily ruled off limits.
Similarly, any problem involving the structure and processes of management
above the shop floor is also ruled out of bounds. In contrast, with Xerox,
leaders of union and management agreed that any problem affecting productivity and costs could be pursued through all its ramifications in the structures,
policies, and processes of management.

There are also enormous differences in the frequency and duration of
worker participation. At one extreme, there are quality circles or employee
involvement groups that meet for an hour once a week or every two weeks. At
the other extreme, with Xerox, CSTs composed of workers and members of
management worked together full-time during a period of up to six months.

How can such a wide variety of forms and situations be homogenized to
yield a single variable called *participation*? That sleight of hand is achieved
by survey research. Instead of observing, interviewing, and documenting the
human interactions and activities making up the participation process in any
particular case, researchers have commonly fallen back on indirect measures:
survey items asking workers whether they *feel* they have been participating.

This practice enormously simplifies the conceptualization and measurement problem, but science cannot be built on oversimplifications that lump
together vastly different behaviors. Although survey measurements of worker
perceptions of degrees of participation can be useful supplemental information, they cannot be taken as adequate proxies for the behavior of the parties
in the case under study. For that purpose, we need systematic descriptions of
the participative activities that have been occurring. Those reports should be
based on field observation of the participation process or at least upon
intensive interviewing of some of the key participants so as to document in
some detail the nature of the interactions and activities under study.

Those considering themselves hard-nosed scientists reject this kind of data
as being simply "story telling," but we should not accept this put-down. It is

hardly scientific to accept numbers measuring perceptions and attitudes that have arisen in response to the behavior experienced by workers as superior scientifically to data on the interaction and activities in the participation process that have given rise to those attitudes and perceptions.

To be sure, it is more difficult to measure interactions and activities than attitudes and perceptions, but some very solid measurements are possible. To take the most obvious example, the difference between a group of workers meeting once a week or every two weeks for an hour to discuss problems with their supervisor and the participation of a CST for 40 hours a week for up to six months provides a very simple but also very important measure of the nature of the participation process.

How do we conceptualize productivity? The most common approach is to count the number of production and maintenance workers involved in a given operation and to divide that number into the number of units produced in a given time period or into the value of the products produced in that period.

For this measure to make sense, we must assume that worker output is primarily dependent on worker knowledge, skills, and motivation. That assumption flies in the face of what we know from research and what has long been recognized by practitioners in industry and labor: The output of workers is strongly influenced by management—by the supervisors, by staff people, by the organization of the work flow, by technology, and by the flow of orders into the plant, among other variables. To be sure, where there is a strong and active participation program, worker involvement will have an impact on management, on the work flow, on the technology, and so forth. If that is the case, why then look solely at output in terms of workers?

Consider the following hypothetical case. In plant X, production is 1,000 units per week. In plant X some years later, the same number of workers is putting out 1,000 units per week, but the number of managerial, staff, and clerical people has been reduced by 50%. According to conventional standards of measurement, worker productivity has not changed. Does that make sense? As we have seen, this hypothetical case is a simplified version of the changes that actually took place in Xerox over several years.

This analysis led us to the following question: Why have social scientists been so interested in measuring worker productivity—and also so respectful of the numbers yielded by such measurement? We offer speculative answers along the following lines.

(1) The Department of Labor provides figures purporting to measure worker productivity, so this measure has become part of the conventional wisdom for social scientists as well as for practitioners.

(2)  In conventional terms, productivity is easy to measure. Technical problems arise only when we compare results of two time periods, making adjustments for changes in product mix and in prices.

(3)  Progress in the social sciences depends upon quantitative measures.

The first two justifications obviously have no scientific basis. The third justification is valid only if we assume that what we are measuring has some logical relationship to the question we are seeking to answer.

That brings us to the heart of the conceptualization problem. Instead of relying on conventional measures, we need to go back to the intellectual drawing board and ask: What is the question we are trying to answer?

Let us abandon the conventional conceptualizations and ask instead: What is the relationship between worker participation and *organizational performance*? We then need to devise measures of organizational performance. We do not claim that we have found the *one best way*, but we do claim that the conventional worker productivity measurement is one of the worst ways of answering our reformulated question.

The outputs of the organization are the joint products of all of the people and the material resources used in that organization. Unless we base our analysis upon a holistic view of organizations, we will continue to be frustrated as we follow the standard research model down a dead-end street.

The advantage of a cost focus is that costs are attached to the use of all the organization's human and material resources, so the whole organization can be analyzed in cost terms. Direct labor costs, of course, are part of the total data required for a holistic analysis, but in many companies they account for only 10% to 20% of total costs. This suggests the folly of trying to improve the performance of the organization solely through efforts directed at workers. From a scientific point of view, if what we are really interested in is the performance of the organization, it should be obvious that the most exact measures of the productivity of direct labor are worse than useless because they direct our analysis at only a small portion of the total problem area.

In the Xerox breakthrough, the CSTs gathered systematic data on total costs: wages and fringe benefits for production and maintenance workers; salary and fringe benefits for white-collar workers, supervisors, staff people, and managers; costs of technology (original costs discounted year by year for depreciation); costs of space used in the operations; costs of energy; and so forth.

We can readily link this holistic conception of costs to productivity. For an operational unit, the relationship between the total costs charged to that unit and the value of the output of that unit can be considered a measure of the productivity (or efficiency) of that unit. Changes in that relationship over time would then reflect changes in *total factor productivity*.

This strategy does not provide a direct measure of labor's contribution, but, because that depends so heavily upon material resources and other human resources, attributing the total output to labor is clearly misleading. On the other hand, this strategy does enable us to link major changes in worker participation with marked improvements in organizational performance, as measured by total output in relation to the total costs allocated to a given organizational unit.

Finally, we argue that this advance in our theorizing would not have been possible without our involvement in participatory action research. We had long been aware of the inconclusive findings on the participation-productivity relationship. We had been puzzled by the failure of so many researchers over the years to find the consistent positive correlation that they had expected—and that we would have anticipated. That seemed to us a puzzle, but, not having any new ideas on how to solve the puzzle, we did not pursue this line of research.

It was not until we encountered the dramatic results of participation in Xerox that we were driven to the rethinking of the underlying research question. That in turn led us to see the need for a radical paradigm shift for research on one of the most studied topics in organizational behavior.

Regarding thinking accounting methods in industry, the Xerox experience earlier had led us to recognize a problem along the following lines (Whyte, 1987: 497): "These conventional methods are clearly not well adapted to solving the cost accounting problems of modern industry in a highly competitive environment."

We had recognized a problem, but, lacking any educational background in accounting, we did not then think we might find ways to solve the problem. To be sure, we had been familiar with the frictions commonly arising between people in production and those they sometimes refer to as "bean counters," but we had attributed such clashes to rivalries arising out of differences in educational backgrounds and technical specialties and perhaps to personality characteristics that led people into one or the other field.

To Chris Argyris we owe credit for the stimulus that guided us beyond the conventional wisdom on the relations between production and accounting. Upon reading an earlier draft of this chapter, he urged us to press further on the study of accounting methods in manufacturing and armed us with reprints from the pioneering research of his colleague at the Harvard Business School, Robert S. Kaplan, and his associates.

We had assumed that we lacked the technical tools to understand account-ing in manufacturing. Reading the work of Kaplan and his associates has persuaded us that the problems we were facing were not technical but rather *conceptual*. Cooper and Kaplan (1988: 96) put the case in these words:

Managers in companies selling multiple products are making important decisions about pricing, product mix, and process technology based on distorted cost information. What's worse, alternative information rarely exists to alert these managers that product costs are badly flawed. Most companies detect the problem only after their competitiveness and profitability have deteriorated.

According to the authors, the basic problem is that management has been using accounting methods devised for tax purposes and for supplying overall company financial information to stockholders.

How have the indirect costs of products been allocated in the past? One common method has been simply to allocate them in the same proportion as direct labor costs. According to Cooper and Kaplan (1988: 96):

Distorted cost information is the result of sensible accounting choices made de-cades ago, when most companies manufactured a narrow range of products. . . .

Today, product lines and marketing channels have proliferated. Direct labor now represents a small fraction of corporate costs, while expenses covering factory support operations, marketing, distribution, engineering, and other overhead functions have exploded. But most companies still allocate these rising overhead and support costs by their diminishing direct labor cost base or, as with marketing and distribution costs, not at all.

As the authors demonstrated in a study of an actual case of a plant producing six different products, it makes an enormous difference whether costs are allocated according to the conventional system or according to a system in which management gathers and analyzes system-atic information on the actual costs directly attributable to each product. Following the old system, management estimated that all six products were profitable, producing between 30% and 47% gross margins. Accord-ing to the cost analysis worked out by the authors, three of the six products were actually losing money. In fact, the product that management had credited with the highest gross margin, according to the authors' calcula-tions, yielded a gross margin of −258%!

If indirect costs are allocated in proportion to direct labor—or if some of them are not allocated to products at all—such enormous distortions will inevitably occur. Furthermore, as Kaplan explains, these distortions are not random; they tend to lead to decisions prejudicial to the interests of labor in maintaining jobs. Let us say that a given plant produces a single model of a product. Later, management adds to this line additional products requiring substantial new investments in machines, research and development, and distribution. To the extent that the new, more complex machines displace labor, the direct labor costs in the plant are reduced. As the heavy additional costs of going beyond a single model are allocated directly back to every product in the plant on the same basis, this creates the *illusion* that the costs of producing the initial product have increased very substantially. Now, because the company can sell the more complex products for a higher price, with an apparently increased profit margin—because the development and distribution costs of those products are not charged directly to the products in question—management may decide to concentrate on manufacturing these higher-priced products.

Following what recently became the conventional wisdom, the company now decides to cut the costs of the initial product by shutting down that department and contracting with a vendor in a developing nation that provides very low direct labor costs. The company now has to allocate substantial expenses to having its engineers and other specialists work with the vendor company to provide the technical assistance necessary to produce at an adequate level of quality. In other words, the American company has given the vendor not only the business but also considerable resources in technical assistance. What happens later? In many cases, management of the vendor company decides to build on this knowledge and experience base to compete with the American company in developing related but additional products involving greater complexity and selling for higher prices. In other words, the logic of conventional accounting systems appears to be leading a number of American companies into strategic decisions that not only involve sacrificing workers but also may intensify their own international competition.

This line of reasoning puts the Xerox case in a new context. We now recognize that the cost study teams pushed management to set aside its customary system of allocating indirect costs to products and to work with the teams to develop a system of allocation that appears to be similar to that advocated by Kaplan and his associates: tracing (at least to a first approximation) the percentage of each item of indirect cost that can reasonably be attributed to a particular product. Thus we can say that the CSTs achieved a theoretical and conceptual breakthrough in accounting methods in the same period when Kaplan and his associates were making their own break-through—and making their ideas available to the business and academic public through their publications.

On rethinking the participation/productivity relationship, we claim some credit for originality. For ideas on the accounting/production relationship, we are happy to credit Robert Kaplan and his associates, along with our further reflections on the Xerox case.

The issue here is the question not simply of originality but rather of how one learns to integrate ideas and concepts across disciplines previously isolated from each other in our minds. We still do not claim to be able to do our own cost analyses in industry, but now we know enough to ask management the first critical question: "In estimating the costs to the company of a particular product, on what basis do you allocate indirect costs?"

### On Measurement and Social Science

It is important not to confuse measurement with science. In some highly regarded sciences—evolutionary biology, for example—measurement is impossible or else plays a distinctly minor role.

Where measurement is possible, it can be important, providing it helps us to answer a significant scientific question. Measurement is driven by definitions. Poor definitions generate misleading measurements, which, added together, yield misleading conclusions. Research on the participation-productivity relationship has bogged down under the weight of poor definitions and misleading measurements.

Measuring participation in terms of workers' perceptions tell successes nothing directly about the behavior of workers and management people. Such measures are only useful if they are combined with systematic descriptions of the behavior researchers call *participation*. Some aspects of those descriptions can be buttressed by measurement: how many people were involved in the participation process, how often and over what period of time they participated in it, how many proposals for change were initiated by workers, how many of these were accepted by management, how many proposals were actually implemented, what value (in costs or productivity) can be attributed to worker initiated changes, and so on. Focusing on behavior rather than upon attitudes and perceptions greatly complicates the measurement problem but yields data that are much more realistic and scientifically defensible.

Measuring productivity in conventional ways is also highly misleading. Because for many people, the impetus for studying participation is to determine if more participation is correlated with improved organizational performance, we should return to that general question and then focus on the problems of measuring organizational performance. We conclude with the claim that a holistic strategy focusing on the relationship between total costs and the value of total output is one of the better ways to measure organizational performance—and, in any case, is superior, for both scientific and practical purposes, to conventional measures of worker productivity.

What does this mean for research planning? Mainstream organizational behavior researchers call for more research with more rigorous measuring operations. In terms of the logic of *The Structure of Scientific Revolutions* (Kuhn, 1962), that means pursuing more "normal science" to solve a problem that has so far failed to yield to "normal science" for the past half century.

We believe that progress in understanding the correlates of worker participation depends upon a radical paradigm shift: changing the definitions of variables and the specification of what is to be measured. If a paradigm shift is necessary to advance theory, it appears to us that PAR is more likely to cause such a shift than standard research methods.

This chapter is based on an analysis of two cases and a subset of the literature on participation. This amounts to retrospective theoretical analysis of materials, an analysis aimed at highlighting certain key phenomena and relationships that either explain what happened or suggest new hypotheses about key relationships.

Such retrospective analysis and synthesis is an invaluable element in the scientific enterprise. We know historically that significant scientific breakthroughs have been initiated in this way. It must be emphasized, however, that, valuable as it is, this retrospective emphasis is not intrinsic to PAR as a process; it is a product of the particular circumstances under which this chapter was written.

The normal science mode of approach is taught as a process of theory building, hypothesis generation, and subsequent testing. This may or may not be an accurate description of what goes on, but it is by no means the only way to proceed with valid scientific research. Our experience places PAR in the middle of a process that begins with a combination of theoretical and practical concerns, an extended PAR process in organizations, and the subsequent reformulation of existing explanations (e.g., about the participation-productivity relationship).

In addition to features already discussed above, we are especially impressed with PAR's openness. When involved in a PAR process with many team members contributing to the enterprise, it is often far easier to escape the limitations of theoretically imposed logics that constrain observation and thought. Practitioners often bring the pursuit of irrelevant or ill-conceived lines of inquiry to a rapid halt, correcting or refining the questions asked in ways that lead to sharper formulation and more productive research.

PAR has important qualities as a method for examining the plausibility of theories, as has been argued with the participation-productivity example. It also is productive in formulating new hypotheses about key relationships, hypotheses testable by either further PAR research or through conventional research methodologies. It is not, therefore, an alternative to existing social science but a way of dramatically enhancing our achievement of the goals of theoretical understanding and social betterment by widening the range of strategies at our disposal. Active involvement with practitioners struggling to solve important practical problems is highly likely to open up researchers' minds to new information and new ideas, leading to advances in theory as well as in practice.

## *References*

BRETT, J. M. and T. H. HAMMER (1982) "Organizational behavior and industrial relations," pp. 221-281 in T. Kochan et al. (eds.) Industrial Relations Research in the 1970s: Review and Appraisal. Madison, WI: IRRA.

COOPER, R. and R. S. KAPLAN (1988) "Measure costs right: make the right decision." Harvard Business Review (September-October).

ELDEN, M. (1979) "Three generations of worker democracy research in Norway," pp. 226-257 in C. L. Cooper and E. Mumford (eds.) The Quality of Work Life in Europe. London: Associated Business Press.

GREENWOOD, D. J. (1972) "Tourism as an agent of change: a Spanish Basque case." Ethnology 11 (1): 80-91.

GREENWOOD, D. J. (1976a) "Unrewarding wealth: commercialization and the collapse of agriculture in a Basque town." Cambridge: Cambridge University Press.

GREENWOOD, D. J. (1976b) "Ethnic regionalisms in the Spanish Basque country: class and cultural conflicts." Iberian Studies 5 (2): 49-52.

GREENWOOD, D. J. (1977) "Continuity in change: Spanish Basque ethnicity as an historical process," pp. 81-102 in M. Esman (ed.) Ethnic Conflict in the Western World. Ithaca: Cornell University Press.

GREENWOOD, D. J. (1985) "Castilians, Basques, and Andalusians: an historical comparison of nationalism, 'true' ethnicity, and 'false' ethnicity," pp. 202-227 in P. Brass (ed.) Ethnic Groups and the State. London: Croom Helm.

GREENWOOD, D. J. and J. L. GONZÁLEZ et al. (forthcoming) Organizational Cultures in Mondragón: A Participatory Action Research Study of Change in the FAGOR Cooperative Group.

GUTIÉRREZ-JOHNSON, A. (1982) Industrial Democracy in Action: The Cooperative Complex of Mondragón. Ph.D. dissertation, Cornell University.

HAMMER, T. H. (1983) "Worker participation programs: do they improve productivity?" ILR Report 21 (1): 15-20.

JACOBSON, G. and J. HILLKIRK (1986) Xerox: American Samurai. New York: Macmillan.

KLINGEL, S. and A. MARTIN [eds.] (1988) A Fighting Chance: New Strategies to Save Jobs and Reduce Costs. Ithaca, NY: ILR Press.

KUHN, T. (1962) The Structure of Scientific Revolutions. Chicago: University of Chicago Press.

LAWLER, E. E. (1986) High Involvement Management. San Francisco: Jossey-Bass.

LAZES, P. and T. COSTANZA (1984) "Xerox costs without layoffs through union-management collaboration." Labor-management cooperation brief (July). Washington, DC: Department of Labor.

LOCKE, E. A. and D. M. SCHWEIGER (1979) "Participation in decision-making: one more look," pp. 265-339 in B. M. Staw (ed.) Research in Organizational Behavior, Vol. 1. Greenwich, CT: JAI.

THORSRUD, E. (1977) "Democracy at work: Norwegian experience with non-bureaucratic forms of organization." Applied Behavioral Science 13 (3): 410-421.

TRIST, E. (1981) The Evolution of Socio-Technical Systems: A Conceptual Framework and Action Research Program. Toronto: Ontario Ministry of Labour.

WHYTE, W. F. (1987) "From human relations to organizational behavior: reflections on the changing scene." Industrial and Labor Relations Review (Cornell University) (July): 487-499.

WHYTE, W. F. and K. K. WHYTE (1988) Making Mondragón: The Growth and Dynamics of the Worker Cooperative Complex, Ithaca. NY: ILR Press.

*3*

# Participatory Action Research

## A View from Xerox

LARRY A. PACE
DOMINICK R. ARGONA

In 1980, after several years of thought, study, and preparation, and in response to increased foreign and domestic competition, the North American Manufacturing Division (NAMD) of Xerox Corporation and the Amalgamated Clothing and Textile Workers Union (ACTWU, Local 14A) began a joint quality of work life (QWL) experiment that is still in existence eight years later, although in a much different form. In this chapter we describe the process and its evolution from a highly structured adjunct feature of the work environment to a more integral and flexible approach to solving business problems and enhancing quality of work life. This evolution has not been painless, but our hope is that, by an honest sharing of our successes and difficulties, we will be able to help other companies and unions struggling with similar issues and problems.

AUTHORS' NOTE: We are grateful to Bill Whyte, Don Kane, Pete Lazes, Ron Mitchell, Steve Weber, Tony Costanza, Hal Tragash, and the entire Team Xerox/ACTWU QWL team of managers, trainer/coordinators, shop chairpersons, employees, and consultants for their support, encouragement, assistance, and friendship. The names are too numerous to mention, but the contributions of each individual are deeply appreciated. Critical comments by Bill Whyte, Davydd Greenwood, and Peter Lazes resulted in substantial improvements to the manuscript. The views represented herein are the authors' and do not necessarily represent the official position of Xerox Corporation.

The story of QWL at Xerox is a story of participatory action research (PAR; Whyte, 1987). Much of what we have learned has been through trial and error, experimentation and refinement.

What follows are the reflections of two Xerox internal consultants on the evolution of the QWL process at Xerox, a series of major obstacles encountered by the process, the responses to those events, a summary of the organizational learning that occurred, and a listing of current and anticipated issues and concerns faced as the QWL process is merged with the Total Quality Control (TQC) efforts at Xerox. Finally, we reflect upon the role of internal consultant itself, giving thought to the various subroles and the social processes involved in being an effective internal consultant to the Xerox QWL process.

## *The Need for QWL at Xerox*

In the mid- to late-1970s, Xerox began to suffer erosion of market share and profits as (1) patents expired, (2) foreign and domestic competition increased in Xerox's mainline copier and duplicator business, and (3) customers began to demand higher value and quality and greater choice. Worker values were also changing, reflecting changes on the national and international scene. Workers were demanding a greater say over their work and were searching for more than financial rewards for their efforts.

The company was seeking higher productivity and competitiveness. Xerox management believed that worker skills and contributions were not being fully tapped and that, if this potential could be better utilized, productivity, quality, and worker motivation would increase. The union was not opposed to those goals as long as they did not translate into job loss or speedup tactics, but more important to the union was the search for an approach that would accord more dignity and respect to its members, increase the quality of their lives at work, and secure their jobs.

## *The Beginnings of the Xerox/ACTWU QWL Process*

In late 1979, management approached the union during contract talks with the idea of establishing a joint employee involvement (EI) experiment. The idea ultimately produced the following joint sponsorship clause, which was ratified into the 1980 collective bargaining agreement (this clause was included verbatim in the 1983 and 1986 contracts):

A Joint Company-Union Employee Involvement Committee shall be established to investigate and pursue opportunities for enhancing employees' work satisfaction and productivity. To this end, the Joint Committee shall meet regularly to undertake the following responsibilities:

A. Review and evaluate ongoing programs, projects and experiments, both within and outside the Company, designed to encourage employee involvement.

B. Develop programs, projects, and experiments that might ultimately be broadly applied.

C. Establish subcommittees to develop suggested programs for specific areas. Hear and review reports from these subcommittees.

D. Submit reports and recommendations to the Company and Union regarding the implementation and subsequent progress of specific programs.

To implement this contractual language, in April 1980, the parties founded the Joint Planning and Policy Committee, which consisted of top union officials and company executives. This committee established ground rules for the process and authorized the formation of Joint Plant Advisory Committees (PACs) in each of three major manufacturing facilities covering roughly 5,000 union members. The PACs formed Joint Business Center Steering Committees (BCSCs), which were chartered to guide the EI process in their areas of the plants. EI was conceived as a bottom-up, grass-roots effort to get workers involved in problem solving and decision making at the shop floor level.

Union and management trainer/coordinators (T/Cs) were selected to team teach a 40-hour participative problem-solving and group development curriculum to Problem Solving Team (PST) members. The T/Cs were trained by a third party (first Sidney P. Rubinstein and then Peter Lazes).

The authors were internal consultants who worked closely with the T/Cs, with the external consultants, with line management, with corporate headquarters, and with the union in establishing, maintaining, and expanding the QWL process. Additionally, Argona was appointed manager of the employee involvement function, within the Human Resources Department. The EI function was chartered to develop EI strategy in conjunction with the union, to administer the day-to-day operations of the QWL process, and to report periodically to the Joint Planning and Policy Committee. Argona's union counterpart was Anthony J. Costanza, then general shop chairman. Together these two individuals, who later received Xerox's highest honor, the President's Award, were the daily personification of the QWL process.

In the summer of 1980, the T/Cs conducted intensive orientations with the work force and solicited volunteers for PST membership. The rallying calls for QWL were these: "Let's work smarter, not harder," "If Japan can, why can't we?" and "The choice is ours." Enthusiasm was high, and at first the supply of volunteers far outstripped the capacity of the organization to train and support PSTs.

PSTs were formed of six or seven union members and a supervisor, all of whom were volunteers from the same work area. (It must be admitted that the union members were far more likely to be true volunteers than were the supervisors.) By the end of 1980, 10 PSTs had graduated and 14 were in training. By mid-1982, there were over 150 active PSTs.

This era of process discovery and diffusion was one of very high excitement among top managers, union officials, and especially PST members. They were given management attention, were allowed time away from their regular jobs to select and solve problems, and were enabled to expand their horizons through participation in decision making.

## PST Accomplishments

Problem Solving Teams, as a form of parallel suggestion involvement (Lawler, 1988), were very successful for Xerox and the ACTWU. Millions of dollars worth of cost savings and productivity improvements were documented. Team accomplishments were mainly in the form of improvements to working conditions, work flow and process, quality, safety, and workmanship. Although the traditionally organized job and work design and organization structure were initially unaltered, worker commitment and productivity were enhanced, especially in areas where the process had middle management support.

## 1981 to 1983: Four Major Hurdles

Between 1981 and 1983, four difficult and unexpected situations were faced by the QWL process. The responses to those situations challenged and ultimately changed the design of the QWL process.

(1)  There was a potential outsourcing situation in the Wire Harness Assembly Plant, part of the Components Manufacturing Operations in Webster, New York. It was determined after a year-long competitive benchmarking study conducted by management that the wire harness assemblies for the new 1075

copier could be purchased on the outside at a saving of over $3 million but a loss of 150 to 180 union jobs.

(2) From 1981 through early 1983, Xerox, driven by increasing competitive pressures, went through a substantial "resizing" effort that led to voluntary and involuntary reductions in force in both salaried and hourly ranks. It was very difficult to separate the layoffs from QWL in the minds of those affected.

(3) The QWL process reached a plateau. Job movement driven by the rolling production plan disrupted team membership and necessitated the training of replacement members. Additionally, the pool of new volunteers for PSTs evaporated.

(4) In 1983, Xerox initiated a TQC process called Leadership Through Quality. This was conceived as a top-down corporate culture change that required managers to learn, use, teach, and inspect the practice of Total Quality Control before cascading the training and application of Leadership Through Quality to the next level. The organizing structure for Leadership Through Quality consisted of a manager and his or her staff. It was hoped that this structure would support the managerial behavior changes that proponents of EI had so often said were lacking. The union had been actively involved in the QWL efforts as a joint partner, but the Leadership Through Quality effort was solely a corporate management initiative.

### Overcoming the Obstacles

*The Wire Harness Study Team.* The union, supported by Lazes, approached management and asked if, in the spirit of QWL, the workers could be given a chance to save their jobs by taking the surplus costs out of the harness plant. This project was given management approval, and a team of six union members and two management employees was selected from a list of 160 volunteers. The team was given six months in which to develop its recommendations, access to all company information, and office, clerical, and travel budget support. The story of the original Wire Harness Study Team has been reported elsewhere (Lazes and Costanza, 1984), but suffice it to say here that the results of the study team were successful beyond either party's initial hopes. The work and the jobs were kept in house, and recommendations were implemented that ultimately saved the company more than $4.2 million annually.

*1983 collective bargaining agreement.* Because of the success of the Wire Harness Study Team in taking surplus costs out of an internally manufactured commodity, the company was desirous of using the same methodology in all areas of the business in which it was not competitive. Following the layoffs from 1981 to 1983, the union was reluctant to give the company carte blanche to form cost study teams without some measure of employment security. Thus the parties entered the 1983 negotiations with a mix of motives, some complementary, some conflicting. The result was a trailblazing collective bargaining agreement that provided protection against economic layoff for all union members (Local 14A) for the life of the contract (three years). In return for (1) stricter absenteeism control measures, (2) some deliberalization of benefits, (3) containment of wage rate growth, and (4) the ability to duplicate the Wire Harness Study Team approach in any area deemed to be uncompetitive, the company was able to provide the employment security union members sought (Costanza and Pace, 1985). This provision was extended in 1986 for another three years. Although the 1983 contract provided job security for union members, the strict no-fault absenteeism measures were not well received by the membership. The problems with the no-fault absenteeism arrangement were corrected to some extent in the 1986 contract, which provided incentives for good attendance rather than simply punishment for absence.

*Refocusing the involvement process.* As the number of teams increased, two phenomena occurred. The pool of volunteers began to evaporate, and the ability of the traditionally designed organization to absorb more teams began to diminish. A "balance point" was reached in most of the plant operations at around 15% to 25% involvement. (One plant, a continuous process operation, proved to be an exception in achieving the involvement of 60% of its employees on PSTs.)

The biggest problem presented by the leveling-out phenomenon was that it created polarized "in-" and "out-groups". This split into divided camps produced two very different ways of looking at the employee involvement process. To those who were active participants, the process was very meaningful and fulfilling and tended to be evaluated in terms of its potential to increase member satisfaction and loyalty as well as to lead to superior solutions to organizational problems.

Members of the out-group, however, evaluated the process from an outcome perspective, asking such legitimate questions as how much the process cost and what its return on investment was.

Moreover, those outside the process often had to work harder to cover the jobs of those who were off at meetings, which often had refreshments served. This led to some frustration and resentment toward the process and its participants. It has often been observed, of course, that participants are more favorable in their evaluations of the participative process than are nonparticipants (see, for example, Nurick, 1985).

The need for a change in approach became obvious. The Quality Circle model would never produce 100% involvement in the traditionally organized operations. We made two joint decisions in early 1983. All hourly and salaried employees would be trained in problem solving and group dynamics. Regardless of whether a person volunteered to be on a team, he or she would need to speak the "problem-solving language" to operate in the new work system.

The second joint decision concerned the nature of the EI process itself in the plant organizations. The Divisional Planning and Policy Committee instructed each PAC to sponsor off-site strategy sessions with both participants and nonparticipants in the QWL process to answer two basic questions: Why weren't people volunteering to join QWL teams? How could the process be reorganized so that business and human needs could be simultaneously met?

These joint strategy sessions led to a complete restructuring of the EI process through an interesting application of PAR (Pace and Mitchell, 1985). The plants were encouraged to perform participative, stakeholder evaluations of their EI processes. In the Components Manufacturing Operations, a stakeholder survey was constructed by the PAC with the assistance of Ron Mitchell from Cornell. Pace and Mitchell analyzed the responses to the survey, which was administered to nearly 1,000 employees, and fed the results back to the PAC, which then restructured the EI process. The focus shifted away from Quality Circles and onto problem solving and participative decision making as fundamental ways of organizing work. This led to the formation of Business Area Work Groups as a superior approach to EI (Mitchell and Pace, 1986).

Business Area Work Groups blanket an entire organization with a 100% involvement structure. Consisting of from 15 to 50 people, all of whom are connected with a particular product or service, these groups meet regularly on company time (usually for one and a half hours every other week) to discuss their work area's performance, company business information, and union information and to recognize individual and group accomplishments. These groups then discuss problems of quality, cost, or delivery schedules and either solve the problems immediately or commission ad hoc teams to take the problems off line for resolution. Ad hoc teams usually consist of 3 to 5 people rather than the usual 8 to 10 in a Quality Circle. After an ad hoc team solves a problem, the team disbands.

The Business Area Work Group strategy solves the in-group versus out-group problem and enables a traditional work system to migrate toward a high-performing, self-managing work system.

These two decisions resolved the problem of the loss of volunteers for Quality Circle activities and paved the way for integrating the QWL efforts with the Leadership Through Quality strategy.

*Creating a desirable future: Horizon Teams.* Another effort at refocusing the involvement process was an experiment in participative strategic planning for Xerox Manufacturing (Pace, 1987). The so-called Horizon Teams involved the union and many hourly employees. These teams developed projections and recommendations in the areas of factory automation and robotics, product and process quality, materials management, business scenarios, and human resource management. Pace served as team leader for the Human Resource Management Horizon Team.

*1984 to 1986: Integrating TQC and QWL.* In late 1983, Argona moved to Xerox Corporate headquarters as manager of EI for the entire corporation, and Pace replaced Argona as organizational effectiveness manager for manufacturing. The corporation was developing its Total Quality Control process, which came to be known as Leadership Through Quality, and Argona and Pace were asked to integrate the ongoing EI activities with the corporate-driven Leadership Through Quality approach.

Although the philosophies of TQC and QWL are mutually supportive and highly compatible, a major concern in Webster, New York, was the lack of involvement of both the union and the local manufacturing management in the development and rollout of the Leadership Through Quality strategy.

Recognizing the problem, and agreeing that it was a potentially severe one, Xerox corporate management sponsored and supported the following steps:

The union and management T/Cs, who had developed and delivered the initial QWL training, were asked to modify and deliver the TQC curriculum to the industrial work force. This modification reestablished the concern for human needs at work and also firmly placed the union in an equal status with management in the TQC process wherever bargaining unit employees were involved.

The T/Cs were reclassified as organizational effectiveness specialists (OESs) and given an expanded role as internal consultants to the combined TQC/QWL process. Simultaneous with this development, the OESs were centralized and reported directly to the organizational effectiveness manager. This gave a central focus to the process, which was highly favored by the union.

The Joint Planning and Policy Committee was chartered with overseeing the combined TQC/QWL process in NAMD (which by this time had been renamed the Reprographic Manufacturing Operations—RMO).

These steps provided the organizational base for the TQC training of the entire RMO work force. Union and management OESs trained management employees and union employees alike, just as had been done with the original QWL training. The implementation of the TQC process following the completion of training was, and is, an issue of joint union/management concern.

### *1987 to the Present: Current and Anticipated Issues*

In 1987, upon completion of the TQC training, the OESs were once again returned to the line organization as internal consultants and facilitators for the TQC/QWL process. Simultaneously, their ranks were reduced because of the completion of the heavy training schedule. Currently, the organization is facing (and dealing jointly with) the following issues:

(1)   The decentralized OESs, while being more closely tied to the actual deliverables of the business by reporting directly to operations managers, may lose their "organizational effectiveness" and "joint process" perspectives.

(2)   While the TQC process assumes, and expects to be built upon, a healthy QWL process, this assumption is implicit rather than explicit. The implicit assumption regarding employee involvement may lead to a reduction in emphasis on the  human needs of the members of the organization and too heavy an emphasis on the bottom line (Jacobson, 1988).

(3)   The role of the production supervisor is undergoing radical change in Xerox's manufacturing operations. One plant in Webster (New Build Operations, the assembly operation) is instituting an improved work system that fully integrates QWL and TQC with the day-to-day operation of the business. In support of this work system, supervisors are being trained with a 360-hour curriculum covering their new roles as coach, counselor, resource person, teacher, and facilitator.

(4)   The next steps for the joint QWL process are not currently clearly defined. The ACTWU, along with other progressive labor organizations, is seeking a redefined role in the industrial enterprise. What form this role will or should take is not immediately obvious.

## Reflections on the
## Internal Consultant Role

The role of internal consultant in the QWL process at Xerox was a very challenging and exciting one for us. At the same time, the role was very demanding and often quite frustrating. In the early days of QWL, 60- to 70-hour weeks and even longer were quite common for us.

We lived through eight years of the process, nursing it in its infancy and helping it grow to its current stage of development. In what follows, we reflect personally on our experiences by identifying several specific responsibilities (subroles) of the internal consultant and then describing our approach to integrating these various responsibilities.

*Human resource strategists.* Although case studies abound on the Xerox/ACTWU QWL experiment, few even mention the role of the internal consultant team as strategists. This is a major omission.

In response to increased foreign and domestic competition, Xerox management had developed a three-phase business effectiveness strategy to lead the company from a position of competitive disparity (Phase I) to a position of parity (Phase II) and finally to a position of competitive leadership (Phase III). This business strategy focused on new product development, technical superiority, strategic planning, competitive benchmarking, and financial control but was largely silent on human resource issues.

Yet Xerox was aware that the skills and talents of its work force were being underutilized on the job, and, as early as 1975 for Argona and 1979 for Pace, we began producing and implementing strategies for developing the human potential of Xerox workers and managers. These started with a series of studies by Argona of technical obsolescence in manufacturing engineers and culminated in 1979 in a document coauthored by Argona, Dr. Robert W. Mann, and Pace that laid the groundwork for the QWL process.

In this strategy document titled simply "Project 90," employee involvement was shown to be a necessary ingredient for achieving and maintaining a competitive business advantage. As early as 1979, we had charted a 10- to 15-year course for QWL at Xerox. This human resource strategy provided a blueprint for moving the Xerox Manufacturing organization from a traditionally organized bureaucracy to a high-performing, high-involvement system.

The three phases, each projected to last from three to five years, consisted of a parallel suggestion involvement process for the process entry phase, a job and work group involvement strategy for the competitive parity phase, and a high-involvement work system for the competitive advantage phase. Recognizing the current operating system, and working within the "arc of the possible," we initially shared only the first phase of the QWL strategy with Xerox line managers.

Although some developments were unexpected, the QWL strategy outlined in Project 90 was amazingly prescient in predicting both the *kinds* of problems that would occur during each phase and the appropriate response to those problems. The actual development of the QWL process is still tracking almost perfectly with the original strategy.

*Applied researchers.* Based on the approval of the strategic thrust of Project 90, we were given the responsibility to visit our counterparts in other companies and to interact with outside organizations, including consulting firms, universities, governmental agencies, and research organizations.

The purposes of these visits were (1) to learn the strengths and weaknesses of various involvement approaches, (2) to identify likely problems with process implementation and ways to overcome such problems, (3) to learn the strengths and weaknesses of various outside consultants, and (4) to develop superior approaches to training problem-solving team members, steering committee members, and trainer/coordinators.

With the learning that occurred through these visits, we developed a presentation for communicating both internally and externally. For each phase of Project 90, we projected approximately a year of applied research *during the height of success* of the phase, during which the plans could be formulated for the next generation of activity. We deemed this research necessary because we had adopted a "product life cycle" notion of the involvement approach used in each phase, expecting it to diminish in effectiveness over time.

*Salespersons/process champions.* Another of our roles was to "sell" unconvinced line managers and shop representatives on the benefits of the QWL process. In this role, we worked closely with Costanza of the ACTWU and Lazes of Cornell. This activity was most successful when all three parties worked together, for example, by coconducting presentations and training sessions for managers and shop chairpersons. Much of the selling in the early days involved assurances and reassurances to the parties that their own prerogatives would not be undermined by the process, at least not in the initial stages.

A distinct frustration in this role was that, by frequently associating and collaborating with the external consultants and the union, as required and even demanded by the internal consulting role, we lost credibility with many traditionally oriented line managers, especially middle managers.

This highlights one of the key problems of this role. The internal consultant must develop a coproducer/partner relationship with management, with the external consultant, and with the union. All of these relationships must be continually refined and developed, yet, at the same time, none of them can predominate. Juggling and balancing multiple relationships requires a healthy dose of tolerance for ambiguity.

This ambiguity was exacerbated by the fact that we had multiple "bosses." As manager of the EI function, Argona worked for the human resources vice president, but, in just as real a sense, he worked for the Joint Planning and Policy Committee, and also for the VP of manufacturing operations.

Simultaneously satisfying the requirements of multiple bosses was difficult at best and sometimes downright impossible. This situation was initially somewhat easier for Pace as an individual contributor because he knew that Argona was his *manager,* while the union, the management, the OESs (T/Cs), and the hourly employees were various *"customers"* who had requirements that should be satisfied as much as possible. Pace, however, later experienced the same role conflict Argona had as the OE manager for manufacturing.

Another aspect of the sales role was that of coach, counselor, and cheerleader for the OESs, who often were at odds with the system as a result of their change agent status and needed to hear an encouraging word from someone who understood.

*Corporate interface.* In addition to our other responsibilities, we were given the task of interacting with the corporate office both to keep the headquarters informed of progress and problems with the process and to transfer learning from Webster to other parts of the corporation. This required frequent travel to corporate headquarters and participation on various companywide committees, teams, and task forces.

*Integrating the various subroles.* The various roles of the internal consultant—change agent, facilitator, strategist, researcher, and salesperson, were integrated by us into a sort of "phantom" role in the process. By this we mean that, to the extent that all the roles were being performed appropriately and at the right intensity, the internal consultant role was largely transparent to management and the union, who were, after all, the joint partners in the process.

When the subroles were out of balance or when crises arose, the overall role became visible, but our approach was to submerge the internal consultant role as soon as we could. If the QWL process worked, we believed the credit should rightfully go to the union and to line management, not to the internal or external consultants.

In addition to requiring a high tolerance for ambiguity, the low profile we took meant that personal career ambition for the internal consultant had to take a backseat to the desire for the QWL process to grow and prosper.

## Conclusions

We have shared an insider's view of the evolution of the joint QWL activities at Xerox during an eight-year period. We show that the QWL process has had its share of expected and unexpected events and that the organizational learning occurring through the PAR approach was quickly internalized within the process.

Over time, the QWL process had become a decentralized, contingent involvement structure. While this was desirable from a management perspective, it presents significant problems to the union, which would like to speak with one voice about and to the QWL process.

Some of the words we and others have used in describing the QWL process at Xerox are "robust," "a learning experience," and "evolutionary." The common thread is that the PAR approach has allowed quick, although by no means painless, adjustments to the process that have helped it to survive, grow, and develop.

Being principal stakeholders, change agents, coproducers, salespersons, researchers, coaches, counselors, and strategists for the QWL process placed multiple demands on the internal consultants. These demands were exacerbated by the ambiguity of multiple and sometimes unclear reporting relationships and customer requirements. On balance, however, we have found the job of internal consultant a fulfilling, challenging, and exciting role.

## References

COSTANZA, A. J. and L. A. PACE (1985) "A cooperative approach to job security at Xerox." Invited address to the American Productivity Center Employment Security Conference, Washington, DC, July.

JACOBSON, G. (1988) "Employee relations at Xerox: a model worth copying." Management Review (March).

LAWLER, E. E. (1988) "Choosing an involvement strategy." Academy of Management Executive, pp. 197-204.

LAZES, P. and A. J. COSTANZA (1984) "Xerox cuts costs without layoffs through labor-management collaboration." Labor-management cooperation brief (July). Washington, DC: Department of Labor.

MITCHELL, R. and L. A. PACE (1986) "Company-wide quality control programs: are quality circles the best vehicle?" Presented at the 40th annual American Society for Quality Control Conference, Anaheim, CA, May.

NURICK, A. J. (1985) Participation in Organizational Change: The TVA Experiment. New York: Praeger.

PACE, L. A. (1987) "Creative management through employee involvement in strategic planning." Journal of Creative Behavior 21 (2): 127-135.

PACE, L. A. and R. MITCHELL (1985) "Participative evaluation and organizational change." Presented at the meeting of the Evaluation Research Society, Toronto, October.

WHYTE, W. F. (1987) "From human relations to organizational behavior: reflections on a changing scene." Industrial and Labor Relations Review 40 (4): 487-500.

# 4

# *Participatory Action Research*

## *A View from the ACTWU*

### ANTHONY J. COSTANZA

During the time when the employee involvement program was getting started in the Webster, New York, plants of Xerox in 1981 and until 1986, I was shop chairman. In that role, I had the principal union responsibility for the program and, therefore, had an intimate view of its problems and progress. That experience has led me to these reflections regarding the evolution of participatory action research and specifically the cost study teams at Xerox. I shall also set those activities in the context of the evolving relationships between union and management and the changing role of the union.

### *The Transformation of Labor Relations*

By conventional standards, for years our union had enjoyed a reasonably good relationship with Xerox Corporation. Nevertheless, the employee involvement program represented a major change, going far beyond these conventional standards. It has involved a transformation of the role of union leaders. No longer do we concentrate exclusively on wages, benefits, and working conditions. Without neglecting those fundamental elements, we have had to learn to understand a different language, that of costs, quality, and delivery, as essential to business success and, therefore, also essential to the welfare of our members.

70

The employee involvement program has also had a major impact on collective bargaining. We have gone beyond traditional issues to focus on job security and on the sharing of gains flowing from improved business performance. Negotiations have become less adversarial and are becoming a mutual problem-solving process. We have gained increasing flexibility, to the advantage of both parties. We renegotiate our basic labor contract every three years, but it makes no sense to wait to solve problems that come up in the intervening months. We solve those problems either through informal discussion or through negotiating side agreements that modify the existing contract.

The Xerox "comeback" against foreign and domestic competition has been widely reported in the press. Our workers have made impressive gains. In job security, we have gone far beyond the contractual guarantees described in the Whyte, Greenwood, and Lazes report. In 1978, employment in our bargaining unit had reached a high of 4,650. By 1982, employment had dropped to 3,354, and, in 1983, management projected that in five years the number of jobs would drop further to 2,600, largely through attrition. On the contrary, by July 1, 1988, employment had rebounded to 3,702.

We still support our members vigorously in processing grievances. Our records for 1976 through 1979 show an average of one grievance for every 19.5 workers. For the 1980 to midyear 1988 period, that ratio had dropped only slightly to an average of one for every 25 workers. Although this change would appear to reflect only a minor improvement in the union-management relationship, it must be borne in mind that the 1980s have been a period of wrenching readjustments in response to intense competitive pressures. This has increased the need to move workers from one job or department to another, a condition in which the union must be vigilant in safeguarding the rights of individuals while still supporting the long-run interests of the collective body. These days, in general, we do not feel that grievances reflect bad faith on the part of individual managers but rather reasonable differences of opinion in interpreting the contract and the needs of a rapidly changing business.

There are also important but less tangible benefits to workers and the union. The program has provided greatly enriched learning opportunities. As they face new intellectual challenges, workers find their work more interesting. The program also provides an excellent training ground for future union leaders, as they are grappling with the new problems that must be solved for the union and management to progress together.

To be sure, the enrichment of the experience of workers who get involved in cost study teams (CSTs) or other problem-solving activities also raises new problems. Following their involvement in a CST, many workers are content to go back to their regular jobs, but others are so stimulated by the experience that they are no longer satisfied with their regular jobs. We believe that the more workers on the shop floor gain new knowledge and skills, the better off we will all be. Nevertheless, there is a continuing challenge for management and the union to devise ways of continuing to support the kind of job satisfaction and commitment that goes with increasing knowledge and skills.

### How Did We Get There?

In explaining the gains we have achieved in recent years, we need to recognize that the program was building on a good relationship with management over many years. Furthermore, our union had never been opposed to cooperating with management, provided that a real partnership could be achieved. In fact, notable cases of cooperation were developed as early as the 1920s by our union.

To go beyond a good but conventional relationship, we had to establish ground rules for building the employee involvement program. Top management and union leaders recognized the importance of this new program and also its innovative nature. For Xerox, we had the strong commitment of chief executive officer David Kearns. For our union, we had the strong commitments of Les Calder, then manager of the Rochester Joint Board, and of Jacob Sheinkman, then secretary-treasurer of our international union and now president, and Murray Finlay, then president.

It was clear from the outset that this was to be not simply another management program but a real partnership between the union and management. Both parties recognized the need for outside assistance to get the program started. Although Xerox paid the bill for the consultants, management agreed that those consultants would be *jointly* responsible to both union and management.

We agreed to begin focusing on shop floor problems to build up worker participation at this level, but at the same time members of both parties recognized the importance of learning as we went along and, therefore, of developing new strategies to meet new problems.

We agreed that it was necessary to have third parties come in to help us get started. Once well established, such a program can continue without third parties, but this may not necessarily be the most effective way to go. There is a danger of complacency and a loss of momentum as the novelty of the process wears off and new ideas are not as frequently developed.

## The Role of the Third Party

To some extent, the third party plays the role of mediator, helping members of each party to understand the position and problems of the other and thus strengthening their ability to work together. With responsibilities to both parties, the consultant/facilitator has access to higher levels of management and the union. This enables him or her to intervene to eliminate roadblocks.

In the CST case, Peter Lazes had the basic idea but laid it out to us only in general terms. He invited us and the management people to work with him to find ways to make it happen. In our lengthy and continuing discussions, he stimulated us to use our imaginations. Rather than giving us solutions, he would sometimes comment, "That's a great idea. Now, how can we build on it?" He also helped us get from the general to the particular, focusing on the details. We worked out the steps to be taken, but he insisted we write them down and determine when action was required and who should take it. He was very effective in making ideas grow. We felt that he was stimulating us but that we were in control of the process—in fact, at times we got so interested in what we were doing that we wondered whether we really needed an outsider.

We all agreed that we needed a training program, particularly for the cost study teams. Peter Lazes did not tell us what the content of that program should be. He got union people and management people together to plan that content, balancing the technical information in engineering and cost accounting with the orientation and training in the social process of problem solving.

## The Role of the Union in
## Intensified International Competition

We recognize that our union must be prepared to meet increasingly intense competitive challenges. It is often assumed that a unionized company is at a competitive disadvantage with nonunion American companies and even more so in competition with foreign nations, where wage rates are substantially lower. We believe that we have certain compensating advantages to help us withstand competition.

Against foreign competitors, and particularly competitors in Third World countries, where wages are a dollar an hour, more or less, we don't believe that we can always overcome such extreme wage differentials for unskilled labor. On the other hand, we believe we have comparative advantages in the flow of information and the sharing of ideas between union and management. We reject the idea that American workers are not able to work as fast and as efficiently as workers elsewhere. We also question the commonly held view that our competitive disadvantage is due in large part to deficiencies of our educational system. We are well aware of these deficiencies and want to do our part to improve education. Nevertheless, apart from the content of material imparted by teachers in countries with which we compare ourselves, Americans generally have an advantage of education that is more likely to stimulate imagination and initiative than that which we see in many other countries. We need to find ways to harness American creativity at the worker level rather than just depending upon the information and ideas possessed by management.

In competing against American nonunion firms, we believe that we have compensating advantages that can overcome wage differentials. In the nonunion firm, management can hardly be expected to share technical and financial information with workers. Because nonunion workers have no organization to represent them, if management really wanted to share information as freely as does Xerox, how could this be done? We would hardly expect management to spread technical and financial information broadside across the whole work force. Even if management undertook to do so, management would only be communicating the information that it thought workers needed to have, whereas we have often encountered situations in which workers and union leaders have called for information that management had not thought to provide.

There is also a problem of management instability. One manager may develop a participative program, but the person who succeeds him or her in that position may have quite a different personal style. In that case, the unorganized workers have no means of insisting that the previous ground rules be honored. In our case at Xerox, we regard the union as the primary guardian of the philosophy and policies of labor-management cooperation. Today, none of the leading figures in management who participated in the building of the CST program and related activities remains in his or her position in the Webster plants. The commitment to cooperation with the union has remained firm at the top levels of the corporation, but it has been the role of the union to socialize new people as they move into the key management positions regarding the policies and philosophy underlying the cooperative program.

The union's contribution is not limited to stimulating the flow of information and ideas. The facts do not simply speak for themselves. Workers and union leaders and managers often have different interpretations of those facts.

holders
of the +
process
philosophy

When that happens, it is important for workers and union leaders to have the ability to argue with management people on important issues. That can hardly be achieved in a nonunion situation. Furthermore, progress in the sharing of information and ideas and in implementing changes that come from them can often be blocked at the level of the immediate supervisor or the middle managers. Workers in a nonunion plant have little opportunity to get to higher levels of authority. We have found it important to be able to reach the highest levels whenever we appeared to be blocked on an important issue by people in middle management.

This does not mean that at Xerox the union always wins its arguments with management regarding CSTs or other issues. Nevertheless, in some cases, management has been willing to go along with the union on an issue of major importance to the workers, even when the management people felt that they were risking a somewhat negative outcome. This does not mean that management people would yield on an issue for which they were convinced the results would be strongly negative. It does mean that they have often been willing to take small risks in order to reach an agreement with the union that would continue and strengthen the cooperative relationship.

In most cases, our arguments with management have not been on crucial issues, but there was one case worth mentioning because it threatened to undermine the whole process. This issue arose in the early stages of establishing our CSTs. We found the union competing with the Procurement Department. These were individuals whose salaries and bonuses depended upon their effectiveness in outsourcing items that had been previously produced at Webster. In this situation, we did not trust people in procurement. We believed that they might be leaking technical and financial information regarding what our CST would be able to bid on a given item. This would then give the outside sources essential information to enable them to underbid our own people. To meet this problem, we negotiated an agreement with management specifying that the internal CST would have the opportunity to make the final bid. If our bid was then lower than those received from competitors, we would retain the jobs; otherwise, they could be contracted out.

Sometime later, we learned that management was about to outsource some products on which no internal cost study team had had the opportunity to make the last bid. I met with our shop committee to discuss it. We agreed that this was serious enough that, if management did not reverse this decision, we would pull the union out of the employee involvement program. I then arranged to meet with the vice president for manufacturing to discuss the problem. He agreed that a mistake had been made, promised to block the outsourcing that we had protested, and went on to reaffirm the previous policy decision.

I do not believe in threatening to pull out of a program just because we disagree with a position taken by management. We made this threat because we felt that we could not live with an agreement made in good faith if the company was going to violate it.

Much later, we had a similar problem that was easier to resolve. This time we were involved in bringing into the bargaining unit work that had previously been contracted out. This involved a trucking contract. We had set up our own CST and had submitted a bid that was below bids from outside contractors. We thought we had the business and the jobs, but then people in procurement went out and found a contractor to underbid us. We called a foul on that one. We reminded management that our own CST must have the final bid on any item. Procurement can take its best shot first, but that would be their only opportunity. We refused to compete against a moving target.

In Xerox, I do not believe that key management people will deliberately violate agreements, but they are busy people under lots of pressures externally and internally (from procurement), so it can sometimes be necessary to remind them of a particular agreement.

### An Evolving Program

The cost study team program was a giant step forward in employee involvement. Since that beginning, a number of different versions of involvement have developed, along the following lines:

(1)  We now have study teams to bring in work we never did before—as in the trucking contract case and now on assembly jobs that we are studying for bids. In the beginning of the program, the CSTs were entirely defensive, struggling to hold on to jobs.

(2)  We have teams formed to solve problems that were never addressed together with management before.

(3)  Shop representatives attend operations review meetings with management on a regular basis.

(4)  Shop representatives attend manpower planning meetings.

(5)  Employees make trips to other companies in the United States and abroad as a means of broadening the base of our knowledge of the competition.

5

# Participatory Action Research

## A View from FAGOR

JOSÉ LUIS GONZÁLEZ SANTOS

The Participatory Action Research (PAR) project that was carried out in FAGOR beginning in July 1985 has been most stimulating for the members of the Department of Personnel of the group of 12 firms and 6,500 employees that belongs to the Mondragón Cooperative Group in the Basque provinces of Spain. As an effort at collaboration between the university and the private sector, between research and action in an industrial context, it has been enriching. Yet in presenting my own analysis of the process, I do not wish to overlook the difficulties that emerged. One learns as much from the problems as from the successes, and reflection on the practical limits encountered improves our ability to advance.

The initiative arose in the Central Personnel Department of FAGOR, more as the expression of a general interest or curiosity than in response to a specific set of problems in the factories. There were three aims:

(1) to create the capacity for social science research in the personnel department

(2) to gain more systematic knowledge of the human experience of FAGOR in order to build personnel policies on a more solid foundation

(3) to identify culture and underlying values affecting the logic of decisions in order to take these dimensions into account in developing or acquiring management techniques

To set the context, it is important to recognize the personnel department's responsibilities. Personnel focuses on structural and functional issues, intervening only marginally in questions of the organization of administrative processes. It participates with engineering departments in the conceptualization of workstations, although engineering is responsible for leading this process. Although personnel has a different qualitative focus compared with other aspects of businesses, leadership in the cooperatives is in the hands of marketing, production, and research, with personnel and finance having less influence.

The expertise of Davydd Greenwood, codirector of the project, and the intellectual support of W. F. Whyte contributed to the resolution of problems as they arose and assisted in bringing this PAR collaboration to a constructive conclusion, planting in FAGOR the seeds of greater intellectual and methodological discipline. This discipline is helping us to manage change in a more self-conscious and systematic form.

## The Process

Viewing it synthetically, we can see three phases of action: The first, intensive phase, which centered on one of the firms, had the character of a theoretical-practical apprenticeship. The second phase involved research at the level of the whole cooperative group and took approximately two years. The third phase centered on specific, short interventions aimed at testing the possibilities of PAR and the ability of the team to utilize it.

### Phase One: Initial Contact with PAR

This was developed intensively during July 1985, when we devoted the mornings to class debates and the rest of the day to reading and discharging the participants' ordinary professional duties. During this phase, lowering the barriers between the internal team members and the outside collaborator gradually led to an integration of their agendas and perspectives.

Part of the month was devoted to the analysis of general information and learning about basic conceptual approaches, for instance, how emphasis on process is essential in the analysis of organizations, the importance of attention to heterogeneity and contrast, the role of dichotomies in creating models of organizations, and so forth. Then these methodological fundamentals were put to use in the analysis of two particularly significant situations in the history of one of the firms. This permitted both research practice and the reinforcement of the concepts that had been discussed.

A critical reading of the most significant writings published about the cooperatives of Mondragón permitted comparison of internal and external perspectives, the role of different types of determinisms, projections, and epic foci in thinking about Mondragón. The reflections and debates that took place during this phase were limited to a group of personnel department members.

The month ended with the writing of a monograph that was presented to the general manager of the group. He authorized the continuation of the project into a phase involving research and analysis of greater breadth and depth.

**Phase Two: Application of PAR in FAGOR**

In this phase, the research expanded to cover the 12 cooperative firms of FAGOR, all of which are located in the same geographic location but each having important differences in technology, size, and economic situation.

An initial, modest, pilot questionnaire provided the first approximation of the problems of cooperative life and the perceptions of the members. Although some differences appeared in the results, the image we captured seemed to us more homogeneous and positive than we would have expected in any organization. This caused us to move to an extensive set of interviews. After defining the questions to ask, we selected a sample to obtain the most heterogeneous responses possible, to provide members the opportunity for personal catharsis on important issues, and to gather abundant, diverse, and extreme information. We found the sometimes harshly formulated responses important but noted that they lacked the subtlety gained through the expression of views in more ordinary social contexts.

Some of the limitations of the interviewing technique were overcome through holding roundtables involving persons from different parts of the organization with different views, educational backgrounds, and experiences. These roundtables centered on the most significant issues that came up in the interviews, permitting us to capture the subtlety of different views but assuring that these views were tested in a social context, with each person obliged to support his or her statements. This gave clear evidence of the existence of a variety of different discourses regarding the same facts in FAGOR and also showed the existence of schematized worldviews, replete with prejudices and stereotypes.

The roundtable debates were focused on issues such as the problematic relation between the economic and social dimensions of the cooperatives.

Participants debated the relationship between equality, solidarity, and hierarchy, efficiency and participation, authority and power, cooperation and conflict, and centralization and decentralization. But in the roundtable format, these debates were carried out not in terms of dichotomies but as a challenge to the participants to achieve some degree of integration.

Ancillary to this process, the collection and analysis of abundant existing information in the form of the minutes of the various social bodies, documented positions taken prior to making key decisions, lists of issues dealt with in the different social bodies, and so forth permitted the reconstruction of the historical process followed in the business and institutional development of the cooperatives. Through this process, we identified certain basic questions that underlie or dominate the socioeconomic dynamics of FAGOR.

Subsequently, we engaged in the process of jointly writing the chapters of a book about FAGOR, as a process of synthesis, internalization, and conceptualization. Without doubt, this was one of the most difficult parts for the team, the one that required the greatest personal effort.

A briefer report-synthesis was directed to all those who had been involved in the process, to the members of the Management Councils, and to the plenary Personnel Committee. Its objective was immediate feedback, taking our reflections to different levels of the organization and outlining orientations, objectives, and future action plans.

All of this phase took place in an atmosphere of open discussion, continuous questioning, and the wish to get to the bottom of things, to touch the reality as it is lived in the workplace by different people. In this way, it represented a change in our conception of culture, a move toward a more dynamic and multifocal vision of the cooperative group.

The various parts of this process were carried forward by differing groups, dedicating varying amounts of time and attention to it. The key groups were as follows:

- A team of seven persons, including the external collaborator, who acted as the principal leaders in the research, dedicating special effort to the final phases of writing and synthesis: Although these were members of the Department of Personnel, their educational backgrounds differed: law, psychology, economics, education, and so forth.

- A broader group of around 20 people who worked on the interviewing process, defining the questions, doing the interviews, and discussing the results: This included members of the personnel department and representatives from many different levels in the cooperatives.

**Phase Three: Specific Interventions**

These interventions undertaken as we were finishing up the general research process and were intended to test the new skills of the team and the PAR method through specific, short-term activities. By developing them, we tried to reinforce the idea of creating within the organization the habit of approaching problems from a variety of angles, of sitting at the table with all those who have something to contribute—independent of department or rank. We wanted to accustom people to becoming conscious of the complexity and interrelationships and to press the groups to arrive at solutions, making them co-owners of the problem, the analysis, and the solutions. We also wanted to sensitize them to the many blind alleys that can deflect change processes.

On a smaller scale, the process followed was basically the same as in the larger project: problem identification, search for information, getting those affected together, and collaborative attempts at analysis and suggested solutions. In the interventions, we learned to take special care not to permit the passing on of responsibility for solution of the problems to the cooperatives in general or to the PAR leader in particular.

These applications happened to coincide with the initiation of a program of Total Quality. As a result, this type of intervention has been integrated into that process, as a generator of cooperation, reflection, analysis, and actions for improvement.

## *A Critical Analysis of the Experience*

The general impact on the participants has been favorable, and I would particularly highlight

> the development of a more open mind-set, the explicit awareness of diversity in the system, the will to arrive at the root of problems, the enhanced capacity to listen and get beyond the obvious, the development of a greater capacity for analysis and reflection

> awareness of the possibility of learning from everyday events, learning to conceptualize problems on the basis of local realities through the use of simple methods like roundtables

> a better knowledge of the human experience of FAGOR, of the implicit values, of characteristic ways of dealing with problems, and of the importance that immediate, everyday experiences have for the members

In addition,

> Learning to think counterintuitively (asking "what if?" questions, taking a non-parametric view, appreciating the heterogeneity of organizational reality) was the dimension that had the most impact on us.
>
> Becoming aware that, because approaches using qualitative methods are more natural and fluid, but less precise and accountable, greater conceptual solidity and breadth of personal experience is required. The simplicity of qualitative methods turns out to be only apparent.

On more than one occasion, however, we wondered if we really had assimilated the methodology, if it were truly possible to apply social research in the firm. Throughout the process, there were moments of enthusiasm, absenteeism, perplexity, loss of interest, exhaustion, coldness, renewal—all due to reasons such as the following:

> Overwork caused by having to combine regular professional duties with the research: There is a clear choice here, and we are clear that it is preferable to be less perfectionist and demanding in job definition in order to maintain the capability of research-action in our people.
>
> The feeling of uncertainty, of not participating in a project that was laid out rationally in advance with perfectly defined steps and ready tools: The tactic we adopted of beginning the research process and then going along, providing concepts and methods when the research process required them, generated a triple reaction:
>
> > The perception that the outside collaborator, who was perceived as the "expert," exercised insufficient control over the process.
> >
> > The positive sensation of joint progress and of co-ownership of the research, along with the realization that social research is not an occult science but that, given some concepts and an appropriate context, it makes good use of intelligently applied common sense.
> >
> > The perception that providing concepts and methods to enable action, method, and concept to coincide as an inseparable reality converts social research into a process of ongoing apprenticeship.
>
> The external collaborator and the internal team had different agendas, which showed up as differences of rhythm, priorities, mutual expectations:
>
> > Review was ongoing throughout the different phases of the process about the true role of the external collaborator: expert, cheerleader, facilitator, director, . . . ?

The external collaborator was repeatedly being converted into the catalyst at any meeting. The group reflexively tended to free itself of responsibilities for the direction of the process.

The group suffered occasionally from the impression of not gaining ground, of using tools and concepts that were too loose, of taking too long to arrive at conclusions and action plans. It also became evident that the PAR process may be too open because it offers the possibility of arriving at basic issues through the analysis of simple situations, but it can also cause much time to be wasted on subjects that lead nowhere.

There was considerable difficulty in accounting publicly for improvements made, a common enough circumstance in the social sciences. This made the external collaborator nervous, because he wanted to present visualizable results; it bothered the internal cooperative manager, who found it hard to perceive the positive results of the budgetary costs and time dedication of his personnel; and it worried the team itself, because its members were evaluated by other standards and were needed by the organization for other, more immediately definable tasks.

The final effort of writing the monograph was particularly hard because of the lack of practice. This generated some insecurities and accentuated the desire to finish.

## Conclusion

The contrast between internal and external perspectives has been basic to the process. The rapid integration of the external collaborator, because of his knowledge of the cultural reality of our country, was complemented by significant differences in our educational backgrounds, habitual work environments, and personal views. This polarization between proximity and difference was present throughout the process in differing proportions and provided us with varied practical results.

Important space for and habits of reflection have been created. Yet it would be too bold to affirm that the entire team could define exactly what PAR is, what its basic focus is, and what its specific, differentiating tools are.

It is reasonable to affirm that PAR's impact on the Department of Personnel has been uneven. In part, it has followed the degree and intensity of involvement of particular individuals, particularly taking into account our need to combine PAR with other activities and other management tools.

Why not?
P. 44
How did it solve issue of opportunity

No formal restructuring of the Department of Personnel has occurred, but it does now operate with a different perspective. The personal and professional impact has been particularly important for the small group that worked most closely on the project.

There currently is no project or specific objective of applying PAR to our strategic planning. Rather, its ideas and methods have become implicit in the orientation of the department. The department has received no express requests from the cooperatives, the social bodies, or management for specific PAR interventions. Nor am I optimistic that such explicit requests for applications of PAR will be formulated. Our organization tends to blend things, to integrate them. This is as true of personal protagonism as for the use of any particular methodology. Syncretism is evident in all aspects of FAGOR life.

At this time, we now propose three levels of action:

Meeting specific objectives and jobs of each section, including the personal effort of reflection, by synthesizing the experience in paths of action, follow-up, and evaluation, and adaptation of specific PAR tools.

Working through teams on interdisciplinary projects, dealing with particularly important subjects where different disciplines flow together: These involve short projects, of three- and six-month lengths.

Developing larger-scale, multiyear projects, taken on by interdisciplinary teams, through which we attempt to identify the interrelations and repercussions of certain major facets of cooperative life, such as technological change and industrial redevelopment in FAGOR: This will enhance the Department of Personnel's ability to intervene more actively, consciously, and professionally.

In this triple way, we are assimilating participatory action research into our system.

*6*

# Participatory Action Research and Action Science Compared

## A Commentary

### CHRIS ARGYRIS
### DONALD A. SCHÖN

### The Dilemma of Rigor or Relevance

Whyte, Greenwood, and Lazes frame their discussion of PAR in terms of the desirability of pluralism in social science. They argue for the incorporation of PAR, along with normal science, in the social scientist's "kit of tools." We take a different tack. In our view, social scientists are faced with a fundamental *choice* that hinges on a dilemma of rigor or relevance. If social scientists tilt toward the rigor of normal science that currently dominates departments of social science in American universities, they risk becoming irrelevant to practitioners' demands for usable knowledge. If they tilt toward the relevance of action research, they risk falling short of prevailing disciplinary standards of rigor.

From the action researcher's perspective, the challenge is to define and meet standards of *appropriate* rigor without sacrificing relevance. And, for this purpose, action research needs three things: a way of representing research results that enhances their usability, a complementary way of construing causality, and an appropriate methodology of causal inference.

In our review of the Whyte, Greenwood, and Lazes chapter, we shall explore the meaning of these three conditions. Let us begin, however, by defining *action research, participatory action research,* and *action science. Action research* takes its cues—its questions, puzzles, and problems—from the perceptions of practitioners within particular, local practice contexts. It bounds episodes of research according to the boundaries of the local context. It builds descriptions and theories within the practice context itself, and tests them there through *intervention experiments—* that is, through experiments that bear the double burden of testing hypotheses and effecting some (putatively) desirable change in the situation.

Hence, action researchers are always engaged in some practice context. In Geoffrey Vickers's phrase, they are "agents experient," and their research results tend to be couched in everyday language—often in metaphors of "optimal fuzziness," such as Kurt Lewin's "gatekeeper" or his distinction between "democratic and authoritarian group climates." Although action researchers may make claims to generalizability across local contexts, their generalizations are unlike the "covering laws" to which normal social science aspires; they do not describe relationships in which the values of a group of dependent variables are uniquely determined by the values of a group of independent ones. Rather, their generalizations tend to describe thematic patterns derived from inquiry in *one* setting, the valid transfer to other settings of which depends on confirmation there by further experiment.

*Participatory action research* is a form of action research that involves practitioners as both subjects and coresearchers. It is based on the Lewinian proposition that causal inferences about the behavior of human beings are more likely to be valid and enactable when the human beings in question participate in building and testing them. Hence it aims at creating an environment in which participants give and get valid information, make free and informed choices (including the choice to participate), and generate internal commitment to the results of their inquiry.

*Action science* is a form of action research that, although it shares the values and strategy described above, places a central emphasis on the spontaneous, tacit theories-in-use that participants bring to practice and research, especially whenever feelings of embarrassment or threat come into play. These theories-in-use we call "Model I." They include strategies of unilateral control, unilateral self-protection, defensiveness, smoothing over, and covering up, of which their users tend to be largely unaware (Argyris and Schön, 1974). And these strategies tend, in turn, to undermine attempts to implement inventions based on the discoveries of action research; indeed, they often distort the discoveries themselves—all in ways of which researchers and practitioners tend to remain unaware not because of ignorance but

> *theory of resistance*

because of a skillful adherence to Model I theories-in-use and virtues such as "strength" (construed as dominance or unwillingness to be swayed by others) and "caring" (construed as unilateral protection of others) learned early in life.

In our commentary on the Whyte, Greenwood, and Lazes chapters, we shall use the action science perspective to point out certain practical limitations and conceptual gaps. We want to emphasize, however, that we see action science and participatory action research (PAR) as members of the same action research family. In the broader world of social science, PAR and action science are aligned in a basic and consequential conflict with normal social science. What they have in common far outweighs their differences. Nevertheless, as we shall try to show, an understanding of their differences illuminates both the potentials and the limits of PAR and the future development of action research as a whole.

We shall illustrate these differences by reference to the Xerox case described in the Whyte, Greenwood, and Lazes chapter. We begin by reviewing its main features.

## *The Xerox Case*

The authors place the Lazes intervention within the framework of attempts by organizational researcher-consultants to bring workers and managers together to diagnose and solve organizational problems. Starting with the proposition that interventions "limited to the shop floor" tend to yield only marginal increases in productivity and quickly exhaust participants' interest, the authors ask, How do you get from the conventional shop floor focus to the much broader sociotechnical economic focus and how do you do so without opening up Pandora's box?

The breakthrough occurred, the authors tell us, when Xerox proposed to close its wire harness department, outsourcing its production and eliminating some 180 jobs, to save $3.2 million dollars per year. Lazes proposed an alternative: creating a cost study team that would "study the possibilities of making changes internally that would save the $3.2 million and retain the 180 jobs." To gain the willingness of labor and management to participate in this venture, Lazes built on the "relationship of mutual trust" he had previously established with them and on their prior experience as participants in regular meetings in which management had invited union leaders to discuss its strategic business plans. Lazes interviewed labor and management representatives to draw out their sense of the risks involved in the CST venture and to help them "think through . . . the potential advantages and disadvantages of accepting the proposal."

Once the CST had been accepted by both labor and management, a joint team of eight people was set up and charged with working on the problem over a six-month period. Lazes then operated as a "consultant/facilitator" "to identify the problems . . . caused primarily by blockages, the development of adversarial positions, turf issues, immobilization, and a general loss of the sense of control and ownership of the organization's activities."

> Behavior had become largely reactive. To address this, he emphasized "changing the shape of the box"—throwing out a broad array of options and tactics that temporarily disorganized the blocked system and might eventually lead to a sense of joint responsibility, openness, and control and ownership, if properly handled. In other words, he attempted to facilitate a transition to a more reflective and active mode of organizational behavior.

Management offered the team access "to all financial information they might require" and invited them to consider "any and all possible changes." Solutions were found, we are told, in two areas. First, the team discovered data that revealed the high costs of training new workers—in response to the "bumping" by seniority that was sanctioned by the labor contract—and was able to project a substantial savings through "stabilizing the . . . personnel—provided that the parties would then negotiate contractual changes to make this possible." Second, the team discovered inappropriate allocation of overhead charges to the wire harness division, the removal of which would also achieve substantial cost reductions. The two measures, taken along with other changes, promised to achieve savings in excess of the required $3.2 million.

As a consequence, CSTs were established in three other units at Webster, resulting in productive changes that included worker participation in the R & D process and in plant redesign. These successes "made it possible for the union and management to work out a new labor contract providing employment security for workers in the bargaining unit" and led management to commit to establishment of a CST before any large-scale layoffs were undertaken.

The authors note that this "powerful process of organizational learning" did not spread to Xerox plants in locations other than Webster. They cite the "exceptionally favorable circumstances" at Webster: a history of labor and management relations of "mutual trust and respect built over years of joint problem solving" coupled with "urgent economic needs" that "had not reached the crisis stage" that "demanded quick and drastic rescue measures."

## The Xerox Case from an Action Science Perspective

At least three kinds of important consequences are claimed for Lazes's intervention. They are (1) cost savings to Xerox and retention of employee jobs, (2) restructuring of the cost accounting system and labor contract, and (3) experience that would act to up the ante as to the kinds of changes that would be possible in the future (this is what the authors refer to as "the intensification of organizational learning" at the Webster plants).

We want to raise two main issues about these claims. The first has to do with the inferences, explicit and implicit, by which the authors link Lazes's intervention to its consequences. They do not consider alternate explanations and thereby miss an opportunity to demonstrate the kind of rigor appropriate to action research.

The second issue has to do with certain questions the authors do *not* ask: Why was the "shape of the box" so narrow to begin with? Why was the organizational system so "blocked"? In short, why did the organizational learning system of the Webster plants have the features attributed to it prior to the Lazes intervention described in their chapter? If these questions were taken seriously, we believe, it would suggest important limits to Lazes's intervention and cast doubt on the likely durability of the organizational changes he is said to have facilitated.

There is a distinction between these two issues, but they are also interdependent in certain ways, as we shall try to show.

*The authors' treatment of causal linkages.* We reconstruct the following causal chain associated with Lazes's intervention, drawing on explicit or implicit elements in the authors' chapter:

Lazes intervention + "favorable circumstance"
↓
intensified organizational learning process: breaking open the box, holistic, cooperative
↓
achieved (at least one-time) savings of over \$3.2 million at wire harness plant, saved 180 jobs, significant increase in organizational productivity
↓

established CSTs at three other Webster departments

↓

further organizational improvements: more efficient R & D cycles through worker involvement, more efficient plant redesign

↓

management commits to worker security at Webster, agrees to CST before layoffs

What we seem to have here is a threefold claim:

(1)   Important shifts in organizational learning occurred: Hidden sources of data were opened up, participants' thinking was broadened to include the entire sociotechnical system of the firm, and cooperative problem solving took place among groups (especially labor and management) that were usually in an adversarial relationship to each other.

(2)   These shifts in organizational learning caused the favorable first-order results: cost savings, job retention, and the like.

(3)   Lazes's intervention, coupled with "favorable circumstances"—an impending crisis clearly visible to all concerned and a prior history of labor/management relations characterized by "mutual trust and respect"—caused these shifts in organizational learning.

 Let us take item 1 as given by observation, although even here we may wonder whether *all* relevant observers—other management and labor participants—saw the matter as Lazes did. We have no information on this point because the authors tell their story only from the interventionist's perspective.

With respect to item 2, the causal attribution is supported in this chapter only by the authors' claim. There is no consideration, as far as we can see, of other plausible causal accounts of the first-order effects. One possibility is the following: The change was really a political one; management made a decision to open up hidden data, and so on, in order to achieve labor peace. In other words, the story was really one of adversarial pressure rather than organizational learning. The authors may easily be able to refute this alternative on the basis of evidence available to them. (We shall suggest another version of it in the following section, when we have introduced some additional terms.) Our point here is that the authors do not try, on the basis of their special knowledge of the case, to construct and test plausible alternatives to their "organizational learning" hypothesis. Indeed, they do not treat it as a hypothesis at all but as an obvious interpretation of the data of the case. In this, we believe, they follow the practice customary in most published papers written in the traditions of organizational development and sociotechnical systems. We are not arguing that their interpretation is mistaken but that a failure to seek out countervailing evidence leads too easily to a belief in the efficacy of organizational learning—in effect, to an ideology of organizational learning.

With respect to item 3, we are in worse shape. We know very little about what Lazes actually did. We are told that he proposed the structure of the CSTs within which the new organizational inquiry occurred, facilitated the process by which management and labor considered the risks and benefits associated with the CST venture, and thereby increased the likelihood of its acceptance. We are told that he facilitated the work of the CSTs through process consultation—that is, he "provided training in group methods and in problem analysis," and in the early stages of the intervention sat in as an observer in meetings of the CSTs but "never intervened except to help the parties to resolve an impasse."

We do not know, however, *how* Lazes trained the participants or how he helped to reduce resistances or resolve impasses. Lazes's way of intervening remains, for the most part, a black box, and there is no attempt to present other accounts of his intervention and its role in organizational change at the Webster plants. In our experience, participants and observers of an organizational intervention often see things in very different ways. The "Rashomon effect," whereby different observers tell internally compelling but incompatible stories of organization change, is a hallmark of organizational reality. The surfacing of such stories provides an opportunity for testing the interventionist's story or reconciling it with others.

The authors make a brief reference to "quasi-experimental method" and to management's interest in testing claims made for intervention. But it is clear that at least what Donald Campbell describes as quasi-experimental method, which very much involves proposing and testing alternate causal accounts of phenomena, has not been carried through here—or at least is not recorded in the chapter.

The issue of "appropriate rigor" is important from the point of view not only of research methodology but also of learning from the experience of the intervention. Prospective imitators of the Lazes intervention would need both an operational description of what Lazes did *and* a critical inquiry into the causal attribution of his achievements to certain features of his way of intervening.

We wish, finally, to comment on the theoretical advance the authors describe and attribute to the intervention. They were led, they say, to pose a new question and to propose a new theory in answer to that question. The question: "How can it be that the . . . studies of several decades have found no consistent relationship between participation and productivity, whereas in . . . Xerox we could report participation leading to cost savings of 25% to 40%?" And the answer: an interesting elaboration of various kinds and levels of participation, and a proposed shift in the definition of "productivity" from "productivity per worker" to "organizational productivity," meaning "the relationship between the total costs charged to (a) unit and the value of the output of that unit." The main thrust of the chapter, as far as Xerox is concerned, is really this shift toward a more broad-gauged, sociotechnical approach to participation coupled with the shift toward a more holistic definition of productivity.

There is certainly an interesting observation, with which we have no quarrel, except for the question of how we know that the shift toward "holism" really did account for the first-order effects described (as above) and how we are to understand the relationship of this theory building to the intervention itself.

Was the new idea about productivity *suggested* by the intervention, or was its development an important part of the intervention itself? Surely there is nothing wrong with the former. But it is the latter that characterizes some of Lewin's best examples. In these instances, the development of the theory is critical to the effectiveness of the intervention, and it is the intervention that *tests* the theory. Did this happen in the Xerox case? The case might be made that it did, but we can't tell for sure. The issue seems to be important for what we intend by the relation between "action" and "research" when we speak of action research (or action science, for that matter). It is not merely a question of *temporal priority* but rather one of the *function* of "research" (theory building and testing) within and in relation to "action" (organizational intervention). On one view, organizational intervention is said to be suggestive or evocative of theoretical insights. On the second, it is said to have a distinctive function as a context for theory building and a means of theory testing.

*Questions the authors do not ask.* As mentioned above, we do not have access to what Lazes actually said and did in the course of his intervention at Xerox. We do not have relatively directly observable data of what actually happened during the meetings. The reason we seek such data is that only by having access to actual behavior can we infer the interventionist's theory-in-use. At the moment, the most we can infer is what Lazes (and others) believe he did. To use our language, we can only develop a picture of Lazes's espoused theories. Moreover, if our knowledge is limited to espoused theories, we are also limited to the reasoning that underlies these theories. It is difficult to provide an independent test of causal relationships embedded in the case if we are limited to the ideas and reasoning espoused by the interventionist.

As we read the material, we find that we can piece together a more complex causal account than the one described in the case. This account, if valid, suggests that Lazes may well have produced successful first- and second-order consequences, as claimed, but that as he did so he bypassed the organizational contextual factors that helped to create the problem in the first place.

Because we do not have transcripts or notes of Lazes's actions, we will build our case upon the text provided by the authors. We hope to show that our conclusions are plausible by using their statements as our premises and by making inferences that they, and the readers, will find worth consideration. For example,

(1) The authors state, "It was obvious from the outset that such a plan would involve abandoning the rules that declared certain topics of study or discussion out of bounds." They state that the CST was formed with individuals who were not handicapped by "preestablished interpersonal hostilities."

Abandoning rules that declared certain topics out of bounds makes sense. But we would wish to peel the causal onion by at least one more layer. What were the causal factors that made it possible to have rules the effects of which were antilearning? What rules existed in the organization that sanctioned making such topics undiscussible?

If it is possible to abandon the rules, as Lazes was able to do, we would wish to explore how he was able to accomplish this feat. Our inference is that he used the crisis situation to say to both sides, "OK, if you want to save jobs, or reduce unacceptable costs, then the undiscussibles have to be discussed." This intervention "works" because everyone's back is up against the wall, and is, in our terms, a "Model I" intervention. It does not require the players to explore how they got themselves into such a crisis in the first place.

What were the causal factors that produced the "preestablished interpersonal hostilities"? It makes sense to reduce these factors, as Lazes reports he did. The method used to reduce these factors was, in effect, to get rid of the old broom and start fresh—again, without leading the players to explore how the "old broom" (or the old "shape of the box") had been created and sustained.

(2)  The team discovered that there were high training costs caused by the bumping procedures required by the existing labor contract. The team was able to show that these costs could be reduced by stabilizing the work force, which could be done by altering the contract. Moreover, the CST identified allocations of overhead charges that were inappropriate and recommended their removal.

The question arises in both cases: What were the factors that had made these issues undiscussible prior to Lazes's intervention? What did management and labor do that made it likely that these discoveries would *not* be made and that solutions to the discovered problems would *not* be found without the threat of an impending crisis?

In our own research, we find that, whenever undiscussibles exist, their existence is also undiscussible. Moreover, both are covered up, because rules that make important issues undiscussibles violate espoused norms of managerial stewardship and union practices (in George Meany's terms, "helping management act more efficiently").

These cover-ups, and their cover-up, are indications of organizational *defensive routines*, which may be defined as any policy or practice that prevents organizations (and their agents) from experiencing embarrassment or threat *and* at the same time prevent them from identifying and reducing the causes of embarrassment or threat (Argyris and Schön, 1985). Defensive routines, at any level, are antilearning.

Yet the Xerox case is described as one in which organizational learning occurred. The puzzle can be solved by introducing a distinction between "single-loop" and "double-loop" earning. In the former, the actions that produce errors are identified and changed. Thus, for example, the action, inappropriate allocation of overhead charges, was changed and costs allocated to the wire harness department were reduced. Double-loop learning would ask: How come the inappropriate allocations were allowed to go on for years? Did the cost accountants know the allocations were unfair? If so, how did they get away with making them? Did the management sense that the cost allocations were arbitrary? If so, what led them to continue the practice?

In the case of bumping, what led the union and the management to continue a process that led to unnecessary and costly training? Was this due to a tacit labor-management agreement to keep the peace? If so, what theory of industrial relations was served, if its propositions have to be renounced precisely when they are most needed, namely, during a crisis?

There is an interesting feature about organizational defensive routines that stems from their being undiscussible and the undiscussibility being undiscussible. It is very difficult to manage them. They continue to exist and proliferate because they are relegated to the realm of "underground management" and all sides tacitly agree to this state of affairs. As a result, organizational defensive routines often are very powerful, yet there is, to our knowledge, no formal managerial policy protecting them.

Under these conditions, defensive routines can only begin to be managed if they are surfaced. To date, the most likely condition for surfacing them is a crisis that requires that they be engaged. Because it is difficult to get management or labor representatives to admit that they have been colluding in such activities, it is not surprising that in the Xerox case the surfacing occurred when a new team was selected and when corporate management promised immunity.

Now back to Lazes's intervention. It is plausible that he succeeded in getting the two parties to make discussible the hitherto undiscussibles because of an impending crisis plus the apparently genuine commitment on the part of management not to punish local managers or workers for collaborating to solve problems. If so, the basis for his success is an intervention theory that has been practiced for many years. Its premise is this: "Wait until there is an undeniable and unhideable crisis, then bring in a fresh team, give them the power to look into the box and change its shape if necessary." Lazes could apply genuine pressure on all sides because there was a crisis that no one could deny. But crisis management is not new (although the kinds of organizational learning described in this case are by no means the only or the usual response to crisis). Moreover, there is little reason to expect that changes effected in anticipation of a crisis would endure for very long beyond that crisis.

The authors frame Lazes's task as one of getting from the conventional shop floor focus to the much broader sociotechnical economic focus "without opening up Pandora's box." It is our hypothesis that the moment Lazes chose not to open up Pandora's box, he chose to bypass the organizational defensive routines we have described above. From a single-loop learning perspective, this choice made some sense, because the players are probably not skilled at dealing with the challenges that arise when double-loop learning is attempted. The irony, however, is that double-loop skills can be learned, in our view, so that the Xerox case could have been used by those involved not only to save jobs but to help the Webster plant, corporate management, and union leaders to build an organizational system in which continued learning—of single- and double-loop kinds—would be possible.

## *References*

ARGYRIS, C. and D. SCHÖN (1974) Theory in Practice. San Francisco: Jossey-Bass.
ARGYRIS, C. and D. SCHÖN (1985) Strategy, Change and Defensive Routines. Cambridge, MA: Ballinger.

# 7

# *Comparing PAR and Action Science*

## WILLIAM FOOTE WHYTE

Because I agree with Argyris and Schön that PAR and action science are closely related, this chapter is not a rebuttal but simply an extension of the discussion. I compare the two strategies in the following terms.

Action science (AS) focuses more heavily on interpersonal relations and intrapsychic processes. AS calls for a detached observer to document in detail the intervention process. AS assumes that beginning to learn new ways of thinking and feeling should precede embarking on new courses of action. AS requires the intervention team to gain more control of both the intervention and the research processes.

As I see it, PAR focuses more heavily on social structures and processes. Without rejecting the value of preformed hypotheses, PAR is likely to depend more on what I call "creative surprises"—new ideas that arise unexpectedly during the intervention process. In PAR, it will be more difficult to arrange to have a detached observer to document the intervention process objectively and in detail; the key practitioners in the project are not likely to see the need for such an observer or to be willing to help pay for the additional costs detached observation would involve. Without claiming there is only one way for organizational learning to occur, I would reject the idea that the only pattern of new learning that remains in place after the intervention is that which is preceded by learning new ways of thinking and feeling. In both the Xerox and FAGOR cases, new lines of action emerged first, and then practitioners found those new lines of action to be effective in solving problems and to be personally satisfying. This experience fostered the emergence of new ways of thinking and feeling, which further reinforced and supported the continuation of the new lines of action. Finally, PAR is designed for a greater sharing of control between practitioners and researchers than AS.

Lacking an independent observer, we did the next best thing: We asked the key practitioners to interpret their own cases. Their accounts suggest that they saw themselves as active participants in the PAR process.

Finally, I have suggested to Argyris that it is useful to recognize two possible sources of undiscussibility. As I see it, social undiscussibility involves participants' reluctance to get into topics that might prove personally embarrassing or likely to cause hard feelings. Structural undiscussibility involves reluctance to broach topics that have been defined as out of order, according to the ground rules mutually agreed upon by the parties. Argyris and Schön focus their attention particularly upon social undiscussibility, whereas it was structural undiscussibility that was involved in the Xerox case. It was not concerns about personal embarrassment or hard feelings that prevented the parties from taking up matters involving the labor contract or managerial prerogatives; they were simply following the ground rules customarily governing employee involvement programs in that era.

To be sure, for organizational learning, it may be important to make either type of undiscussibility discussible, but the social process needed to eliminate the barrier may be quite different for the two types. In his response to my suggestion, Argyris has indicated that this may be a useful distinction.

*8*

# Research, Action, and Participation

## The Merchant Shipping Case

### RICHARD E. WALTON
### MICHAEL E. GAFFNEY

This chapter focuses on one international industry—merchant shipping—and explores a variety of strategies employed to promote organizational change during the past two decades. We emphasize the advantages that the worlds of knowledge and action can derive from combining their forces in imaginative ways, especially when they also provide for broad participation.

Although most action researchers in industry are more familiar with manufacturing applications, and in spite of the relative obscurity of merchant shipping (particularly in the United States), we have chosen this particular industry as our case study for a number of reasons:

*Time depth:* Merchant shipping was one of the first industries addressed in Norway's Industrial Democracy project, a pioneering effort in action research.

*Cultural exchange:* The merchant fleets of all industrialized countries (and some Third World nations) have since had some experience with variations on the action research model.

*Diffusion:* The results of action research in this industry have widely penetrated the worlds of both action and knowledge. If you were to travel to any seaport and interview any active merchant seaman, you would undoubtedly hear of dramatic changes in the nature of shipboard organization—changes that are directly traceable to the action research tradition. Similarly, action research in merchant shipping has also contributed to the world of knowledge in the form of numerous scholarly books and articles dealing with both the content and the process of organizational change.

For these reasons, it could be convincingly argued that this particular industry offers perhaps the best case for a review of the symbiotic interactions of action, research, and participation.

Not incidentally, merchant shipping also happens to be the industry that brought the coauthors together in 1982, when we worked on a National Research Council (NRC) project on this subject of effective manning—an activity that will also serve as an element of this current case study analysis. Following the NRC assignment, Gaffney became active as an action researcher promoting change in the U.S. shipping industry. Walton continued to examine the process of organizational change in shipping internationally, comparing the records of eight countries in their implementation of shipboard work innovations from the late 1960s to the early 1980s (Walton, 1987).

We can briefly summarize the pattern of organizational innovation in this industry, which has come to be known as "effective manning." In the early 1970s, several Norwegian ships successfully experimented with elements of a new shipboard organization that has served as a model for innovative shipping companies in many countries. They examined role flexibility between deck and engine room personnel, delegation of shoreside management functions to vessel officers, participation by the crew in work planning, continuity of employment and vessel assignment, and measures to reduce the social gap between officers and unlicensed crew members. By 1983, similar shipboard innovations had been introduced in a number of companies in Norway, Holland, and Japan, in a few companies in the United Kingdom, and in one company each in Sweden, Denmark, and West Germany. This form of innovative change began somewhat later in the U.S. flag fleet, in the early to mid-1980s.

The participative and flexible shipboard model continues to evolve in slightly different forms in different countries. While the sustained pattern of development and international diffusion testifies to the strength of the new shipboard model, the uneven pace of change suggests weak strategies for promoting change.

In this industry, as in others with which we are familiar, the reason for differential rates of change is to be found partly in the way practitioners from the world of action (managers and trade union officials) and researchers from the world of knowledge often fail to combine their efforts effectively. Typically, managers and union officials have agreed on changes and implemented them, leaving researchers to document aspects of the change and to advance theories about the new organization and change process. These two worlds have carefully maintained an arm's length relationship, and both have paid a price for it.

We propose that innovative change efforts by practitioners that incorporate the spirit and techniques of inquiry, discovery, and invention produce more significant and lasting innovations and greater understanding of why they do or do not work. We also propose that fact finding and theorizing that tap the wisdom and knowledge of those who work in the system under consideration produce knowledge that is more relevant to practice and, therefore, in certain respects, of greater validity. Finally, we emphasize the advantages of broader rather than narrower participation in both the action and the research aspects of change. While the separateness of action and research in industrial organizations is the norm, examples of imaginative integration are available.

## Enriching the Action Cycle by Drawing on the World of Knowledge

To identify the potential for integrating action and research processes, it is useful to set forth the action cycle as a separate activity. Action involves a sequence of activities that starts with identifying a problem or opportunity, and the factors that may influence the solution; proceeds through several steps to formulate, implement, and assess the required change; and culminates in actions to institutionalize and diffuse the change (Figure 8.1).

Steps in this action cycle sometimes are omitted or addressed only superficially, such as diagnosis in the first step and assessment in the fourth. Often, the institutionalization and diffusion steps are recognized as important but are addressed with weak techniques. Important lessons from the shipping story, as we shall see, are the positive differences that a research component and appropriate participation can make at each step in the action cycle. We explore the contributions of researchers to the action cycle in this section and the importance of participation for effective action in the next.

### The Norway Case

The concept of action research developed during the 1960s. Some academic researchers who served as consultants to industry began to explore how to bring their scientific attitudes, research skills, and theoretical knowledge to bear on problems within the framework of the action cycle. It is an accident of history that action research methodology was being developed at a time and location (northwestern Europe, particularly Norway) in which the shipping industry was experiencing a need to undergo dramatic change. From the early 1960s to the mid-1970s, the push for change came from a shortage of seafarers

1.  Identify problems to solve and other opportunities, causal factors, environmental constraints, and relevant practice.

2.  Formulate proposed changes and the implementation plan.

3.  Initiate changes in targeted areas.

4.  Assess changes and implementation methods.

5.  Deepen, institutionalize, and diffuse changes.

**Figure 8.1.** Action Cycle

because employment opportunities and standards of living on shore outstripped the attractions of the seagoing profession.

We review the early history of shipboard change in the Norwegian shipping industry to examine contributions of third-party researchers (the Oslo Work Research Institutes, led by Einar Thorsrud) throughout the change cycle. This case also indicates how the integration of researchers into the action cycle can enhance the quality of the knowledge they contribute to the public domain. Our account is based on our personal observations and several secondary sources (NRC, 1984; Thorsrud, 1981; Walton, 1987).

In 1969, when new legislation permitted smaller crews, a new industry mechanism was formed to consider changes in staffing concepts. It had been suggested by the Work Research Institutes (WRI) researchers, who had previously established relationships with a few shipowners and the seamen's union. This mechanism, called the contact group, comprised representatives from four unions, the shipowners' association, and three government directorates. WRI researchers participated in all of the group's meetings. During the first six years, some 25 key people in Norwegian shipping were involved in 30 half-day or full-day meetings, discussing in detail plans, results, and their policy implications. The contact group was an open forum for exploring options, confronting differences, and clarifying—if not endorsing—organizational principles.

Hoegh, the shipping company chosen to conduct the first field trials, formed a project group of managers and seafarers, assisted by the WRI researchers. The seafarers selected were designated as future crew members for the project ship. The project group visited the sites of work experiments in industry to learn from workers, managers, and union officials the issues they would face. Committees composed of top and middle managers also met, sometimes with the researchers, to hammer out the objectives of the project: to better develop and utilize seafarers' capabilities, to improve the work culture, and to adapt to technological, economic, and social changes. They also identified constraints on the organizational options that could be considered. These were safety rules, regulations, labor contracts, and certain operational requirements. Only a broad outline of alternatives was developed before the project group began planning changes.

The experiment onboard the Hoegh *Mistral* started in February 1970. It had the following experimental features: general purpose ratings (unlicensed seamen), crew (unlicensed) involvement in work planning and supervision, common recreation room, delegation of new responsibilities to shipboard management, and a new personnel planning and salary system designed to enhance crew continuity. *Mistral* confirmed the advantages of the above changes but also indicated the need for more involvement of junior officers.

After one year, this project was evaluated at the ship, firm, and sector levels. The crew members themselves decided they wanted to continue their way of working. The company also was satisfied and proposed a second and more advanced project. The contact group members expressed approval of *Mistral* and endorsed the second Hoegh project ship, *Multina*, on the basis of quarterly progress reports they received on the *Mistral*, meetings they had with three observers who sailed with the ship, and personal visits they made to the vessel in Rotterdam.

The Hoegh *Multina* project started in 1971 and included all the features of the *Mistral* plus role flexibility for officers. Engineers were given nautical education (deck department skills), and mates were given additional technical (engineering) training to enable them to operate and maintain all technical equipment on deck.

A third major Norwegian experiment occurred aboard the *Balao*, a new ship of the Klaveness company launched in March 1973. The involvement of WRI helped ensure that this effort built on the lessons from the two Hoegh experiments. It gave additional emphasis to the development of participative work planning. Officers and ratings had common dining and recreation rooms and similarly appointed individual cabins. Other features of the initial organization, decided by the crew during the first summer in 1973, were the conversion of the foreman position into that of a manager of training, application for approval of a fixed annual salary for all crew members, and flexible staffing levels during various seasons of the year while maintaining an agreed-upon annual average staffing figure.

Meanwhile, at the industry level, the contact group began playing a more direct role in the policymaking process. Its activities sometimes became contentious.

One confrontation occurred early on about crew members alternating between deck and engine work. Another focused on the introduction of a common mess room and dayroom for the whole crew. The confrontations produced a compromise to allow the trial of these ideas on the ships without attempting to agree on their merits first.

Basically, by 1976, these three experiments had demonstrated the feasibility of most of the advanced crew concepts employed in Norway (and elsewhere) a decade later. They also had been judged safe, socially effective, and economical.

Demonstrating feasibility, even effectiveness, was one matter. Diffusing the new operational model was quite another. In 1972, when Hoegh management and the unions tried to extend the new concepts to two additional ships, the *Merit* and the *Mallard*, they encountered some difficulty. The planners learned the source of the difficulty—too little participation by the new crews and hence too little identification with the new policies. Hoegh adjusted implementation practices to allow more participation and proceeded to slowly diffuse the innovations to other vessels in its fleet.

One important development in the spread of the new practices throughout the Norwegian fleet started in 1975, more than three years after the first ship had been evaluated. The crew on *Balao* requested an opportunity to compare experiences with the crews of other project ships in the industry, including the two Hoegh vessels. Seafarers from a number of the ships planned a conference in which direct participants from six ships in the Norwegian fleet met to exchange what they were learning. Researchers, company representatives, trade union officials, and government officials were invited as observers. The agenda for these ship-meets-ship workshops, as they were called, included issues related to participation, role flexibility, and layout of cabins and common spaces. The agenda also covered labor contract changes and new forms of education that were required to support shipboard reforms. Reports of the discussions were sent to the crews, the contact group, and the companies involved in the change projects.

By the early 1980s, the Norwegians associated with the shipping industry believed they had built a capability that was an even more important asset than the products (the actual shipboard innovations) of their efforts. To paraphrase one Norwegian, "We have built a network of people and companies who have expertise and know how to exchange it, and more importantly we have created a tradition of experimentation." The capability of Norwegian industry was an aggregation of the competencies possessed by seafarers, managers, union leaders, government officials, shipowners' representatives, social science researchers, and maritime educators.

How did third-party researchers contribute to the industry's increased capacity for innovative change? Both Thorsrud, who worked with the Norwegian industry, and his Dutch colleague, Jacques Roggema, who worked in Norway, Holland, and the United Kingdom, were associated with the WRI during critical periods of change. One is struck by the pervasive presence of these two researchers and their colleagues throughout the period studied. They participated in all five steps of the action cycle, bringing values and ideas from the world of knowledge to each. They were involved in diagnosing the recruitment problem and redefining it in more systemic terms (action cycle Step 1). They were involved in designing, implementing, and evaluating the three major project ships and went to sea on them (Steps 2, 3, and 4). They helped form and participated in the interinstitutional contact group. They assisted the diffusion activities at the industry level (for example, ship-meets-ship) and at the company level (Hoegh conferences; Step 5). They consulted with many individual companies and with the seamen's union. They helped reshape the maritime educational institutions and worked with particular schools or colleges to adapt to the changing needs of the industry (Steps 1 through 5).

The WRI researchers made contributions to both the content, or substance, and the process of the innovative changes. Even their initial agreement to assist the shipping industry in dealing with manpower shortages in the late 1960s carried with it two preconditions that reflected their findings from previous action research. One condition was "that no single element in the organization of a ship could be understood or changed . . . unless it was seen as part of the total system onboard (as a sociotechnical system)." A second was "that the ship must be seen as a twenty-four hour society and not only as a workplace" (Thorsrud, 1981: 5). Thus in effect these two conditions were an insistence that whatever change was contemplated must be systemic and embrace interrelated policy areas. A third condition for assisting the industry reflected their independence as researchers: "No public authority should be allowed to direct or sanction the research or utilization of results" (Thorsrud, 1981: 5). They envisioned the type of forum process that was later developed to represent all stakeholder groups.

In the contact group, the WRI researchers helped to establish objectivity, empiricism, and a learning climate that reflected the norms they brought from the world of knowledge. The contact group was established apart from existing tripartite committees and was vested with limited formal power. It became a forum in which the parties could engage each other. The researchers facilitated this engagement and helped shape group norms. One norm enabled parties to confront each other and to modify views on the basis of dialogue and new information. Another norm permitted a trial to go forward to create concrete experience for learning purposes rather than attempt to reach a consensus in advance on the probable merits of the proposed innovations.

The WRI researchers, including both Thorsrud and Roggema, have made highly regarded contributions to the literature on change, in the shipping industry in particular and in knowledge about social change in general. We believe their research products were enhanced by their intimate working relationships with practitioners in the action research projects. Their observations and findings about a particular aspect of the system they studied invariably recognize the rich context—historical, cultural, and political—in which the focal problem is embedded. In reading their work, one never has any doubt that these authors knew the territory. Their writings also reflect a deep understanding of the dynamics of the change process, including, for example, how learning by participants and researchers continually changes what is feasible.

### The Second-Tier Issue

It is remarkable that a number of innovations from the early 1970s in Norway have now spread throughout the fleets of many nations. Although the terminology may be a bit different, the basic concepts are surprisingly uniform. In many instances, the process, as well as the content, of change has also been diffused, particularly the use of industrywide tripartite committees, company networks, and company-specific workshops and project ships.

However, that has not always been the case and it sometimes relates to the inadequacy of the transfer of knowledge from the pioneering experiments to would-be followers. Some companies have adopted only bits and pieces of the content of effective manning innovation—for example, reducing the numbers of seaman onboard without simultaneously lengthening their period of assignment (continuity), or providing a social climate onboard conducive to the development and maintenance of a high-commitment ethos, or providing substantial cross training in support of a general-purpose crew structure. Moreover, such operators often spend little time on the process side of the equation, whether the use of project ships or workshops.

This sort of piecemeal or selective approach to both the content and the process of organizational change may be attributed to the fact that this second tier of ship operators is less sophisticated than the early innovators, having less knowledge of the importance of the integration of content changes and the significance of process issues, and possessing fewer resources to spend on research (internal or external consultants), training, and development. It is also possible that some of them are also taking shortcuts, not so much out of ignorance but in the pursuit of short-term profits.

An analogous situation can be observed within manufacturing. Early innovators, employing action research methods, demonstrated the utility of reconfiguring manufacturing organizations in the direction of multiskilled and self-managing teams of employees. This success (fueled by Japanese parallels in content innovation receiving wide publicity) has resulted in pressures within corporations, and between original equipment manufacturers and their suppliers, to move dramatically in the direction of "the new manufacturing." However, such diffusion is often content focused and fragmented and does not always live up to expectations. Katz et al.'s (1988) research shows that, for one major U.S. auto assembler, the pursuit of flexibility through work rule modification and job classification reduction in the absence of significant employee participation has resulted in a net loss in productivity and quality.

The point is that inclusion of a research component in the adoption of these new work designs is recommended for two reasons: (1) It increases the likelihood that the immediate application will take into account what has already been learned about sound organizational models and effective change processes, and (2) it ensures the continuation of learning so that unique characteristics of the immediate application will be taken into account.

The presence of a third-party change agent does not necessarily guarantee a meaningful research component. Particularly in an environment characterized by many second-tier adopters looking for assistance, there is a tendency for outside assistance to be limited to the dissemination of information regarding the content of changes, particularly if the third party defines his or her role as an "expert in content" rather than an "expert in process." Providing content assistance can be helpful to the consultant in gaining entry to the organization (credibility) and in getting the organization thinking and moving. It should not be pursued too far, however, or adopted innovations may prove not to be the best fit for a particular organization or may not be sufficiently owned by the organization. Because organizational learning is primarily experiential, the third party must assist organizations in developing activities that will enable many individuals, departments, plants, firms, and so forth to gain direct involvement in the change process.

## *Strengthening the Action Cycle by Broadening Participation*

The role of participation in the management of change has become part of conventional wisdom, although it is often neglected in practice. Our particular interest is in providing for participation throughout the action cycle that is broader and more systematic than often occurs, even in action programs guided by the participation principle. We draw our examples primarily from the Norwegian case already described and from change efforts in the United States that espoused participation.

The problem of providing for appropriate participation becomes more complex as one moves from change within a single unit (a vessel) to companywide change (a company fleet) and to domains (an entire national shipping industry). Although the challenge becomes progressively more complex at each level, participation remains equally important for effective action.

### Change Within a Unit

The initial action research approach was that of single-site experimentation. In the shipping industry, this takes the form of the "project ship." With a single-site focus, change agents usually regard it as essential (1) to obtain a buy-in from the minimum number of authorities required to proceed with the proposed experiment and (2) to involve the direct participants in the experiment.

To minimize the number of authorities and interest groups that must sign off on the proposed changes, the effort is characterized as a "sheltered experiment." This is an attempt to insulate the experimental unit and the rest of the organization from each other. As we shall argue below, this limits not only mutual influence, which would otherwise complicate the change task, but also mutual learning between the experimental unit and other interested groups—but this latter point is getting ahead of the story.

One key to the success of these single-site experiments is the involvement of members of the unit. We find instances in which the objectives of an action research effort have been set without the involvement of all the groups directly affected. Recall that in Norway the initial research agenda emphasized expansion of the job content and improvement in the job satisfaction of unlicensed seamen. This may have been due to the Norwegian concentration on industrial democracy—the unlicensed seamen being at the bottom of the hierarchy—and no doubt was contributed to by the fact that the officer unions (particularly the deck officer union) resisted participation in national and company-level steering committees. In any event, the comparative lack of participation of ships officers (and their representatives) was eventually recognized to be a serious drawback. Officers resisted pushing responsibility and job content down to unlicensed seamen when no corresponding improvement was being made in their own lot. This blockage was less evident in those projects for which the content of officer jobs was first addressed (or simultaneously addressed) through greater delegation of authority from onshore management. (There is a lesson here for action research in manufacturing, in which the initial and primary focus has been on improving the situation of hourly employees, with little or no attention to, or participation of, middle managers.) Trist notes that the Industrial Democracy Project experienced this same problem when it tried to diffuse sociotechnical change throughout Norshydro, the largest enterprise in Norway. A total of 500 middle managers, not having been participants in the action research effort, saw little in the way of improvement for them and said no (Trist, 1981: 48).

A similar problem occurred in an American shipping firm in the mid-1980s when proposed changes did not adequately address the needs of the licensed engineers. The engineers were hoping for more flexibility in the assignment of tasks to unlicensed engine room personnel to cope with a significantly smaller work force and a constant work load. Because of the multiple unions involved (five, representing a crew of 21), issues of jurisdiction were paramount, and the issue of flexibility was explicitly excluded from the action research agenda, resulting in an attempt to operate a reduced manning ship largely on the basis of improved attitude onboard (rather than improved work organization). As a result, the licensed engineers viewed the effort as being a deck department administrative/morale (soft) concern rather than a technical/engineering (hard) issue and subsequently held back on the extent of their participation in the project (Gaffney, 1989).

Another lesson was learned in Norway, and elsewhere, with regard to the inclusion of both shipboard and onshore operations. With the success of the concept of a shipboard management team (in which deck and engine officers jointly administer a budget for the entire ship), the departmental boundaries and conflicts (deck versus engine), so significant in merchant shipping, began to soften. However, this traditional division aboard ship was mirrored in the onshore organization (port captains/marine superintendents from the deck side and port engineers from the engine side). Although the adoption of shipboard management teams resulted in much greater cohesion and coordination between deck and engine specializations aboard ship, their now unified recommendations and requests to onshore management were segmented at head office and dealt with separately by their onshore counterparts still untouched by any redesign.

Not until companies rectified this situation by first involving onshore stake-holders and then creating new structures, such as "ship superintendents" (a new cross-functional billet responsible for the ship/shore interface regarding any and all technical specialties), did the shipboard management team innovation come closer to realizing its potential.

In sum, it is desirable to involve all the groups who will be directly affected by the unit's change. This will improve not only the range of data available (and the likelihood that the most technically correct changes will be made) but also the likelihood that the interests of these groups will be addressed and their support forthcoming.

We have emphasized instances of omissions in managing participation. In fact, if participation is reasonably well managed and appropriately broad participation is provided for in all of the first four steps of the action cycle, the single-site experiment has proven to be a powerful way to elicit the energy and imagination of those directly involved and to demonstrate relatively quickly the feasibility of a new model and the new dynamics associated with it that must be managed. The disillusionment with this approach has developed among action researchers and practitioners primarily because of the subsequent difficulty in action Step 5, diffusing the new model. We turn next to this and other issues in managing companywide change.

### Change Companywide

Initially, a few daring ship operators in Norway experimented with one or two of their vessels. With the success of these ventures, other shipowners established their own project ships, to the point at which project ships became a familiar topic at industry gatherings—"How's your project ship doing?" Experimentation was often limited to only one or two ships per company for a number of reasons. Initially, of course, the parties were not sure the content changes would work and were, therefore, not inclined to involve the entire fleet. Additionally, diffusion was slowed by the laws specifying the size of crews (based on vessel tonnage and horsepower). Because the shipboard experiments often incorporated a reduction in the number of seamen actually carried, each ship required specific exemption from the law to operate in nonconventional fashion.

The limitations of launching companywide change with single-site experiments became apparent when companies attempted to diffuse learning from project ships to the remainder of their fleets. After-the-fact conferences, seminars, and training sessions had very limited success. The managers and seafarers not involved in the projects, in fact, developed a resistance to the content of the changes. They often resented the special attention given to project ship personnel by management, union officials, and researchers.

The thriving but isolated experimental units continued for some time as long as there were external forces (consultant, top management, and union attention) preserving the experimental groups. However, once that external force was gone (end of "project," transfer of senior management, new union leadership), those dispossessed (shipboard officers, onshore department heads) gradually restored order and normalcy.

The problems associated with containment of some single-site change efforts were confounded when change agents saw themselves in the role of "expert" and provided ready-built models for client organizations. Such projects often were initiated with an "outside" assessment of the client organization conducted by the consultant. These assessments, based on interviews and participant observation, would be followed by a written report describing the problems, potential solutions, and recommendations for action. Although, at first blush, these may seem like appropriate research components to an action research endeavor, the participation level was generally quite low (being interviewed does not amount to participation, although it can lead to raised expectations), and most of the connections made in the process were dyadic (employee to researcher), rather than multiplex, service to establish or reinforce ties of expectation and obligation among members of the organization.

An alternative to the sheltered field experiment as the beginning phase of a change effort is the "workshop approach." The workshop approach has seen many applications in shipping, from company-focused efforts (Royal Dutch Shell in Holland being perhaps the best case) to industrywide events (such as ship physical design workshops both in Britain and in Norway). In the United States, the workshop approach has been employed with senior shipboard officers and onshore managers in two companies (Exxon and American President Lines) and in the design of the superstructure of the largest containerships ever built (American President Lines and several West Coast maritime unions; Gaffney, 1989).

There are a number of variations to the workshop approach, but it usually contains the following central features:

Much greater responsibility for analysis and recommendation rests with the client organization (rather than with the consultant).

An attempt to get a cross section of the whole organization in a room: With larger organizations this was accomplished either by means of a diagonal slice of the organization—tapping the major functional groups and hierarchy levels—or by a series of workshops.

An attempt to have the extant functional interest groups be explicit about the problems and solutions as they see them from their different vantage points: Often these differences are consciously muted in participative activities because it is felt that voicing them would be contrary to the spirit of cooperation and might be disruptive. In contrast, the workshop approach recognizes that these special interest groups exist and that to pretend that they don't will likely result in half-hearted participation or even eventual sabotage. Interfunctional conflict is managed by permitting questions of clarification only at the early stages of the workshop rather than rushing to consensus. This element of the workshop approach recognizes that provisions for making explicit the observations and expectations of special interest groups also increases the quantity of information available for subsequent design.

An attempt to move the organization from a definition of current problems and opportunities to a definition of a desirable and attainable future: In some instances, workshops focus first on the definition of attainable and desirable futures (rather than reviewing present difficulties), following the logic that turning first to the future is energizing while an initial concentration on current problems might be depressing.

The end product of the workshop approach is the identification of solutions to problems in which all of the major interest groups have had a hand. Concrete activities to move the organization in the direction of the solutions are generally produced, with named individuals taking responsibility for accomplishing specific tasks by particular dates. Conflicting values have been made explicit, consensus has been attained where possible, and members of the organization have taken responsibility themselves for further exploration of innovations and subsequent implementation. The action program often involves several pilot projects—not only one or two—and they proceed within an organizationwide consensus regarding their importance and meaning for the future.

Thus, compared with launching a change effort with a single-site experiment, the workshop approach emphasizes broader participation and a much more thorough exploration in Step 1 of the action cycle. The development of a broad and informed consensus about the forces requiring change and the general direction of change increases organizationwide interest in, and ownership of, the pilot change efforts (relevant to Steps 2 and 3); enhances interest in, and the objectivity of, assessment of the pilot efforts (Step 4); and provides the groundwork for subsequent diffusion and adaptation of the changes (Step 5). Although it often delays somewhat more the beginning of

concrete change, it usually results in better change and a more rapid transformation of the whole company.

### Change at the Level of Domain

In industries in which each company, together with its unions, is free to
establish a unique solution to its shared problems, companywide participation may be adequate. However, organizations that find themselves in tightly
woven relationships with other firms, government regulatory bodies, central
training institutions, central labor organizations, and so forth must bring these
other players along on the same journey if indeed they are going to be able
to continue themselves. Trist (1981: 54) refers to such organizational aggre-
gates as "domains" among which he identifies industrial sectors and singles
out the Norwegian shipping industry as exemplary of an industrial sector in
which problems associated with work redesign could not be effectively
tackled at the level of a single company. Roggema and Smith (1981) make
the same point when they observe that the shipping industry may be rather
unique in the extent to which laws specify the training, qualifications, and
service periods of all employees. In U.S. shipping, laws go even further to
specify work assignments by watch (shift) and to proscribe assignments
outside a seaman's department of assignment. And while some organizational innovations (such as crew continuity) were not much constrained
in Europe by such central institutions, the American situation is even more
difficult due to the more pronounced role of the national unions (in fact,
there are no local unions in American shipping). Not only is rotary assignment to vessels a central value of a number of the American seafaring unions
(which works against the achievement of crew stability), the absence of locals
makes difficult the collaboration of unions with individual experimenting
companies. The national unions try to deal with all their contract companies
on an equal basis and are uncomfortable in working closely with only one or
a few innovating companies.

Internationally, the solution to this puzzle has largely taken two forms:
informal networks of experimenting companies and formal tripartite (labor,
management, government) steering committees. (The Norwegian contact
group appears to be a hybrid form containing elements of both.) Roggema
and Smith (1981: 75) report their dissatisfaction with the formal tripartite
approach on the basis that this approach in European shipping has tended to
protect traditional arrangements as much as it has encouraged innovation.
Their preference was for company networks that offer encouragement to
members who might, at some point, exert some joint influence on the central

institutions. At the time of their writing, Roggema and Smith were unaware of the dramatic influence a tripartite structure was having on the redesign of work in Japanese shipping, through the Committee on the Modernization of the Japanese Seafaring System (Yamanaka and Gaffney, 1988). In the United States, there has been no attempt at an industrywide tripartite committee to deal with this subject; neither has there been any sort of network established between companies. The closest parallel came during the past year in the form of an industry workshop and its aftermath. A review of that event will be instructive.

In recent years, one of the central institutions of this industry, the state and federal maritime academies, has been confused by signals coming from various employers and unions. Traditionally, an understanding existed within the industry about the shipboard organization and seafaring skill requirements for which the schools trained. The traditional consensus has been eroding recently as various companies and unions have begun to experiment with elements of effective manning. Some employers have expected the academies to produce graduates with more general management (rather than technical) expertise (to pick up the decentralized shipboard management team functions mentioned earlier). Others asked the schools to establish or beef up their human resource management curriculum so that their graduates could do a better job in developing and maintaining a high-commitment culture onboard. In still other cases, the schools were being asked to provide more crossover training between deck and engine disciplines so that their graduates could work more flexibly between departments. Additionally, the academies were sometimes being asked to scrap or redesign their paramilitary regimental systems—structures and behaviors that are now seen by some to be antithetical to industry efforts to reduce the barriers between officers and unlicensed seamen and between deck and engine departments.

The Coast Guard (another central institution) is also having some difficulty in that some segments of the industry are asking for relaxation of some of the legislative and regulatory restrictions on the number, qualifications, and use of seamen, while others see no need to change. And these different viewpoints are not divergent only on the basis of management versus union. Frequently, companies have very divergent views, as do the many unions that represent American seafarers. A similar situation existed in West Germany, where one major company, Hapag Lloyd, pushed very hard for the government to switch the training schools over to training general-purpose ratings only. Another line, Hamburg (Sud), worked just as hard against the proposed change. Why the conflict? Hamburg (Sud) runs a fleet of tramping bulk carriers in which hull fabric maintenance (chipping rust and painting) is important because all vessels are always for sale. That firm wanted to employ larger crews of less expensive (less mechanically skilled) traditional seamen. Hapag Lloyd, on the other hand, is a liner (containership) operator with a steady requirement for a fleet of ships. Because these latter ships are not continuously on the market, there is far less concern for how they look and more concern for economy of operation, hence the desire to carry fewer, but cross-trained, seafarers, even at a premium labor rate.

Returning to the U.S. case, this confusion led the federal maritime academy (Kings Point) to send one of its faculty around the country to find out what the industry wanted. The conclusion: Very little agreement existed about the future shipboard organization, and there was, therefore, very little agreement about the type of officers the academies should be training. To move the industry a bit closer to consensus on the topic of future maritime education, the academy asked the Maritime Administration to assist in hosting a conference. The Maritime Administration saw this proposed event as an opportunity to move the industry along on the subject of effective manning generally (not just with regard to training considerations) and suggested that Kings Point involve Gaffney in designing the conference—as they saw this event as a follow-on to an earlier (1983) National Research Council conference for the effective manning study in which Gaffney was the staff officer.

In subsequent meetings between the Maritime Administration, Kings Point, and Cornell University, it was agreed that the objective of the event would not be well served by a traditional conference design in which an industry audience would be invited to hear experts from Europe and Japan relate the wonderful things that were being accomplished overseas. The shortcomings of such a design would have been as follows:

The industry doesn't need more information—they know what is happening abroad.

Being lectured to by overseas experts is beginning to grate a bit on the industry (just as American manufacturers joke about having to sit through another presentation on the Japanese miracle).

Given the "dog and pony show" nature of such presentations (emphasizing the successes and minimizing the difficulties), industry people tend to leave such conferences feeling depressed rather than energized: "That could never work over here—they have so many advantages (laws, unified industry, government assistance, single unions, culture) that we lack—we have too many obstacles (laws, fragmented industry, government neglect, multiple unions, culture, and the like) to overcome in this country."

Therefore, the planners decided to use a search conference workshop design in which the principal objective would be to stimulate action. (Gaffney and his colleagues at Cornell recommended this approach on the bases of experience with somewhat similar activities at the company level and the influence and direct assistance of a visiting scholar from Norway, Morten Levin of the University of Trondheim.) With that action focus in mind, the conference planners designed in the following elements:

All the principal industry elements were to be present (government, management, labor).

Only principals within those elements were to attend (CEOs, union presidents, agency heads), with no cameo appearances—all attendees would participate for the whole time.

Conference designers would attempt to visit all participants in advance of the conference (both to gather suggestions about the design of the conference and to begin a discussion of the issues).

Minimal presentations would be made by "experts." Partly from concern that all participants may not be entirely familiar with developments abroad but also out of the host's desire to focus the discussion on the topic of effective manning (and to avoid digression to such topics as the need for more government subsidy), the workshop began with a review of related developments throughout Europe and Asia. Although no recommendations were made in this opening presentation, it was clear that the unstated message was that effective manning is the important topic for industry to address; this later proved to be a problem.

Aside from the opening address, all information and recommendations were to be developed by the participants.

The special interest groups would first meet to summarize their particular viewpoints as to problems and solutions. The workshop would later progress to mixed groups attempting to reach consensus on solutions.

The workshop would move from identifying current issues to formulating a shared vision of the future.

An intended outcome would be the formation of groups of named individuals who would take responsibility for further action on issues that the industry as a whole had agreed were important.

Letters of invitation from the acting secretary of transportation were mailed to three dozen industry leaders, almost all of whom attended.

At the conclusion of the day-and-a-half event, the conference goal of stimulating action was realized. Five rump groups were formed to continue the discussions begun at the conference. They were charged with considering (1) the means to improve the use of shipboard manning without reducing the size of crews, (2) legislative and regulatory reform required to permit more advanced forms of effective manning, (3) jurisdictional issues associated with multiple unions, (4) how additional cargo might be generated for the U.S. flag fleet, and (5) technological opportunities offered by various "ship of the future" programs.

Some 12 months later, only one of the groups had stalled completely (the multiple-union issue group). Other groups had held a number of meetings, one issuing a report, another holding larger industry review meetings on specific legislative and regulatory reform proposals.

It is too early to thoroughly evaluate this attempt at working the domain issue by means of a search conference approach, but some preliminary observations can be made. In general, the industry participants felt very good about the meeting. They said that, for the first time, the industry was actually doing something about advancing the cause of effective manning.

However, it appears that the lack of follow-on structure may have been a problem. At the conclusion of the conference, the participants were asked if they wanted to form some sort of infrastructure/staffing arrangement to organize and support the five activities they had just sanctioned. The answer was "not yet," probably because they were somewhat enamored of the notion that they had advanced this far by themselves and were concerned that a staff arrangement might remove the principals from active engagement. A year later, some participants are wondering whether that was the right decision, in that some of the activities have slowed, stopped, or at least not been well reported. There has been no coordination of the activities of the rump groups and little communication between them—a role played in Norway by the contact group and WRI. In hindsight, some support structure may have been needed.

But for the most active group, the problem was of a different kind, created by a dramatic change in the composition of the principals. The participating union president died and the Coast Guard admiral was reassigned. The death of this particular union leader was also a major blow to the effort as a whole. He, more so than the other participating union presidents, had been a leading voice on the national scene (he was president of the AFL-CIO Maritime Trades Department) and took a leading role at the conference. The Coast Guard admiral also had been very vocal within the industry and had played a dynamic role at the conference.

Another problem surfaced after the conclusion of the conference. One of the more influential unions withdrew from the rump groups. This was the only union not represented at the conference by its president. Because a scheduling conflict prevented his attendance, he sent both his East Coast and his West Coast vice presidents. The conference designers considered postponing the event, but, given the difficulty of coordinating so many personal schedules, the decision was made to proceed without him. As the conference proceeded, it became clear that these vice presidents could not speak for the missing president. And subsequently it became clear that this president did not share the consensus of the conference participants that the five issues assigned to the rump groups should be explored as they had been.

In retrospect, beginning the conference with an extensive presentation reviewing effective manning developments abroad may have been more of a problem than anticipated. Although it was explicit that participants were not limited to discussions strictly of effective manning (and, in fact, one of the five rump groups focused on the topic of cargo generation), the very focused setup to the conference may have discouraged wider consideration of the ills and cures for this industry. Clearly, some of the unions felt that manning was important, but not to the exclusion of other things also requiring attention. This viewpoint may not have received the time it needed. The conference probably could have elicited more energy and commitment with a broader search.

One other design decision constrained the range of salient topics actually discussed: The union leaders were together for only one rather than two breakout sessions. Some members of the conference design group (and participants interviewed in advance on this issue) felt that two special interest sessions would have locked people into their standard postures and would have stifled creativity and mutuality. In fact, paying insufficient attention to special interest concerns here may have contributed to the fact that at least one of the unions later felt that the conference was somewhat rigged to advance the cause of effective manning (in which labor is often viewed as the main villain) without also examining other areas for industry improvement (in which management and government might take the brunt of blame).

Again, as in the company-level workshops, the design and management of industry-level forums to perform the first step in the action cycle are crucial. They determine whether the necessary energy and consensus are generated to proceed with confidence to the next four steps in the change process. And, while the obstacles to enlisting the right industry participants with the most appropriate discussion agenda can be formidable, there is no substitute for trying and trying and trying again.

| | |
|---|---|
| 1. | Identify topic to study and review relevant knowledge. |
| 2. | Operationalize hypotheses. |
| 3. | Select sample to observe. |
| 4. | Select other research methods, gather data, and generate findings. |
| 5. | Derive and disseminate implications for theory and practice. |

**Figure 8.2.**  Research Cycle

### *Grounding the Research Cycle by Including Elements of Action and Participation*

We have explored how the world of knowledge can be drawn upon to enrich the action cycle. Another strategy toward integrating these two worlds is built on the research cycle presented in Figure 8.2.

The research cycle starts with the identification of a topic or issue to study as well as a review of the relevant knowledge. It proceeds by operationalizing hypotheses or research questions, identifying the sample to study, selecting research methods, gathering data, and generating findings. Finally, it concludes by deriving and disseminating the implications of the study for theory and practice.

What is usually meant by "applied research" relevant to social change is that the researcher in Step 1 identifies a practical problem and in Step 5 emphasizes the implications for practice rather than for theory. These also are the two steps that more frequently include participants from the world of action; however, participation can occur at any of the five steps.

We explore these possibilities by reviewing the evolution of policy research efforts in the U.S. shipping industry. We are interested in how research grounded by the participation of the actors themselves can complement the action research strategies already reported.

Some research efforts to promote organizational change in shipping did not employ action research methods of any kind and were noteworthy in the degree to which they were not acted upon. More common in the late 1960s and early 1970s in Europe, and more recently in Japan and in the United States, these research projects consisted of stand-alone attitude surveys, interview studies, and work load modeling (all of which culminated in the form of written reports) and engaged practitioners not at all or only to a very limited extent. The reports of such research were usually ignored by industry. More dramatically, they sometimes resulted in political disputes that further polarized the various industry interest groups.

The NRC Committee on Effective Manning represented a modest departure from the strict research model, but its gestures to participation and action were relatively weak and, therefore, its impact was limited. In 1982, the Maritime Administration, concerned with the dwindling size of the U.S. fleet, asked the NRC to propose more effective crewing structures for American merchant vessels. Contributing factors to that decline, it was felt, were the comparatively large size of American crews, the transient nature of employment, and the relatively inflexible manner in which work was organized and accomplished aboard ship. The Maritime Administration and some parts of the industry had become aware of progress being made by other high-cost maritime nations in the development of new and more efficient crewing structures.

The NRC established a committee with both industry and academic participation to work the problem. Unfortunately, the practitioners were in the minority on the committee and were selected partially on the basis of their remove from industry. One of the two participating managers was retired, and union concerns were to be voiced by a lawyer for a union-supported lobby group.

Members of the effective manning committee felt keenly that the committee would not have significant impact on U.S. manning practices by merely issuing the report on its findings and recommendations. They persuaded the NRC and the Maritime Administration to hold a conference for representatives of interested industry groups before the report was finalized. This did not entail much arm-twisting, as NRC was, at this time, actively encouraging its committees to make presentations of its recommendations to sponsors.

The conference was fairly well attended by shipowners, top union officials, and representatives of the Maritime Administration and the Coast Guard, and the discussion was productive. A search conference model was proposed for this conference, but the NRC felt that this relatively open-ended design might not produce enough industry comment on the draft contents of the committee's report. Therefore, a more tightly scripted design was employed in which the conference participants heard two keynote presentations by members of the committee (researchers), and then broke up into small groups to address a number of issues identified by the committee in its trip to Europe and earlier distributed to the conference attendees in the form of a working document. There was no attempt to get this industry group to develop its own agenda, arrive at a consensus, or take personal responsibility for following through on any such decisions. However, the conference did play a role in encouraging action research, which prompted two of the participating CEOs subsequently to initiate projects in their companies.

The committee also saw the need for a series of industry-level forums to identify and address common problems, including the need for reform in the shipboard organization, and, therefore, it hoped that this initial conference would be followed up by further industry-level meetings over the next two years. Unfortunately, no follow-up in this spirit occurred until the Kings Point search conference described earlier.

Thus the NRC Committee on Effective Manning followed basically the research cycle in Figure 8.2, with only token participation of stakeholder group representatives at research Steps 1 through 4. In the future, such projects, which have as their primary objective the production of general knowledge that will be acted upon, should include more influential representatives of more of the stakeholder groups. At Step 5, the breadth of participation was meaningful but insufficiently sustained to have any impact. This shortcoming underscores how the dissemination of knowledge and diffusion of innovation can depend upon the existence of continuing mechanisms that enable stakeholder groups to deal with each other on matters of common interest.

The bottom line is that knowledge produced in the NRC manning study and other research projects with little or no industry involvement (other than as subjects) tends to produce little or no action. That observation, and corresponding recommendation, were made by another National Research Council study: "The review of research programs overseas suggests that their success depends critically on the degree to which companies—both individually and jointly—initiate, manage, and review them" (NRC, 1983: 44). "The ship operations R & D program of the Maritime Administration has not achieved wide acceptance of its project results, principally because of insufficient industry participation in the direction and management of research" (NRC, 1983: 2).

A recommendation of yet another National Research Council committee is that "MarAd should broaden its efforts to stimulate industry to form collaborative mechanisms for the support and conduct of research and innovation" (NRC, 1987). This is easier said than done, however, as the fragmentation of this industry in this country has proven to be a formidable obstacle in achieving collaboration on a number of issues, research being only one.

It appears that the NRC now appreciates the need for a differential approach to practitioner involvement based upon the nature of the question being asked and an awareness of who it is that might be expected to act on the results of a study. The composition of a current NRC committee (working on the safety implications of reduced crews) is a definite improvement in terms of practitioner involvement, although, in this case, the sponsor (the Coast Guard) might have more opportunity to act on the results than did the Maritime Administration in the case of the effective manning study. In any event, this latter committee is constituted primarily of practitioners—active managers and trade union leaders.

Both the Maritime Administration and the NRC have attempted to encourage industry (and government) action by providing for industry review events at the conclusion of their studies, such as the one pioneered by the Committee on Effective Manning. The Maritime Administration now builds into its research contracts requirements for researchers to make presentations to industry conferences; and, as indicated earlier, the NRC actively encourages its committees to make personal presentations of its recommendations rather than to rely strictly on the written report.

In recent years, the Maritime Administration has shifted its focus in this matter of manning innovation from sponsorship of applied research to promotion of action research. In those applied research projects that remain, the agency has attempted to increase the extent of practitioner involvement by adding to the evaluation criteria used to judge competing proposals the presence and strength of "industry advisory groups" established by researchers to guide and contribute to the project. This is an improvement, no doubt, but, because it is the researchers who sanction the industry advisory groups and not the other way around, the efficacy of this approach to gaining practitioner involvement is somewhat in doubt (NRC, 1983: 13). But, once again, easier said than done; unfortunately, there is no preexisting industry reference group to play the more desired proactive role.

### *Lessons for a Theory of Participatory Action Research*

To summarize the potential for integrating action and research cycles, it is useful to lay them out in parallel (Figure 8.3).

Each step of the research process can be viewed as potentially contributing to, or being informed by, the corresponding aspect of the action process. At each stage, broadening the pattern of participation can potentially strengthen both the knowledge and the action outcomes.

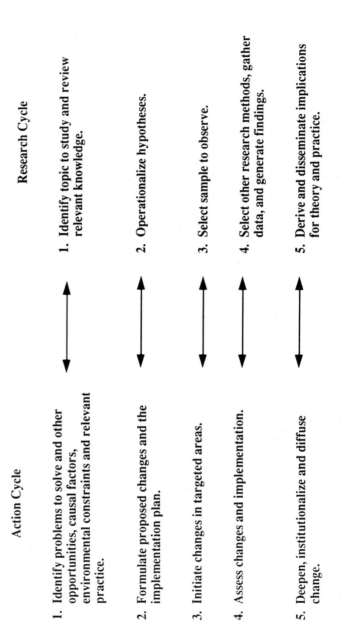

**Action Cycle**

1. Identify problems to solve and other opportunities, causal factors, environmental constraints and relevant practice.

2. Formulate proposed changes and the implementation plan.

3. Initiate changes in targeted areas.

4. Assess changes and implementation.

5. Deepen, institutionalize and diffuse change.

**Research Cycle**

1. Identify topic to study and review relevant knowledge.

2. Operationalize hypotheses.

3. Select sample to observe.

4. Select other research methods, gather data, and generate findings.

5. Derive and disseminate implications for theory and practice.

**Figure 8.3.** Action, Research, and their Potential Integration

**Why Action Research?**

The shipping industry story demonstrates the potential reciprocal flows between social theory and social change.

First, the Norwegian and American change efforts provide powerful examples of how researchers can draw upon theory and prior research to propose hypotheses, such as the systemic nature of organizations, that guide action. These cases illustrate how researchers can inject the spirit and techniques of inquiry that enrich the search for solutions and can shape norms that provide for objective and credible assessments. Researchers also have facilitated events, such as the ship-meets-ship conferences, that provide for direct transfer of social technology. In addition, the researcher role has provided continuity, sometimes serving as the social memory when turnover occurs among managers and union officers.

Second, the shipping case demonstrates how third-party action roles can contribute to the research process and the knowledge it generates. We have already noted the intimate familiarity with an industry that action researchers can gain in their dual roles and how it enhances the validity of their research. Also, the realization by action researchers that they will be judged first on relevance (by the world of action) and only later on elegance (by the world of knowledge) galvanizes their concern about the validity of their observations.

A pattern of intellectual activities with dual purposes has certain efficiency and practical advantages, not the least of which is access. One may have better access to certain types of data as an action researcher consultant than strictly as a researcher. Participants who view themselves as "clients" (rather than as "subjects") often are more highly motivated to ensure that all of the relevant data get on the table; moreover, the amount of investment that "clients" are willing to make and the quality of their attention are often higher. The tendency for participants in an action research project to be active and challenging and to provide on-line feedback about the relevance of ideas can be an asset for the party interested in formulating general knowledge. In addition, resources are saved by shortening the feedback cycle by which general ideas are formulated, tested, and revised. Much of the data gathering has dual relevance, and so does some of the analysis and conceptual work.

The WRI researchers' role in Norwegian shipping and Gaffney's role in American shipping both illustrate these practical advantages. In addition, Walton's role in assisting the NRC Committee on Effective Manning to make policy recommendations contributed greatly to his research effort to build a theory of industrial innovative capability. It was clearly more efficient: He was totally freed of concern with the logistics of arranging travel and scheduling three dozen meetings with approximately 100 practitioners in six countries. It was also more effective: He gained direct personal access to labor leaders, shipowners, and government officials in those six countries—access of a quantity and quality he could never have arranged as an independent scholar. And in that respect, his theory-oriented agenda clearly benefited from the dual-purpose nature of this particular action research project.

## Why Participatory Action Research?

It is now conventional wisdom that broader participation can lead to stronger consensus for change and sounder models—because models arrived at through broader participation are likely to integrate the interests of more stakeholder groups. Participation also promotes continual adjustment and reinvention—because there is greater overlap in the populations involved in the planning, execution, experience, evaluation, and modification of the organizational innovations.

The shipping industry case demonstrates that participation has not only a horizontal dimension (entailing interest groups at the level of the firm) but also a vertical (cross-level) dimension. Thus the lesson of both the Norwegian and the American change efforts is that broad and inclusive participation at the pilot ship level is necessary but insufficient. Effective change in the long run requires the involvement of company-level actors and industry-level actors. Moreover, participation at both the company level and the industry level must be sufficiently broad to ensure that actions taken on these two levels support the shipboard innovations. In the shipping industry, these actions range from supportive company policies to appropriate national training curricula to enabling legislation.

## The Future Challenge

We believe that we are still low in the learning curve regarding our knowledge as to how the action and research cycles can benefit from one another—and from greater participation. In the relatively short history of action research, there may be something of a progression in the variable weighting of the elements of action, research, and participation—at least at the level of an industrial sector:

First, there is research—but little action. We might call this stage *learning without practice,* and it is characteristic of a pretakeoff stage in which increased participation of companies and unions is required to generate action.

Then there is a period of action research in which the principal issue seems to be the degree of participation within experimental units, between experimental units, and at the level of domains. *Limited participation* at this stage extracts a cost in terms of the quality of the content innovation and the likelihood of implementation or diffusion.

Finally (especially if the domain issue has been well addressed), there is a tendency to shift into a largely action mode, with the research component given short shrift. Such *innovation without spirit of inquiry* may lead to losses in organizational performance (safety, productivity, quality, job satisfaction) in that content changes are adopted piecemeal, out of context, or without ownership on the part of those who are most directly affected.

For action researchers working in industrial sectors that are in, or are approaching, this third stage, the agenda is clear: to develop methods of participatory action research that are less expensive and then to get the information out to the second tier.

## *References*

GAFFNEY, M. E. (1989) Effective Manning at American President Lines. Washington, DC: Department of Transportation, Maritime Administration, Government Printing Office.

KATZ, H., T. KOCHAN, and J. KEEFE (1988) "Industrial relations and productivity in the U.S. automobile industry." Brookings Papers on Economic Activity 3: 685-715.

National Research Council (1983) Requirements for a Ship Operations Research Program. Washington, DC: National Academy Press.

National Research Council (1984) Effective Manning of the U.S. Merchant Fleet. Washington, DC: National Academy Press.

National Research Council (1987) Strategies to Improve R & D and Its Implementation in the Maritime Industries. Washington, DC: National Academy Press.

ROGGEMA, J. and M. H. SMITH (1981) "On the process of organizational change in shipping," in Proceedings of Ergosea '81. London: Nautical Institute.

ROGGEMA, J. and M. H. SMITH (1983) "Organizational change in the shipping industry: issues in the transformation of basic assumptions." Human Relations 36(8): 765-790.

THORSRUD, E. (1981) "Policy-making as a learning process in working life," pp. 313-326 in B. Gardell and G. Johanson (eds.) Working Life. London: John Wiley.

TRIST, E. (1981) The Evolution of Socio-Technical Systems: A Conceptual Framework and an Action Research Program. Toronto: Ontario Ministry of Labour, Ontario Quality of Working Life Centre.

WALTON, R. E. (1975) "The diffusion of new work structures: explaining why success didn't take." Organizational Dynamics (Winter).

WALTON, R. E. [with C. ALLEN and M. GAFFNEY] (1987) Innovating to Compete: Lessons for Diffusing and Managing Change in the Workplace. San Francisco: Jossey-Bass.

YAMANAKA, K. and M. E. GAFFNEY (1988) Effective Manning in Asia. Washington, DC: Department of Transportation, Maritime Administration, Government Printing Office.

# 9

# *Cogenerative Learning*

## *Bringing Participation into Action Research*

MAX ELDEN
MORTEN LEVIN

> If you want to understand what a science is you should look in the first
> instance not at its theories or findings and certainly not at what its apologists
> say about it; you should look at what the practitioners of it do.
>
> Geertz (1973: 5)

According to Rapoport (1970), action research (AR) is a strategy for using scientific methods to solve practical problems in a way that contribute to general social science theory and knowledge. This strategy leads to several dilemmas. The two most relevant to our concern here are what Rapoport calls the dilemmas of AR's "goals" and "initiative." Each represents a choice between polar opposites. The first revolves around the choice between scientific rigor (at the expense of practical relevance) versus practical problem-solving relevance (at the cost of scientific validity). The second deals with the problem of who takes the initiative to bring forth the problem.

AUTHORS' NOTE: We would like to thank Richard Ault, R. J. Bullock, Michael Gaffney, Davydd Greenwood, Pamela Kennedy, and Ann Martin for thoughtful and useful reactions to earlier versions of this chapter.

It is either a researcher operating out of a disciplinary/theoretical framework or a person with a real-world problem stated in everyday language. Involvement of the participant from the research situation in the action research process moderates both these dilemmas. So one source for understanding participatory action research (PAR) is understanding AR.

In this chapter, we describe one way of defining and doing PAR. We have our doubts about the possibility and utility of general, abstract theory in solving real problems in a specific context or situation. As in AR, knowledge in PAR is context bound (Susman and Evered, 1978). Thus we reflect on, systematize, and generalize from our own experience as researchers in the context of doing PAR. We develop a model, new terms, and a set of concepts for describing what we do in situations where we attempt to create new knowledge in active collaboration with the people who live in that situation. They are not "subjects," or "clients," or "data sources," they are "colearners." In trying to understand our own reality as PAR researchers, we hope to contribute to the ability of others trying this approach to democratizing work life.

We believe that our approach is typical and quite consistent with that of our Scandinavian colleagues (see, for example, the chapter by Karlsen in this volume and references to the work of Gustavsen and Thorsrud). We cite their work as well as that in other countries that supports and illustrates our "language."

### What is PAR in Scandinavia?
### Notes on a Model

Political values concerning increased democracy, political equality, and social justice are at the center of PAR efforts in Scandinavian work life. To realize these values, PAR researchers in Norway use sociotechnical systems (STS) thinking (often in projects with a strong component of technological change) to create more workplace democracy and self-management. We have contributed to and been influenced by the evolution of AR into PAR in Norway as a part of a strategy to reform work life since the early 1970s. This is more fully described elsewhere (Elden, 1979; Gustavsen and Hunnius, 1981; Gustavsen, 1985) but we can note here some of the key features of work life research in Norway.

As Scandinavian PAR professionals aiming to contribute to major reforms in work life, we are a long way from being detached, "value-neutral" individual scientists. For us and many of our colleagues, PAR in Norwegian work life means researchers who have

(1) clear value commitments to democratization as well as economic improvement—people have a right to "good"-quality jobs;

(2) a vision of the "good organization"—that is, one based on self-management, development of human potential, power equalization, and democratic principles;

(3) well-developed and proven tools, concepts, and ways of working founded on sociotechnical systems thinking that can be used to (re)design organizations to achieve our visions and values;

(4) a shared tradition of a way of working, a vocabulary, and a network of collegial relations and support structures mostly in the form of well-financed public or nonprofit research institutes;

(5) a researcher role of "colearner" rather than of "expert in charge of change" in which the researcher's expertise includes the ability to "fade out" as participants take charge of their own learning; and

(6) an extensive formal political infrastructure supporting participation in work life as reflected in specific labor legislation, national labor-management agreements, and industrial relations and traditions in Norwegian work life.

Our model of participatory action research should be understood in this context. Most of the projects we have done were institutionally based, involved long-term relationships with the participants, and were to some degree publicly financed. No project lasted less than two years, and we have had relationships that have lasted as long as five years. We have worked in cooperative labor-management projects (Elden, 1979; Levin and Skorstad, 1975), in projects exclusively for unions (Elden et al., 1980; Levin et al., 1980; Levin, 1981; Levin and Kaul, 1984; Levin and Havn, 1985), and in local communities (Levin, 1988; Levin et al., 1989). Our projects do not generate "data" in the usual sense of what independent reviewers can use to validate our conclusions. They are the basis for the concepts and ideas that we have developed and systematized in the form of a model of PAR. Our main purpose is to create concepts that clarify PAR and its praxis and not to prove a position through empirical evidence.

**Cogenerative Learning in PAR**

Our model of PAR rests on "insiders" (local participants) and "outsiders" (the professional researchers) collaborating in cocreating "local theory" that

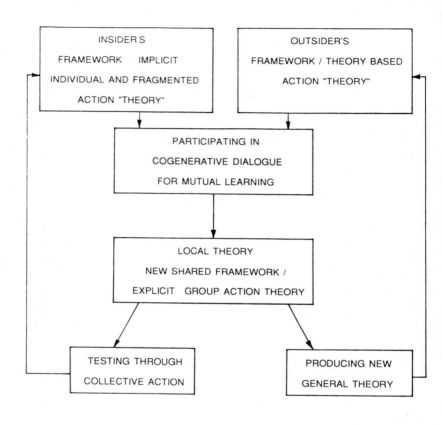

**Figure 9.1.** A Model of A Participative Action Research Scandinavia Style: The Cogenerative Way

the participants test out by acting on it. The results can be fed back to improve the participants' own "theory" and can further generate more general ("scientific") theory. The elements in our PAR model are illustrated in Figure 9.1.

The basic idea behind our version of PAR is that those who supply the data have their own ideas, models, or frameworks for attributing meaning and explanations to the world they experience. Those who spend their work lives in a particular organization get to know more about it and have more ways of making sense of their world than would be possible for an outsider to appreciate without in some way becoming an insider. But "going native" is an expensive, time-consuming, and unnecessarily indirect strategy for researchers to reform work life. Our point is that the researcher has no legitimate monopoly on explaining social worlds or making sense or reality interpretations.

In Berger and Luckmann's (1971) apt phrase: Reality is socially constructed. This means that a scientist's theory about your world is not necessarily more valid or true than your own theory of your world. Both theories are social products that can be improved through investigation and testing. The difference between the two socially created realities is both the methods used to create them (everyday, "espoused" thinking versus data-based scientific methodology) and their formal presentation (informal, "natural," everyday language versus highly stylized, formal forms of scientific discourse). Theory is influenced by the local situation in which it is created. PAR is a way of learning how to explain a particular social world by working with the people who live in it to construct, test, and improve theories about it so they can better control it. We are interested in theories that help people learn how to better control the circumstances of their lives. Workplaces can be powerful sources of learning for empowerment and democratization.

Research is a particular way of systematic learning. PAR gives us a new answer to the question: Who learns from the research? The answer in nonaction, nonparticipatory research is clear. Only the researcher or those who can extract meaning from research reports (largely other researchers) learn, not the "subjects." Participatory action research means that all relevant stakeholders do what only researchers usually do. It can be seen primarily as a learning strategy for empowering participants and only secondarily as producing "research" in the conventional sense.

PAR as learning empowers in three ways. First, it empowers because of the specific insights, new understandings, and new possibilities that the participants discover in creating better explanations about their social world. Second, participants learn how to learn. This is what Argyris and Schön (1978) identify as deutero-learning. Third, PAR can be liberating in Brown and Tandon's (1983) sense of participative research when participants learn how to create new possibilities for action.

Compared with conventional research, in PAR, the roles of practitioners and professional researchers are quite different. This makes analyzing and assessing or even talking about the equality in inquiry that we experience in PAR difficult. We have tried to overcome this in other contexts by talking about "colearning," "participant-managed inquiry," or "client as consultant." In this chapter, we think the terms for describing what the two different kinds of participants bring to the party should be *insider* versus *outsider frameworks*. By *framework* we mean a way of understanding, a language, or a cognitive map. The richness and quality of the research depends on the ability of the insiders and the outsiders to play their different frameworks and expertise against each other to create a new, third explanatory framework. This new way of looking at things would not necessarily have been predicted from any of the initial frameworks. PAR is a way of generating new knowledge where the participants in the research process function as equals because of their different kinds of expertise and frames of reference. Each of the two types of participants in the research process has its own expertise and "frame" as the point of departure in creating a shared framework or "local theory."

*Insiders* (employees and others who experience the workplace directly) are expert in the specifics of the setting or situation and know from personal experience how things work and how the elements are connected to each other and about values and attitudes, local company culture, and so on. This knowledge tends to be highly individual, nonsystemic, tacit, and unreflected upon. Insiders are primarily concerned about a "science" of their own particular situation. They want to solve practical problems and achieve personal and organizational goals. The initial framework of what will become local theory comes from how individual organization members make sense out of their situation. They are experts in the particular situation but their theories are not systematically tested.

*Outsiders* (researchers and the external "experts") have what's missing: training in systematic inquiry and analysis, in designing and carrying out research, and in recognizing patterns and creating new knowledge irrespective of content. Our PAR professional must also have a high level of interpersonal skills and be able to design and manage learning events. The researcher's initial framework of what will become local theory is based on general theory or a particular way of thinking about the problem at hand. How do researchers and social scientists make sense out of this kind of situation?

The insider comes to the inquiry because of a personal interest in a specific practical problem. The outsider, in contrast, comes because of an interest in solving particular kinds of problems (in theory and/or practice), methods, general knowledge, or values. The researcher's framework will be different:

more explicit, full of ideas about how things could hang together, with lots of abstract concepts, and a high degree of formalism. The outsider's concern is basically relating to the research community in creating scientific theory, using acceptable methods, and communicating through publication (Kalleberg, 1989). The researcher is the linchpin so that what he or she learns contributes to accumulation of knowledge above and beyond a local, "context-bound" situation.

We have described the "what" and the "who" of participatory action research. Let us now turn to the "how." What is needed is a connection between insiders and outsiders that integrates their different forms of expertise and different initial frameworks to generate a third framework or "practical theory" of the local situation. We aim at a partnership in which insiders become more theoretical about their practice and outsiders more practical about their theory. This occurs by participating in what we call a "cogenerative dialogue."

### Learning Through Participating in Cogenerative Dialogue

"Participation" is a powerful but slippery concept. As Pateman (1970) makes clear, participation is a necessary but not sufficient condition for democracy. In her terms, we mean "full" rather than "pseudo-" or "partial" participation in our definition of participation in PAR. Participation within a nondemocratic structure is possible, and organizational designs for "high-performance systems" and the like can be quite humanizing without being democratizing (Elden, 1981).

Thus the degree and nature of "participation" in all phases of participatory action research is a critical factor. Not all participation is empowering. Participation must be full participation or a form of "codetermination" if it is to be empowering. This is consistent with Brown and Tandon's (1983) emphasis on participants being in charge of the inquiry. Participants create new meaning in their own terms through a learning process that follows the basic tenets of research design and methods. The insiders are not simply sources of data or sanctioners of studies and reports but actively help create and codetermine in every phase of the research process—especially in creating new meaning. (See Elden, 1985, and Jan Irgens Karlsen in this volume.) They are not merely consulted in each phase of knowledge production; they participate as cocreators. We call this *empowering participation.*

Empowering (i.e., codeterminative and with learning) participation in action research does not mean that every single person in an organization is decisively involved in every phase of the research process. Because PAR builds on learning by doing research within the context experienced by participants, the size of most companies poses problems in carrying out PAR. Indeed, in all of our projects dealing with large organizations, the actual research work is done by a small work group. In all but the smallest organizations, PAR is a representative form of participation in which all stakeholder interests and points of view are included. In Scandinavia, this means worker representatives, union representatives, and representatives of several levels of management, including, of course, top management at least at times. We have elsewhere reviewed the new methods and techniques of involving large numbers of participants in PAR (Elden, 1985; Gustavsen and Engelstad, 1985).

Empowering participation occurs between insiders and outsiders in what we call *cogenerative dialogue*. Both insiders and outsiders operate out of their initial frames of reference but communicate at a level where frames can be changed and new frames generated. Exchange on a level that affects one's frame of reference is a much more demanding form of communication than mere information exchange.

In the beginning of a project, participants have little experience in empowering forms of participation. We tend to move from partial to full participation. Participants seem to need some time to learn about their own source of expertise, and its importance, and how to be colearners in creating a new, shared framework. We develop relationships to insiders in the design phase that are like the relations we have to undergraduates. By the end of the design phase in our most successful projects, the insiders act more like graduate students doing their own research. Then comes a period of keeping in close enough touch that we can help them avoid pitfalls they might not know about (e.g., lack of systematic data, bias, incomparability), but, for the most part, they operate so autonomously that we often have to ask to be consulted. Participation means that the researcher also has to participate! In the final stages, the insiders take the lead in creating new knowledge. In this way, the dialogue becomes truly "cogenerative" (Levin et al., 1980; Greenwood, 1989).

What we call *cogenerative dialogue* seems necessary in any form of liberating learning. Paulo Freire (1972: 136) argues for a dialogical relationship that is characterized by "subjects who meet to *name* the world in order to transform it." In the development of local theory, the dialogue between the "teacher" and the participants is crucial. The knowledge generating process should proceed under local control. A teacher-controlled dialogue would never create new local theories based on participants' gradually improved theory-creating competence. The balance between mentoring and the participant's control over the knowledge-generating process is always complex. There is no simple solution for this problem of maintaining a proper balance.

Oddly enough, for a communication process aimed at empowerment, power equality, and democracy, inequality is a hallmark of the dialogical relationship. Insiders and outsiders have different power and knowledge bases. The outside expert has much more powerful and explicit "sense-making" models. Indeed, a researcher could be said to be in the business of being a professional sense-maker. The Norwegian sociologist Bråthen (1973, 1986, 1988) calls this dominance situation "model monopoly." Researchers have the most relevant training and specialized education and the most influential position, so they have a model monopoly in the sense that their way of thinking may dominate the dialogue.

How can the researcher's "model monopoly"—which is part of being a researcher—be overcome? It is not enough to bring insiders and outsiders together and hope for a happy and spontaneously created cogenerative dialogue. Overcoming the researchers' model monopoly is one of the real challenges for a PAR practitioner. The threat of model dominance must always be considered, and planning and action must be reviewed against this challenge.

The question of model monopoly is seldom reflected upon in the literature on dialogical relationships. Nor is it as yet much considered among PAR researchers. Gustavsen's idea of "democratic dialogue" in Scandinavian PAR is quite similar to ours (Gustavsen, 1985). He builds partly on the philosophical thinking of Habermas, postulating nine criteria for evaluating the degree of democracy in a dialogue aimed at democratizing work (Gustavsen, 1985: 474-475):

The dialogue is a process of exchange: points and arguments move to and fro between the participants.

All concerned must have the possibility to participate.

Possibilities for participation are, however, not enough: Everybody should also be active in the discourse.

As a point of departure, all participants are equal.

Work experience is the foundation for participation.

At least some of the experience which each participant has when he or she enters the dialogue must be considered legitimate.

It must be possible for everybody to develop an understanding of the issue at stake.

All arguments which pertain to issues under discussion are—as a point of departure—legitimate.

The dialogue must continuously produce agreements which can provide a platform for investigation and practical action.

His criteria are more systematic and extensive than ours and guarantee a set of procedural rights that protect stakeholders and relevant arguments from being left out, keep the exchange focused on relevant workplace issues and experience, and result in action. The researcher's job is to guarantee procedural purity. He or she does not interfere with content—that is completely the participants' job. In democratic dialogue, the researcher controls procedure but is not supposed to participate in creating content. This is one solution to the problem of researcher model monopoly. But it is costly. Participants may well spend significant resources to discover for themselves what could be easily available from a knowledgeable outsider.

Argyris and Schön (1977, 1978) also have a theory of change based on a special form of dialogue. They have developed specific and elaborate rules for communication between the researcher and the client. People are trained to be more skillfully self-reflective in perfecting a personal action theory. As one develops the ability to minimize the gap between what one says and what one does, one learns how to learn in a way that seems to approximate the scientific method. As a result, one is not limited by the trainer's models. Recently, Argyris (1985) has developed organizationally based action maps that seem similar to our idea of a new shared framework or group cognitive map. A key difference appears to be not so much in the product as in the process of dialogue.

Our theory, based on our practice, is that we intentionally and strongly influence content. We are always seeking opportunities to bring forth more self-managed forms of organization. Our experience indicates that, if we do not contribute ideas from sociotechnical systems thinking and organization design to the dialogue, then they tend not to appear in the results. Of course, this does not mean that these ideas necessarily are accepted. But elements from our initial framework usually appear in the resulting framework.

What's important is that the arena for possible action has been enlarged because ideas from our framework have been seriously considered. In addition, the challenge of model monopoly has to be resolved. The contradiction between the outsider's responsibility for introducing ideas and concepts and planning a learning process and the participants' control and active influence in framing the new knowledge that is developed must always be resolved based on the participants' values and interests. This contradiction is necessary and is actually the core of the cogenerative dialogue.

In brief, in our way of working, the dialogue becomes an arena in which participation by insiders and outsiders enriches all phases of the research process because of the intermingling of at least two sets of frameworks that contribute to creating a new, third framework or "local theory."

### Local Theory:
### The New Shared Framework

The idea of local theory initially emerged in the mid-1970s in the first project exploring the idea of participant-managed organizational self-study and change (Elden, 1979, 1981, 1983). The insiders in dialogue with a team of outside researchers designed an inquiry aimed at diagnosing the insider's organization. The key breakthrough for our purpose here was creating what we now call a "cogenerative dialogue": We all cooperated to generate a concise and coherent explanation of why things were as they were in the organization. This explanation was not the result of a re-searcher model monopoly because making sense out of the data was a joint task. The new explanation did not emerge only from the insiders' or the outsiders' initial frameworks. The two frameworks were merged to create a new framework that went beyond them.

The "theory" that emerged from this early form of PAR showed that frontline workers had a richer cognitive map about their workplace—the subject of the study—than their managers, but they did not have the authority to change things (Elden, 1979). In our collaboration on the first PAR project in the mid-1970s, Phil Herbst called the insiders' explanation a "local" theory. He wanted to distinguish it from a social scientist's explanations, which took the form of more general, abstract theory.

In our model, initial insider and outsider frameworks are the points of departure in generating a new, third framework or "theory" that integrates the first two and more. This new framework could not be predicted from either one or both of the initial frameworks. In sum, a local theory is situation specific but is generated in part from general knowledge and the rules of scientific inquiry. A local theory then is the most direct, simple, and elegant context-bound explanation of cause-and-effect relations in a given situation that makes sense to those with the most local experience. It could be described as a causally focused, group cognitive map (Eden, 1988) using everyday language and meanings generated by "insiders" in dialogue with "outsiders."

The generation of local theory is empowering because those who create it learn why things are as they are, and this naturally leads to ideas about change. It is like problem solving: identifying underlying causes of what is problematic. Given that a good job is done on this, the solution is usually self-evident. So too with the action implications of theory generation in PAR. To implement what the participants think they have learned in more formal terms, "theory testing" becomes a natural next step in learning. Participants want to test their theory in action.

In one of our earlier projects (Levin, 1980), the research question was how the local union should try to cope with problems raised by new technology. We started by helping workers study how the technological changes in the last 20 years had affected working conditions. They found that there had been a reduction of the job skills needed by workers, a sharp reduction of the number of workers, and an improved physical work environment. Another lesson was that technology in itself never determined the working conditions but that the effects were also caused by the organization of work. This evidence generated activity for influencing technological development. The strategic and action-relevant knowledge consisted of several elements. One was to obtain information about planned changes as early as possible. Another was to involve the workers affected by technological change actively in the planning process. A third was to organize the union's work so that workers could develop their own skills and also work out a basis for identifying their own interests regarding the introduction of new technology. The end product of this research was the local union's strategic initiative to develop a new organizational structure in the company, giving workers the possibility to participate in all technological changes.

A lesson learned from our local community development projects was a dramatic change in how the participants viewed their position as actors in a change process. "What we learned was that we could do something by ourselves, and not just sit back and wait for other people to solve our problems" (Levin et al., 1989). This fundamental change in thinking came along through several years' effort to establish new economic activity.

*Theory Testing Through*
*Collective Action*

A new local theory can be viewed as the learning that occurred through cogenerative dialogue. This local theory should be action relevant. It should help solve the practical problems that participants found important enough to study. But action also means testing and improving the local theory. Evaluation of the results leads to new, improved local theory. Reflection and action form a cyclic process that gradually improves knowledge and creates useful results. When we move from reflection and analysis into action and development, the insiders will usually lead the way.

In our experience, testing has always been a form of collective action. By *collective,* we mean that all stakeholders exercise informal choice and that there is a form of consensus about what changes are to be tested. There must be a mechanism to sanction meaningful trials where changes in existing authority relations are not off limits. In Scandinavia, *collective* means virtually automatic union involvement from the very beginning. We are not sure how PAR should function where workers have no independent voice in the form of a union. In our projects, action planning was always based on joint decision making. In our union projects in which management was not part of the research process, collective action occurred because the union could not implement any results of the research without management's agreement.

Our union research produced two important action results (Levin, 1980). First, the union stopped the introduction of new technology both by taking advantage of Norwegian legislation and by agreements on worker participation. Second, the union negotiated an agreement with management to get extensive rights to information and participation in the introduction of new technology. The collectivity—in this case, in the form of union power—was a key to success, seen from the union's side.

*Generating Scientific Theories*

In our model of the PAR process, theory does not remain local. The goal is to solve practical problems *and* develop new or improved scientific findings and theory. A scientist works under a specific paradigm that defines relevant theory, research methods, and ethics; a specified mode of operation in doing research; and a common technical language (Kuhn, 1962). The scientist is expected to produce knowledge according to specific standards and to communicate it to other colleagues in the scientific community. Thus a minimum requirement for the PAR professional is to generate general theory and findings that are communicated in scientific papers, books, and journals.

What scientific knowledge has been produced through PAR?

We can identify three categories of theory production. The richest one is concerned with reflection on metascientific problems regarding the PAR process. Gustavsen (1985), Eden (1985), Levin (1985), and Whyte (1989) all provide examples of "theory" dealing with either the basis for PAR or trying to develop a taxonomy of PAR. The second group of publications deals with specific social problems and the new knowledge generated in this process (Brown and Tandon, 1983; Elden, 1985; Greenwood, 1989; Levin et al., 1980; Walton and Gaffney, 1989). Most of this work is based on case studies, which are the primary source of data in PAR. The third group of work based on PAR is strictly academic-oriented theory production. One example of this is a theory of the fundamentals for trade union influence in the introduction of new technology (Levin, 1981).

### Conclusion

Although PAR and cogenerated learning may help to overcome Rapoport's dilemmas, we have discovered that PAR produces new dilemmas. Our candidates for the most intriguing dilemmas of PAR are control, limited learning, and elitism. The main idea behind PAR is building up more democratic forms of organization and management. The control dilemma is that, even though participants are to be in charge of the research process, the researcher cannot give up control completely. The researcher has other goals beyond local theory and has special competence to achieve them. The dilemma of limited learning is that only a few participants are actively involved in producing new knowledge, but PAR aims at more widespread learning. The dilemma of elitism is that, while PAR intends to empower the many to more self-management, it operates to recruit new managers. At best, this is a form of democratic elitism. We offer these dilemmas as issues for further consideration.

Our main effort here has been to systematize and explicate a model of our way of doing participant-managed action research. In our model, cogenerative learning produces local theory as a basis for collective action. We believe this model to be more generally relevant where people with different forms of expertise and frames of reference collaborate in creating a common conceptual field that makes possible collective action. The key is overcoming the expert's monopoly in defining what is possible for others. Cogenerating local theory opens up new possibilities for the possible.

## References

ARGYRIS, C. (1985) "Making knowledge more relevant to practice: maps for action," in E. Lawler et al. (eds.) Doing Research That Is Useful for Theory and Practice. San Francisco: Jossey-Bass.

ARGYRIS, C. and D. SCHÖN (1977) Theory in Practice Increasing Professional Effectiveness. San Francisco: Jossey-Bass.

ARGYRIS, C. and D. SCHÖN (1978) Organizational Learning. Reading, MA: Addison-Wesley.

BERGER, P. and T. LUCKMANN (1971) The Social Construction of Reality. Harmondsworth, England: Penguin.

BRÅTHEN, S. (1973) "Model monopoly and communication systems: theoretical notes on democratization." Acta Sociologica 16 (2): 98-107.

BRÅTHEN, S. (1986) "Paradigms of autonomy, dialogical or monological," Department of Sociology, University of Oslo.

BRÅTHEN, S. (1988) "Between dialogic mind and monologic reason" in C. Miriam (ed.) Between Rationality and Cognition. Turin, Italy: Albert Meynier.

BROWN, L. D. and R. TANDON (1983) "Ideology and political economy in inquiry: action research and participatory research." Journal of Applied Behavioral Science 19 (3): 277-294.

EDEN, C. (1988) "Cognitive mapping." European Journal of Operational Research 36: 1-13.

ELDEN, M. (1979) "Three generations of work democracy experiments in Norway," in C. Cooper and E. Mumford (eds.) The Quality of Work in Eastern and Western Europe. London: Associated Business Press.

ELDEN, M. (1981) "Political efficacy at work: the connection between more autonomous forms of workplace organization and a more participatory politics." American Political Science Review 75 (1): 43-58.

ELDEN, M. (1983) "Participatory research at work." Journal of Occupational Behavior 4 (1): 21-34.

ELDEN, M. (1985) "Varieties of participative research," in A. Cherns and M. Shelhav (eds.) Communities in Crisis. Brookfield, VT: Gower.

ELDEN, M., J. FJALESTAD, M. LEVIN, G. MYRVANG, and B. RASMUSSEN (1980) "Fagbevegelsen og EDB i prosessindustrien" [Trade unions and EDP in the process industry]. Trondheim/Oslo: IFIM/NR.

EMERY, F. and E. THORSRUD (1976) Democracy at Work. Leiden, the Netherlands: Nijhoff.

FREIRE, P. (1972) Pedagogy of the Oppressed. Harmondsworth, England: Penguin.

GEERTZ, C. (1973) The Interpretation of Cultures. New York: Basic Books.

GREENWOOD, D. (1989) "Collective reflective practice through participatory action research: a case study from the Fagor Cooperatives of Mondragón." Paper prepared for inclusion in a casebook on reflective practice edited by Don Schön.

GUSTAVSEN, B. (1985) "Work place reform and democratic dialogue." Economic and Industrial Democracy 6: 461-479.

142 Cogenerative Learning

GUSTAVSEN, B. and P. H. ENGELSTAD (1985) "The design of conferences and the evolving role of democratic dialogue in changing working life." Human Relations 39 (2): 101-116.
GUSTAVSEN, B. and G. HUNNIUS (1981) New Patterns of Work Reform: The Case of Norway. Oslo, Norway: University Press.
KALLEBERG, R. (1989) "Action research as constructive science." Working paper. Oslo, Norway: Institute for Social Research.
KUHN, T. S. (1962) The Structure of Scientific Revolutions. Chicago: University of Chicago Press.
LEVIN, M. (1981) Fagforeningers handlingsressurser. En studie av grunnlaget for lokale fagforeningers arbeid med å påvirke utformningen av ny teknologi [Trade unions actions resources. A study of local trade unions work on influencing technological development]. Trondheim, Norway: IFIM.
LEVIN, M. (1980) "A trade union and the case of automation." Human Futures 3: 209-216.
LEVIN, M. (1985) Participatory Action Research in Norway. Trondheim, Norway: ORAL.
LEVIN, M. (1988) "Lokal mobilisering" [Local mobilization]. Trondheim, Norway: IFIM/ORAL.
LEVIN, M., L. AKSET, S. ENGVIK, O. HAUGEN, S. J. SLENES, and T. STRØM (1989) "Hitterværinger Vi kan! Vil vi?" [Inhabitants of Hitra: We can! Will we?]. Trondheim, Norway: IFIM/ORAL.
LEVIN, M., E. GUNDERSEN, R. HALVORSEN, and O. ØYEN (1980) Teknisk utvikling og arbeidsforhold i elektrolyse [Technological development and QWL in aluminum electrolysis]. Trondheim, Norway: IFIM.
LEVIN, M. and V. HAVN (1985) De siste skipsbyggere En rapport om tidligere TMV-arbeideres forsøk med å skape nye arbeidsplasser etter nedleggelsen av skipsverftet [The Last Shipbuilders: A Report on How Unemployed Shipbuilders Worked with the Problems of Creating New Workplaces]. Trondheim, Norway: IFIM/ORAL.
LEVIN, M. and H. KAUL (1984) Fra håndverk til hodeverk Teknologisk utvikling og belastningslidelser i grafisk industri [From Handwork to Headache: Technological Development and Work Loads in the Graphical Industries]. Trondheim, Norway: IFIM.
LEVIN, M. and E. SKORSTAD (1975) "Samarbeidsforsøk ved SIENENS A/S I Trondheim" [Experiments in QWL at SIEMENS S/S in Trondheim]. Trondheim, Norway: IFIM.
LINDQUIST, S. (1978) Gräv der du står Hur man utforskar ett jobb [Dig Where You Are: How to Research a Job]. Stockholm: Bonnier.
PASMORE, E. and F. FRIEDLANDER (1982) "An action-research program for increasing employee involvement in problem solving." Administrative Science Quarterly 27: 343-362.
PATEMAN, C. (1970) Participation and Democratic Theory. Cambridge: Cambridge University Press.
RAPOPORT, R. N. (1970) "Three dilemmas in action research." Human Relations 23 (6): 499-513.
SUSMAN, G. and R. D. EVERED (1978) "An assessment of the scientific merits of action research." Administrative Science Quarterly 23 (4): 582-603.
WALTON, R. and M. GAFFNEY (1989) "Research, action and participation." American Behavioral Scientist 32 (5): 582-611.
WHYTE, W. F. (1989) "Introduction to action research for the twenty-first century: participation, reflection, and practice." American Behavioral Scientist 32 (5): 502-512.

# 10

# Action Research as Method

## Reflections from a Program for Developing Methods and Competence

JAN IRGENS KARLSEN

In Norway, research institutes within different disciplines have gradually become interested in the methods employed in action research, with importance being attached to experimentation, participation, and development of the understanding and solution of problems through dialogue. This is quite another form for the development of knowledge, in which the relationship between practice and theory, and between research and action, is significantly more organic and close than in traditional social science. These approaches have gradually spread and been called into service in a number of dissimilar fields: work research, job creation, introducing new technology, planning, housing environments, and so on.

The intellectual roots can be traced through that part of work research that is, and has been, taken up with democratization and organization development. There is a line linking Kurt Lewin's research on social change and social conflicts (Lewin, 1948), through the Tavistock Institute's (Trist and Bamforth, 1951; Emery, 1959) work on sociotechnical theory, to Einar Thorsrud and the Norwegian Industrial Democracy Project (Gustavsen and Hunnius, 1981), to today.

The development of knowledge through this particular approach is not limited to certain professions; we find sociologists, architects, engineers, economists, and psychologists engaged in the endeavor.

143

A recent survey of the field (Saeterdal & Asmerik, 1986) concluded that action research represents a fruitful form of applied social science relevant to a broad area of reform, but the double challenge of action and research creates difficulties in meeting standards of scientific rigor.

One way to help those working in this field is to strengthen their basic methodological competence. I argue that it is necessary to develop methods that, within a good design, achieve both goals. This is an argument in line with Olquist (1978), when he concludes that the evaluation of this form of social science is not a theoretical question but will have to be based on the ability of action researchers to develop effective and efficient methodologies to produce desired results.

In 1988, we started collecting and systematizing methods and experiences with the methods of a number of researchers. In practice, we have been working on the following three activities.

*(1) A collection of articles on methods in action research.* This represents an interest common to a number of research institutes, and there is a great deal of relevant information and experience about methods that have not yet been processed or documented. We aim to systematize this knowledge and experience by involving several of these institutes in our work. The methods we have in mind are open in the sense that they provide valid data and at the same time are practical instruments for advancing the change process. The methods relate to the following main fields:

— design and planning of research and action
— documentation
— the researcher in the field
— analysis and evaluation
— learning and communication
— diffusion

*(2) Research networks.* A basic aspect of the need for a more systematic development of methods is making the field better known and more open and attractive to researchers. There is no formal education for it, and many people feel uncertain about the challenges the field offers. Competence in research or development work is gained as an addition to one's own academic discipline, usually in a rather haphazard way. There is an obvious need for better organized and more systematic training. Several models may be appropriate for such a program. Our approach consists of linking the development of competence

directly to the activities of an ongoing research network (Asmerik and Saeterdal, 1987).

*(3) Seminars for policymakers within the scientific community.* The purpose of the seminars is to further policymakers' understanding of this major approach within applied social science.

## *Action Research*

We are engaged in a field in which knowledge accumulation and learning take place through participation in changes of social systems or what we often call sociotechnical systems. Here the role of research involves the dual aim of theorizing and taking action, with action based on theorizing.

We agree with Lewin's (1948) conviction that it is not possible to understand a social system without changing it. The passive observer cannot learn anything rational about the inner dynamics and conditions of such systems. It is only through an anthropological approach, that is, by becoming a member and making observations over a long period, that the observer can succeed.

The incentive to move into this field is not only founded in a view about how knowledge of social systems can best be obtained; it also is based on the desire to escape from the traditional, passive researcher role. People in this field are typically busy, not only theorizing and describing problems but also contributing to evolving solutions. One is not only a researcher and responsible for the research process, one is at the same time a participant and jointly responsible for the change process.

Whyte provides a good characterization of this action research when he distinguishes three types of research, depending upon the degree of user participation throughout the research process. The first type is the preparation of reports and theoretical analyses of a fairly general problem-oriented nature. The second type is an attempt to make changes to an organization. The participation of users will often consist only of making decisions about solutions developed and proposed by researchers. Whyte's third type, which he calls "participatory action research," engages users in all phases of a research project.

Our research approach is closest to Whyte's third type, but with certain reservations. The researcher has a distinct role and responsibility, which cannot be shared by others, which, therefore, places limits on degrees of participation. I will return to this point.

This approach to research raises many questions concerning methods, ethics, and science. I will confine myself to the following themes:

(1)  Within what many loosely term *action research,* what is it that characterizes our approach?

(2)  Can action research contribute creating anything new?

(3)  What type of design strategies are relevant?

## Clarifying Our Position

I will lay primary emphasis on elaborating our understanding of action research in relation to two closely related approaches: the clinical approach (Schein, 1987) and participatory action research (Whyte, 1989).

*The clinical perspective versus the explicitly value-based perspective.* Schein describes the clinical perspective as involving a professional helping role. This suggests a therapeutic model of the relationship between researcher and system. The researcher knows how to diagnose and treat, and the system is the patient having the illness. This is a model that has certain characterizing hallmarks:

(1)  an easily identifiable client whose problems chiefly relate to him- or herself,

(2)  voluntariness,

(3)  neutrality in terms of values, and

(4)  a joint objective, namely, to become healthy.

The interaction between researcher and system is complex and difficult to handle, and decisive importance is attached to the professional integrity and diagnostic ability of the process consultant.

We view this interaction in a different perspective. One way of describing it is to make the explicitly value-based perspective the point of departure. In our relations to the various systems we work with, we use two key phrases to describe how we view the process of change and our role in it, namely, that the changes are to be *participator based* and *participator controlled.* *Participator based* means that those who are affected will also take part in defining which problems are to be treated, and *participator controlled* means that they will be in a position to participate in making decisions about what measures are to be implemented. One of our tasks is to contribute ways of working that enable this process to achieve a practical form. This may imply the use of mass meetings, project teams with representatives from all sides, conference techniques, voting, and so on. The explicit value aspect is a commitment to democratic ways of working and not to specific outcomes.

Another point involves the objective for the changes. What is to be achieved must be decided by the other participants. Objectives are formulated by looking at those elements on which we have placed demands, that is, the process must take place through a democratic dialogue (Gustavsen and Engelstad, 1986). The dialogue concept is a vital element in Western democratic tradition, and, among others, Habermas argues that rational dialogue should be the fundamental problem-solving mechanism in this set of ideas. The best, or most rational, solution will probably be achieved in open discussions in which all participants are viewed as having equal rights.

This is related to another assumption: a specific structure or form of organization is not valuable from a participation viewpoint but, instead, having influence on the processes through which the new setup is created is valuable.

This emphasis on value-explicit democratic ways of working does not imply that the researcher's professional ability is without significance. But it does imply an alternative emphasis in the sense that that part of the research process for which the researcher is responsible is not the only source of knowledge.

It also implies that caution should be used with methods that are derived from individual therapeutic contexts. We will confine ourselves to applying methods that, in a certain sense, are more "structurally" and sociologically oriented, where the objective is to develop collective resources for action, that is, resources that are developed as a result of cooperation during the mastering of tasks. This is also a position in line with traditional Norwegian work culture and work values (Gullowsen, 1971).

*Participatory action research and professionality.* Whyte defines participatory action research (PAR) as a process in which some of the people in the organization or community being studied actively participate with the professional researcher throughout the research process from the initial design to the final presentation of results and discussion of the action implications.

This is a position that differs somewhat from the traditional approach in Scandinavian work research, in which the task of action research has been to build theories and descriptions that could be tested through intervention experiments, that is, through experiments that bear the double burden of testing hypotheses and effecting some desirable change in the situation.

There are several reasons for rejecting this researcher-fixed way of working. One of the most important is that, with its emphasis on unilateral control, it comes into conflict with the fundamental objective for the action process, namely, democratic change.

On the other hand, there was a lesson to be learned from these early intervention experiments: There are clear limitations in involving practitioners as coresearchers. Action research does not mean that the researcher should or can relinquish his or her specific professional contribution and responsibility by becoming victim to some misunderstood "democracy" in thinking that everyone can take part equally in every step of the research process.

When that is said, we still assume that causal inferences about what is going on are more likely to be valid when they are formulated and tested in a participatory setting. But developing criteria for reliability and validity, and presenting the results to the scientific community, are still the responsibilities of the researchers.

It may be useful to make a distinction between the processes of research and of action. It is natural to argue that research and action are one thing, especially within our tradition, where the ideals of participatory democracy are emphasized so strongly. As a research tradition, that contrasts with the alienating aspects of the traditional research model. Rowan (1981) has pointed out that the relationship of the persons undergoing investigation to the ordinary research process alienates them in all of the four ways Marx describes: They are alienated from the results of the research process, from the research work, from the other research personnel, and from themselves during this process.

Instead, we stress participation in common learning in which action, reflection, and theorizing are part of the same process and take place as a dialogue between equal partners.

In classical experimental research, the researcher goes through all the stages alone (or as part of a research group) and comes into contact with the persons studied only when data are being collected—and then in an alienated manner. In a fully developed coresearch process, the researchers, together with those who are affected by the research/action process, will be fully contributory at every step of the research process. It may be wise to define more precisely what is necessary before we can talk about a participation-oriented research process. Reason (1988) lays emphasis on the following criteria:

— The degree of involvement on the part of the participant must be open to negotiation and dialogue.

— Everyone should contribute to the creative thinking that is a part of the research process.

— The forms of cooperation must aim toward being genuinely cooperation oriented.

This does not imply that the participants must have the same type of expertise as the researchers; neither does it imply that they take part in all the stages. They can, for example, enter when the project is being formulated and leave around the "making sense" and "communication" stages.

There are some kinds of questions that concern the researcher more than other participants. These are questions relating to the theorizing and knowledge accumulating process itself, as a scientific project. Reflecting about and understanding what the action process is all about, documenting and analyzing it, and making use of technical knowledge to confirm what one assumes has taken place all fall within the sphere of responsibility of the researcher. This does not mean that others must not, or should not, participate; quite the contrary. All who participate in an action process have the need to reflect on and understand the process in which they have participated. But ensuring that the basis—data, assumptions, interpretations—is valid in a broader sense, to the research community, falls on the researcher.

There is another distinguishing aspect of the researcher's participation. The researcher is not a permanent part of the field. As soon as the project-defined portion of the action process has been concluded, the researcher withdraws. The changes do not have the same degree of proximity to him or her because he or she does not need to live with them as do the other participants. There is a distinction both in proximity and in responsibility, which means that the research process has a number of peculiarities that make it useful to consider it separately.

It, therefore, seems reasonable to maintain the analytical distinction between research and action. This does not prevent the action process, as a common arena for dialogue, reflection, and learning, from being the central aspect to which the researcher also must relate him- or herself. But the research process is to be understood especially as an instrument and a special responsibility in relation to this main task.

These general points of view may be summed up using the model in Figure 10.1. It provides a summary of one way of viewing the steps in an action process and describes them as being common and relevant to both research and action but having different objectives. What characterizes the situation of the researcher is that he or she has a responsibility for both sides, in contrast to the practitioner.

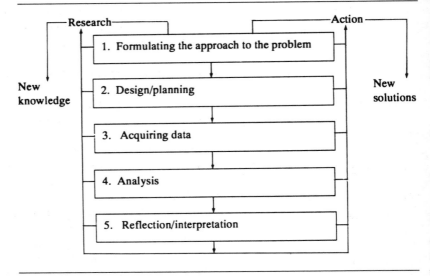

**Figure 10.1.** Steps in an Action Process

This makes certain demands on the type of methods that are useful and relevant at the various stages in this process:

(1) They have to supply data that are input for action at the same time as they are valid.

(2) They have to make participation possible.

(3) They have to be able to provide opportunity for reflection and personal training for other than the researcher alone.

## Can Action Research Create Radical Innovations?

A primary reason given for carrying out action research is the belief that one of the most important professional contributions one can make is to take part in creating something "new," a social innovation, not just testing or reformulating theoretical propositions or ideas. A great deal of learning in such projects will involve conditions for creating and disseminating innovations. Thus, in addition to being concerned with evaluation, the researcher will be interested

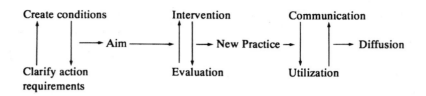

**Figure 10.2.**  Planned Innovation Process

in studying forces that lead to change. Methods suited to such an approach to the problem are of particular interest.

In our context, the innovation will typically consist of the creation of a new practice, or a new way of solving problems, whether it has to do with new forms of leadership and organization, new kinds of planning, or new ways of employing technology.

The planned innovation process covers all stages in a development process, from an idea, through adapting/developing it, and on to its utilization. Reformulated and adapted to our situation, it can be described as in Figure 10.2.

This is another way of describing the change process that we also make use of, in part, to further characterize the methods required and, in part, to emphasize that action research is a method for generating planned social reforms. The process involves three main steps: formulation of aims, development of new practices, and diffusion of results. The way an action is developed and implemented is just as important as the result of the action, in the sense that a reform is tried out with those who are affected, and is adjusted and appraised, before being adopted and diffused. In other words, this represents an alternative strategy for social change, compared with traditional social reform policies that are directed from above, whether based on laws or on negotiated outcomes. In particular, this approach is relevant when it comes to solving complex, problematic situations whose development calls for teamwork and mutual commitment among several interested parties.

We may, nevertheless, ask: To what extent, using this approach, can one create something that is genuinely new, in other words, radical innovations and not just incremental improvements of the existing, or introduction of already well-known, solutions and principles?

The kind of dialogue-oriented action processes we use lay great emphasis on producing genuine problem descriptions and analyses, in the sense that one seeks to circumvent the defensive strategies of the system (Argyris, 1985). On the other hand, it can be argued that the nature of the decision-making process itself implies that all the interest groups will express their opinions and that, through such a process, there will evolve not new solutions but a kind of compromise that will represent a sort of lowest common denominator. In other words, the dialogue itself encourages a form of conservatism and protection of vested interests. Solutions result that people can usually live with but that do not represent any real alternative.

This is an objective I have met in, among others, an action research project in a large theater. There, at the outset, the problems were described as high costs and lack of flexibility, which were said to result from the nature of the agreements between the parties. The wage agreements contained rigid provisions about the fields of activity, with extra payment for the slightest departures from defined jobs and so on.

We kept open minds regarding the way the problem was described, which was anyway strongly contested by others, and arranged a search conference with broad representation to examine the problems on a wide-open basis. During this conference, completely different problems were formulated and given priority. In addition, proposals were put forward for reorganizing, which failed to find support—which also provoked the objection to which I referred.

The problems of flexibility and costs were, nevertheless, dealt with, but without any changes being made in the agreements; it was just the way of interpreting them that was changed.

During this process, a sort of tacit agreement came into being that the wage agreements were too sensitive and difficult to tackle. In fact, they covered not only that particular theater, but all the theaters. And it was instead decided to choose other angles of attack.

The views of the participants concerning the reorganization proposal were that it seemed foreign to them, it would call for too many changes, they were doubtful about how practical it was, and so on. Now, however, three years later, it nonetheless seems to be of interest. Perhaps a sort of maturing process has taken place.

Even though this is only one example, it confirms a common experience I have had in other projects, that the most radical solutions are stripped away during the kind of dialogues for which we are setting the scene. Such experiences pose a challenging dilemma.

In the early phase of action research in Norway, we were working on really radical solutions. It was then that the concept of autonomous groups was created, that multiskilling came into being as an instrument for increasing influence, and that participation in all areas of work was defined as a major element in a national reform wave to enhance industrial democracy. Since then, no really radical ideas have been adopted in this field.

But the point is that these innovations were created by researchers. They were not solutions that came as a result of broad, dialogue-oriented participation processes. Certainly, we tried to create participation when introducing these solutions. But the solutions were formulated beforehand; it was just a matter of getting them tried out.

On the other hand, we also have experiences that indicate that more radical changes may be adopted, given time, even if the initial resistance is great. In one instance, in a company with a long history of wildcat strikes, the time span between proposal and adoption was almost two years. The lag then seemed very frustrating, but it now may be looked upon as a period necessary for discussion and preparation.

Another case, a change process involving the merging of parts of three independent public services, was at one point evaluated as unsuccessful. The researchers resigned, experiencing failure, but, after a period of almost a year, the project was taken up again, not as ambitiously as defined initially but still in the same direction.

It is probably fruitful to make a distinction between proposing and adopting radical changes. I still believe it is part of the action researcher's role to formulate radical alternatives, especially if no one else does. On the other hand, if the practitioners do not agree upon the more radical steps, even when they might be more desirable in the long run, it is not our responsibility to set the agenda for change. We do not "own" the change process. But we can hope for some kind of maturing process that eventually can make new steps possible and even, if practical, prepare for them. There are no clear solutions for these issues, but they certainly present a challenge to the way we define our roles and to the kind of methods we apply.

### The Issue of Relevant
### Design Strategies

I have so far been discussing some thoughts concerning the questions of method from the perspectives of values and innovation. Finally, I will say a little about the problem of choice of methods and design from the perspective of obtaining valid knowledge.

As stated before, the basic problem concerns the close proximity of research and action. However, the practical solution is not merely to choose methods that meet both requirements; it is just as much a problem of design. An important issue is thus how to organize the interaction between research and action in such a way that valid knowledge can be obtained.

Based on traditional demands for rigor, the classical experimental model is unsurpassed. In addition, action research projects often have the character of some sort of natural experiment. The moment when the interventions are implemented will normally be identifiable, and one is usually preoccupied with finding out whether expected effects materialize, that is, one also has some hypotheses. It will, therefore, seem natural to choose this strategy.

The contrast with the classical experimental situation is so fundamental as to require us to reject that model as irrelevant, and we must instead evolve other research models. The experiment makes demands on control through the use of random assignment, which is incompatible with the sort of participation-based processes we use.

There are several possible answers to the questions of design strategies. There seems, however, to be one fundamental point in what one is attempting to do, no matter the strategy—namely, to produce a plan with which one confronts plausible rival hypotheses. The classical experimental model merely represents one answer to the question of how one can ensure that the explanation chosen is the one that best fits the available data.

Yin (1984) discusses the limitation of the experimental model and emphasizes case studies as an alternative. He maintains that the case study strategy is an independent research strategy with its own design criteria and its own methods. In his language, case studies are empirical investigations

— when they study a contemporary phenomenon in a real situation,

— when the boundaries between phenomenon and context are diffuse, and

— when one uses many heterogeneous data sources.

However, this strategy also implicitly assumes a traditional research process with a noninvolved researcher.

If we are to take action research seriously, we must recognize that it represents not only a special type of research but a direct break with conventional models for obtaining valid knowledge. It is only in this way that we can issue challenges so clearly that we will be able to meet them.

This means utilizing the special characteristics of action research for purposes of validity—in a way, turning weakness into strength.

## Pragmatic Validation: Spiral Design

It is important to be aware of the practical limitations that are inherent in change processes. These are real situations in which people are absorbed with solving immediate and pressing problems. The pressure to achieve results is great, and the researcher can seldom grant him- or herself long pauses for thinking or extensive data collecting without the utilitarian value being clear. This suggests selecting simple designs and methods that serve several ends.

Part of the researcher's task consists of collecting data and undertaking analyses that will help people understand their situation and that will lay the basis for formulating new measures. The implementation of the measures will lead to new requirements for analysis and so on. This process in itself contributes to corroboration because the assumptions about the causal relationships on which measures are based will continuously be tested when one is occupied with expected effects and is investigating whether they materialize. It is a kind of recirculation of data sets and derived hypotheses that may provide a control that is scientifically satisfactory at the same time that it makes useful contributions to the action process.

This leads to a kind of spiral design of action and research, closely integrating the two processes through common methods and reflection.

## Consensus Validation

The spiral process may often be disorderly, and it may be difficult to trace a clear connection between data sets, assumed causal relationships, and implemented measures. The type of data and assumptions that we use as a basis in "real-life changes" are not only those that have resulted from observable and controlled processes.

Here, however, there is a third source for corroboration, and perhaps the most important one, namely, that the practitioners take part in evaluating, interpreting, and reflecting on the data generated through the research process. This is also part of the design process, which concerns not only the action process but also the evaluations and interpretations that are connected with the research and tested through action.

This means opening the research process to a kind of validation through consensus. It corresponds to an epistemological view of knowledge as partial and local (Gustavsen and Engelstad, 1987).

**The Need for Reflection:**
**Design for the Devil's Advocate**

In both the research process and the action process, there is a need for time to reflect on what is taking place. This is a need felt by everyone taking part in this sort of activity, but the researcher has a special need, involving both design and validity. Involved researchers need guidance from and discussion with people who are standing outside the project itself. Action-oriented research is exceedingly demanding, and a feature of a properly planned process is ensuring that you have contact with one or more additional experienced research workers who also can pose as the devil's advocates.

The involved researcher can often be so trapped by the situation and his or her own role in it that it may be difficult to get an adequate perspective on what is happening. In such cases, it is an advantage to have ready-established structures that ensure that one is confronted by others and has one's own assumptions tested.

Finally, it involves development and growth in the role of action researcher. In the same way that one throws into focus what is happening in the field, it is at least as important to highlight oneself and one's own role. How does one master this? What can be done to improve it? There is a need for reflecting on and learning about this too, and, again, it is important to have someone with whom to discuss things. The prerequisite is that one is willing to view oneself and one's actions as data sets in the same way that one looks upon others (Schön, 1983).

### Concluding Remarks

Action research has an uncertain academic status, something that is reflected in the research councils. It is not easy to deal with both action and research. One may wish to see them as two completely separate activities and may prefer to leave action responsibilities to others. It is not our task to reject that ideal but to argue not only that there is room within this field of applied social science research for different approaches but also that there is a need for the type of research that we represent. But if we are going to advance further, we must also meet the challenge that lies in building up a more uniform field of knowledge, something that presupposes effort in several fields:

— a further development of the bases of scientific theory,

— a corresponding development of a research ethic,

— an elaboration of the role of researcher, and related training in it,

— development of a store of theory, even though one of the most exhilarating aspects of this field is the eclectic and broad approach, and, finally,

— the need for design and method development.

These are broad questions and I have only touched on some aspects of them in this chapter.

I have been particularly concerned with the last point, for several reasons:

(1)  It is important for recruitment and for bringing new research workers into the field. Good knowledge and methods imbue confidence.

(2)  In this field, there is a great deal of undocumented knowledge about methods among researchers and in the research milieu.

(3)  The methods represent a special challenge because they must contribute to driving the action process forward at the same time that they must supply systematic data as a base for working up the research aspect of the project.

## *References*

ARGYRIS, C. (1985) Toward an Action Science. (unpublished)

ARGYRIS, C. and D. SCHÖN (1974) Theory in Practice. San Francisco: Jossey-Bass.

EMERY, F. (1959) Characteristics of Socio-Technical Systems. London: Tavistock.

GULLOWSEN, J. (1971) Selvstrte Arbeidsgrupper. Oslo: Tanum-Norli.

GUSTAVSEN, B. and P. ENGELSTAD (1986) "The design of conferences and the evolving role of democratic dialogue in changing work life." Human Relations 39: 2.

GUSTAVSEN, B. and G. HUNNIUS (1981) New Patterns of Work Reform. Oslo, Norway: University Press.

LEWIN, K. (1948) Resolving Social Conflicts. New York: Harper.

OLQUIST, P. (1978) "The epistemology of action research." Acta Sociologica 21 (2) 143-163.

REASON, P. [ed.] (1988) Human Inquiry in Action. London: Sage.

ROWAN, J. (1981) "A dialectical paradigm for research," in P. Reason and J. Rowan, Human Inquiry. New York: John Wiley.

SAETERDAL, A. and S. ASMERIK (1987) Forsok og Forsok fru Blum! Oslo, Norway: Byggforshinginstitutt.

SCHEIN, E. (1987) The Clinical Perspective in Field Work. London: Sage.

SCHÖN, D. A. (1983) The Reflective Practitioner: How Professionals Think in Action. New York: Basic Books.

THORSRUD, E. and F. EMERY (1969) Form and Content in Industrial Democracy. London: Tavistock.

TRIST, E. and K. BAMFORTH (1951) "Some social and psychological consequences of the Longwall method of coal-getting." Human Relations 4 (3): 3-38.

WHYTE, W. F. (1989) "Advancing scientific knowledge through participatory action research." Sociological Forum 4 (3): 367-385.

YIN, R. K. (1984) Case Study Research: Design and Methods. London: Sage.

## *11*

# *Participant Observer Research*

## *An Activist Role*

## ROBERT E. COLE

Traditionally, the participant observer role has called for the researcher to exercise a nonobtrusive research style. One conducts research in a way to minimally disturb the subjects under investigation. I chose to conduct my study of the spread of small group activities in American industry by actively participating in the organizations I was studying. I served on the board of directors in two organizations I studied as well as on various committees in these and other organizations. As one thinks about the matter, perhaps the difference is not so great as it might appear. In keeping with the "Heisenberg principle," the mere act of observation can influence outcomes. I would guess that more than one participant observer, not to speak of those using more conventional research methods, has had his or her observations influenced, often unknowingly, by his or her very presence in a social situation.

This was explicitly the case in my research as I was called upon to take positions on a variety of issues that could determine the effectiveness of the organizations in carrying out their missions, the very subject of my research. Moreover, based on my comparative research, I had a sense of what strategies might be effective for these organizations and on occasion voiced these views. Indeed, I was personally committed to having the organizations succeed in their mission of successfully spreading quality circles (QCs). Some might consider that to be a breach of professional ethics and wonder how I could treat my data in an objective fashion. I will treat that issue in more detail below but for now I am reminded of some remarks made by C. Wright Mills. He said that

> the most admirable thinkers within the scholarly community . . . do not split their work from their lives. They seem to take both too seriously to allow such dissociation, and they want to use each for the enrichment of the other [Mills, 1959: 195-196].

In this activist role, it can be said that I was engaging in applied social research; my role could be characterized as a researcher in an organization development framework (see Whyte, 1984: 165-166). However, unlike most researchers in this situation, I was not a paid consultant. Each of us participating in these voluntary associations was active based on our professional expertise (knowledge of QCs). In one of the organizations, I participated as an elected member of the board of directors. In another case, I was appointed to the association's committee concerned with promoting quality circles. Yet, I was not engaged by and large in collaborative research with other members of these organizations. The latter represents still another model of applied social research labeled by Whyte as participatory action research (Whyte, 1984: 168-181). As is typical with conventional sociological research, I had full responsibility for designing the research methodology, applying it, and interpreting my research data.

With this as a rough description, I begin with a brief summary of the research project and my findings. In the late 1970s, I began a three-nation comparative project on the spread of what I called small group activities in industry in Japan, Sweden, and the United States. Specifically, I focused on the spread of quality circles in Japan and the United States and self-managing teams in Sweden. Only in the United States did I use the kind of active participant observation role that I have described. In all three countries, I was interested in finding out what accounted for the speed of diffusion of these new forms of work organization. For the period under investigation, roughly 1960 to 1987, I concluded that these new approaches had spread most rapidly in Japan, followed by Sweden, with the Americans bringing up the rear. In trying to account for these differences, I focused on the role of national infrastructures for identifying and diffusing the best practices. Japan had the most well-developed national infrastructure, represented by the Japanese Union of Scientists and Engineers (JUSE). It was an organization with only corporate members dedicated to quality improvement. Private sector engineers played a large role in JUSE's activities while independent full-time consultants were barely visible. JUSE engaged in mass mobilization of circle members and facilitated intercompany learning from one another primarily through its chapters' activities.

Sweden developed a more modest national infrastructure and had correspondingly more modest success. The Americans developed the weakest infrastructure and had the least success in diffusing circles. In the case of Sweden and Japan, these national organizations may be seen as devices through which employers reduced their transaction cost for developing and deploying this new organizational process technology. In the case of the United States, the key organization under study essentially became an ideal organization not for reducing employers' transaction costs but for reducing the transaction costs of full-time consultants seeking to market their version of small group activities.

My participant observation research in the United States took place primarily at the International Association of Quality Circles (IAQC). In 1988, they took on a new name: the Association for Quality and Participation. I was active in the organization almost from the inception in 1978 until the research was completed in 1988. I was a member of the board of directors from 1980 to 1983 and again in 1985 and chair of the strategic planning committee in 1984-1985.

These vantage points gave me extraordinary access to the organization. As part of the leadership of the organization, I was part of its normal information network. I did not have to struggle to figure out what the normal information network was and then try to access it. My activist role allowed me to collect data of all sorts, ranging from minutes of meetings, focused interviews with individuals, and material in the organizational records. I was even able to carry out organizational surveys of the membership under the auspices of the association. I had "real-time" organizational access to many of the key decision makers. That is, I could interview participants at the time events were occurring and before they had time to forget or reconstruct events. This is an often overlooked advantage of participant observation research.

As an outside researcher, I might perhaps have negotiated access to the board of director's minutes. But these were often sanitized, bare bones accounts of decisions, mostly stripped of the process that had led up to these decisions. I also kept my own reasonably detailed minutes of each meeting. It would have been impossible to deduce from the formal organizational minutes that consultants consistently argued against the IAQC developing its own training materials because it competed with their business. However, this pattern was clearly visible through my own detailed observations and minutes. Moreover, I could then follow up my observations of these processes with interviews of key participants and observers. In short, participation as a full-fledged member of the board allowed me to experience the unfolding of organizational processes and decisions that would have been extremely difficult to capture using only conventional research methods.

By serving as a member of the board of directors, as well as head of the strategic planning committee, I was given a legitimate authorization to collect data. Asking questions was part of my job definition. As an "insider," members found it harder to give me the kind of formal explanation for their behavior that they might have given an outside researcher. Moreover, members often brought data to my attention that I would not have known about otherwise (e.g., a private corporate study of the consultant industry for quality circles). Perhaps the major disadvantage of being in such a data-rich situation was the danger of being overwhelmed by too much data. But it is a cost that most researchers would willingly bear.

It is hard to imagine that the richness of this methodology could have been duplicated by traditional methods. Indeed, in many ways, my approach allowed me to subsume many of the traditional research methods (e.g., interviews, surveys) under the more general activist participant observation approach that I adopted. I talked with a number of key individuals involved in the organization after publication of my research. They said that they hadn't realized the role the consultants had played in the organization, and it was only through my systematic accounting that they became aware of it. Had I used traditional methods of research (surveys, interviews, and so on), it would have been difficult to uncover this role because many members were simply not aware of it.

Above all, I would stress that the participant observation role, as other have observed, allowed me to understand the kind of questions that needed answering. Standard research approaches often assume that the researcher knows the important questions to be asked. Moreover, the activist role allowed me access to a wide range of organizational activities that is seldom possible under the more traditional passive participant observer role.

One of the major findings of this research is the role that full-time consultants played in the professional associations I studied. A search of the social science literature shows that remarkably little attention has been paid to the role of consultants in American life. As a consequence, a conventional researcher would have relatively little reason to pursue the subject. Through "living" with the IAQC for some 10 years, however (as well as with one other organization), I came to appreciate the significance of consultant activities. Thus I could structure a great deal of my research activities to uncover their role and understand their behavior. Longitudinal research of this nature allows one's topics to "ripen."

Any researcher conducting some form of participant observation research faces the question of how to present him- or herself to the research subjects. William Whyte (1984: 30) suggests three approaches: overt, semiovert, and covert. Many participant observers have chosen a covert or semicovert role to avoid influencing the social situation they were studying or negatively influencing their access to data.

My own judgment is that ethical considerations should be paramount. Consequently, I made clear from the start that I was an academic interested in conducting research on the organizations of which I was a member. At various times, I made public statements both to remind organizational members of this fact and also to socialize new members. As far as I could judge, this understanding of my role had little impact on the content of what was said in public meetings, who would talk to me, or what they would say.

Because I behaved in most ways as a normal member of the organization, participating fully in its activities, it was hard for other board or committee members to think of me as a researcher. There was one other academic on the board of directors during much of this time, and he was there simply in connection with his interest in the subject rather than as a researcher. This helped legitimate my presence. Apart from asking a lot of questions (almost always in informal situations), I behaved on a routine basis not as researcher but as an ordinary board member.

There were a couple of board members who became especially good informants (the kind of people I would ask, after some important event, "Well, what did you think of what happened?"). These individuals had a better sense of me as a researcher and actively collaborated in interpreting events for me. To take but one of many examples, one of the more perceptive board members explained to me that the dynamics of board meetings were not simply an outcome of consultant versus nonconsultant members, because many of the nonconsultant board members had been clients of particular consultants and thus were tied to them in various coalitions. Although I was aware of the fact that many of them had indeed been former clients of the consultant members, I had not thought through the implications for board meeting dynamics. Such enlightening conversations with key informants were multiplied many times over and were invaluable in shaping my understanding.

I had become involved in IAQC by virtue of my professional credentials (as a long-term student of quality circles in Japan, I knew a lot more about QCs initially than many organizational members and leaders). As a consequence, I needed no formal sponsor to enter the organization and didn't have to worry about the common problem researchers have of becoming too closely identified with their sponsors in a way that jeopardizes access to other types of individuals. Neither did I have to clear my research publication with any organization or individual. On my own initiative, I did show selected chapters to key individuals, including the vice president of the organization (a permanent staff position akin to managing director) to get feedback on what I had written. However, I reserved the right to act on these suggestions. By and large, I found them quite useful but did not adopt all of them.

In my initial involvement, I was simply another volunteer who had chosen to give his or her time to help this fledgling organization. Given the incredible problems faced in the start-up period, all volunteers were welcome, and I was accepted simply because I was seen as just another board member sharing the work load. Later, I was elected to the board by the membership and thus had as much legitimacy as a board member as any other board member. In summary, given this situation and the relatively unobtrusive nature of my research, I had minimal problems in establishing legitimacy. In that connection, the long time period during which I was associated with the organization, during which I published nothing, led some board members to wonder whether in fact I ever would publish my analysis. Clearly, no one was losing any sleep worrying about it except perhaps a few staff officials just before it became clear that I was actually going to publish something in the next few months.

My analysis of the organization and its accomplishments could easily be construed by some as quite critical of the organization. Yet, I decided to use the real name of the organization and the real names of participants. In the latter case, I tried to minimize the use of names, using only those most essential to the story. This is a somewhat unusual tactic in participant observation studies. Many such studies are done on anonymous individuals in relatively easy to conceal organizations (one more manufacturing company). But the organizations I was studying were one-of-a-kind organizations with national visibility. It would not have been easy to conceal their names.

In the end, we come back to the critical question raised early in this chapter. If the researcher adopts an activist stance, trying to push his or her "data" in certain ways in keeping with his values, how can the reader be assured that the interpretation of the data is not skewed in some fashion to meet these needs? Perhaps I was creating the very outcomes I then sought to explain and attributing to others what I myself was responsible for as an activist researcher. There is perhaps no generalized assurance that can be given to readers in this regard other than the usual proscriptions to make as much of the data upon which one's conclusions are based available to readers so that they can judge for themselves. One can also encourage repetition of new research efforts that could validate past findings.

In my research, however, there was one additional assurance that could be provided. Despite my efforts to push the organization in certain directions (toward a buildup of organizational core competencies that would provide greater service to corporate users), they mostly moved in other directions (toward greater and greater facilitation of consultant activities). Thus my explanations for behavior were mostly in terms of why things didn't turn out the way I had hoped (that is, the way they did turn out in Sweden and Japan). In this situation, I could hardly be accused of producing the very outcomes that I wanted to occur and attributing them to my research subjects.

I did impose limits on my activist stance to ensure that I was getting a balanced reading of organizational developments and also to avoid being put in a position of reporting on my own activities. Thus, even though I voiced views as to the directions that the organization ought to go, I carefully restrained these views so as not to alienate those factions that had different views. Indeed, with the exception of one consultant, I by and large maintained good relationships with all factions in the organization. Thus the need to get information from all sources to carry out my research objectives restrained my activist stance. In the case of the one consultant who was visibly unhappy with me, it was not because of my research status but because our substantive views differed so dramatically. He stridently advocated that we had nothing to learn from the Japanese and transparently pushed consultant interests at the expense of organizational interests.

When board members had trouble coming up with a new president to head the organization, I was approached on a couple of occasions so they could assess my willingness to be a candidate. I turned down these requests, fearing that I would be put in a position of reporting too much on my own activities.

There will be times when the activist researcher is successful in helping the individuals he or she is working with to produce the outcomes favored by the researcher. In such a situation, the researcher does indeed face a different task in convincing the reader that the researcher has successfully located the causal factors in the behavior of his or her research subjects as opposed to their behavior being a function of the researcher's intervention.

In conclusion, I found that, whatever the limitations of the activist participant observer role, it was more than compensated for by the wealth of data that became available to me by virtue of this role. Located in the center of the organizational network, I was privy not just to outcomes but to organizational process in ways that enormously enriched the research. At the same time, by presenting myself from the outset as a scholarly researcher, I avoided ethical problems associated with deceiving my research subjects.

## *References*

MILLS, C. WRIGHT (1959) The Sociological Imagination. New York: Oxford University Press.

WHYTE, WILLIAM. F. (1984) Learning from the Field. Beverly Hills, CA: Sage.

# PART II

# PAR in Agriculture

## 12

# *Participatory Strategies in Agricultural Research and Development*

### WILLIAM FOOTE WHYTE

Participatory strategies were becoming popular in agricultural research and development in roughly the same period as in industry, beginning in the 1970s and spreading rapidly in the 1980s. The academic interest in worker participation in industry arose decades earlier than any comparable academic interest in participation in agricultural research and development, but until the 1970s few practitioners in industry showed much interest in worker participation.

Participatory innovations sprang up in roughly the same time period in Latin America, Africa, and Asia. Here, we will focus primarily on the stream of development in Latin America but note also very active communication internationally to strengthen and support participatory initiatives across boundaries of nations and continents.

Until the development of participatory strategies in agriculture, the paradigm providing the intellectual foundations for development efforts was reflected in the phrase "transfer of technology." This paradigm was based on three major assumptions:

(1) Agricultural scientists of advanced industrialized nations had gained the knowledge necessary to demonstrate to Third World farmers what they had to do to improve agricultural yields and earnings.

(2) This assumption was based on what I call "the myth of the passive peasant": the idea that small farmers have been locked into their traditional beliefs and practices so that they resist changes.

169

(3) Putting these assumptions together leads to the diagnosis that the basic problem is to find ways of overcoming resistance to change.

What came to be called "the green revolution" reinforced this predominant paradigm. Beginning in the 1960s, CIMMYT (those initials standing in Spanish for International Center for the Improvement of Maize and Wheat) in Mexico and IRRI (the International Rice Research Institute) in the Philippines achieved spectacular increases in yields through the development of higher-yielding varieties of wheat and rice. At first, it was assumed that these potential benefits were scale neutral, that they would benefit small farmers as well as large operators. Within a few years, evaluation studies indicated that the main beneficiaries were large farmers, except in those cases where small farmers had access to irrigation. But note that such findings did not discredit the predominant paradigm. Agricultural researchers and other professionals could take the failure of most small farmers to change simply as further confirmation of the belief in the passive peasant. The paradigm could not be effectively challenged until some researchers were willing to speculate that small farmers in developing countries might have developed useful information and ideas that must be utilized in any project.

This willingness to consider alternative explanations for the failure of most small farmers to benefit from the green revolution led to the opening up of a broad new line of research and practice focusing on small farmer participation in decision making. This chapter provides the background for the development of such organizational learning.

### Discovering "What Ain't So" in Agricultural R & D

"It is better to know nothing than to know what ain't so."

The wisdom of Josh Billings, the nineteenth-century American humorist, focuses our attention on one of the basic problems of human learning. If you acknowledge that there is something important that you don't know, then you engage in an open-minded inquiry that is likely to advance your learning. If you think you know something that "ain't so," then you continue to act on this misconception in spite of increasing failures and frustrations.

Discovering "what ain't so" in the basic assumptions underlying the conventional model of agricultural research and development did not automatically reveal what is so in this field, but it was an essential first step that helped to open people's minds to searching for new and better ways of working. In this chapter, I trace the organizational learning process as I followed it through my own fieldwork and in discussion with those involved in the discovery process.

My own reeducation began with a visit to the then-well-known Puebla Project being carried out in the Mexican state of Puebla, with the support of CIMMYT (Whyte, 1982; Whyte and Boynton, 1983).

The Puebla Project was designed not as research but as demonstration, to show small farmers how they could increase their corn yields by following instructions of the experts and through crop loans facilitated by CIMMYT to buy the required inputs. In the course of several years, the farmers who adopted the CIMMYT system achieved yield increases of about 30%—substantial but dwarfed by the more spectacular increases in wheat and rice with the new varieties developed by CIMMYT and IRRI. Furthermore, instead of continuing to grow, the numbers of adopters leveled off at about 25% of the Puebla corn farmers. Puzzled by this lag, some of the Mexican staff members went out to do some fieldwork among the more successful nonadopters. That foray yielded a simple yet striking solution to the puzzle: These nonadopters were raising crops double in value to those possible with the CIMMYT methodology!

The Puebla program was geared to the monocultural growing of corn—that is, planting corn in rows. The most successful nonadopters planted beans between the corn rows. They were making much more intensive use of their small plots of land and also making more efficient use of fertilizer, which now served two crops instead of one.

That discovery led the Mexicans to wonder why they had been insisting on the monocultural strategy. The answer seemed to be that that was the way it was done by the successful Iowa corn farmers. Because they used tractors in working their large tracts of land, intercropping was not practical for them.  In this case, who were bound by tradition and resistant to change: the professional experts or the small farmers?

The revelation that led to my reformulation was put to me by Mauro Gomez, Puebla Project general coordinator (1970-1973):

In Mexico we have been mentally deformed by our professional education. Without realizing what was happening to us, in the classroom and in the laboratories we were learning that scientists knew all that had so far been learned about agriculture and that the small farmers did not know anything. Finally we had to realize that there was much we could learn from the small farmers.

In 1976, I began learning for potatoes the same lesson I had learned for maize and beans in the Puebla Project. I accompanied economist Douglas Horton, head of the social science unit of CIP (the International Potato Center) and agricultural economist Anibal Monares on a mission to ICA, the agricultural research agency of the government of Colombia. CIP was being asked not for biological information or advice but for guidance in establishing a viable seed potato program.

Potatoes were first grown in Peru or Bolivia hundreds of years ago—both countries claim the origin of the plant. For centuries, potatoes have grown along with the diseases and pests that prevail in that region.

This naturally led researchers and program administrators to the conclusion that the production and distribution of "clean" (disease-free) seed potatoes was of fundamental importance for high-yielding healthy potatoes for the consumer market. How could this be done?

This was the third or fourth ICA effort to establish a national seed certification program. The first such effort was launched in the 1940s. In the 1950s, ICA reported the establishment of such a program, but it later disintegrated.

Following this mission, Horton decided to study how Andean farmers grew and selected their own seed potatoes. CIP worked on this study with farmers in the Mantaro Valley of the central highlands of Peru, a major potato-growing area. Farmers were persuaded to purchase seed potatoes from the government potato program and plant them in one plot to compare results with another plot where they had planted their homegrown seed potatoes.

This research led to the following conclusion (Horton, 1948: 5):

In on-farm experiments, the use of improved seed increased yields on average by 15-20%. Due to the high cost of the improved seeds, however, its use reduced farmers' net returns below the level obtained when using their own seed. . . .

In the Mantaro Valley project, two things become clear: first, that there was little "demonstrated technology" that could be transferred to farmers without local refinement or adaptive research; and second, that farmers are not passive recipients of recommended technologies but active researchers and developers in their own right.

The professionals did eventually learn from the frustrations of their past misguided efforts. In Mexico, while the Puebla Project was still going on, the professionals changed their recommendations so as to promote the interplanting of corn and beans, and leaders of Mexico's national agricultural research program began promoting on-farm experimentation, where the professionals at least had a chance to learn from the farmers. In the Andes, under the leadership of CIP, the professionals also changed direction to emphasize participatory on-farm research in working with small farmers.

It is important, nevertheless, to recognize the costs of these earlier misguided attempts at technology transfer. CIMMYT invested enormous sums of money and years of work by highly educated personnel to demonstrate to farmers how they could cut the value of their crops in half. In Colombia, the national government and foundations supporting agricultural research also invested enormous sums of money and human talent in vain efforts to establish a national seed certification program, which would probably not have been cost-effective even if it had been technically successful.

### Innovation in Guatemala

In planning for a new national research program, Guatemalan leaders built on what they had been learning regarding the failures and successes of Mexican programs.

Whereas CIMMYT had earlier been concentrating on a monocultural strategy, developing higher-yielding varieties of wheat and then demonstrating to Puebla farmers how to grow more corn, the Guatemalans planned to concentrate on farming systems research, involving the integration of a variety of crops with animal husbandry.

Whereas CIMMYT had worked exclusively on irrigated land with large farmers in developing the new wheat varieties, Guatemala opted to give special attention to the problems of small farmers who had to depend on rainfall.

The Guatemalans also planned at the outset to build some form of farmer participation into the research process, although the planners had only vague ideas of how this might be done.

In designing ICTA (Instituto de Ciencia y Tecnología Agrícolas, or Institute for Agricultural Science and Technology), the Guatemalan government drew on the guidance and support of the Rockefeller Foundation, CIMMYT, and CIAT (International Center for Tropical Agriculture) in Colombia and the U.S. Agency for International Development. ICTA was created in 1973 with Astolfo Fumagalli as its director general and Robert K. Waugh, an American supported by the Rockefeller Foundation, as associate director. The plan also provided ICTA substantial autonomy within the Ministry of Agriculture.

In 1975, ICTA set up Technology Testing Teams to guide and intensify some on-farm research already under way. These teams worked with small farmers but did not begin with any established methodology to support and guide their participation in decision making.

ICTA's distinctive participative methodology was developed under the leadership of Peter Hildebrand, an American agricultural economist, who joined ICTA in 1974 as director of its recently established socioeconomic unit.

The socioeconomic unit began developing methods along four lines:

(1)  delineating "recommendation domains"—that is, areas where soil and climate and commonly practiced farming systems were similar, thus increasing the likelihood that an innovation successful in one part would also be effective in other parts of that domain;

(2)  building innovations upon the base of common farming practices within a domain; and

(3)  developing research methods for the delineation of domains and for the discovery of the farming systems most commonly practiced within a given domain.

To gather data, the unit devised two methodologies: the *sondeo*, a survey administered through farmer interviews, and *registros,* simple farm management records, to be filled out daily by the farmer or a family member, recording the amount and type of labor, the tools and power used, the amounts of other inputs applied, and so on. The methodologies were developed by professionals who had graduated from the agricultural college or had gone on for graduate degrees. *Peritos*, graduates of technical high schools in agriculture, worked with farmers to help them fill out the *registros*.

(4)  Leaders of the unit chose to try to make farmers active participants in a mutual discovery process. They assumed that the professionals would learn more this way and that farmer participation would strengthen their commitment to the change process.

When early efforts to persuade other agricultural professionals to adopt the socioeconomic methodologies proved fruitless, Hildebrand was able to persuade one regional director to allow the socioeconomic unit to carry out its own on-farm experiments.

In two projects, the socioeconomic unit rented small plots from local farmers and paid the farmers for the labor they provided in the experimental process. The unit proposed to try only those innovations that its farmer-consultants considered reasonable and promising. Any innovation that seemed impractical to local farmers was not likely to gain acceptance.

The first on-farm experiments were carried out under the direction and control of professionals. Any innovation that did not work out at this stage was referred back to the plant scientists in experiment stations for advice and further study. The innovations that yielded good results moved into the second stage of farmer field trials. At this stage, the socioeconomic unit gave up control and shifted into the role of consultant and observer. Farmers now tried out, on their own fields with their own money and labor, the innovation they had tested earlier. Innovations that did not work out at this stage were referred back to the professionals for advice and further study. Those that did work were assumed to be ready for diffusion and general adoption throughout the domain in which the on-farm experiments and farmer field trials had been carried out.

ITCA invested heavily in training programs for its agricultural professionals and technicians. The first trainees were sent out to CIAT in Colombia for a course in agricultural production. Building on this experience base, ICTA established its own training program in Jutiapa in Guatemala by late 1976 or early 1977. This ambitious 10-month course involved a combination of didactic instructions with actual field practice. Each trainee was assigned his own farm plot with instructions to farm it entirely with his own money and labor. Throughout the process, he was required to keep a record of his own labor time and expenditures and the farming practices he used. If he made money from his plot, he was allowed to keep the profits. If he lost money, that outcome provided a payoff in learning.

This practicum has proved a powerful learning experience:

> In the first years, the tendency was for many graduates to use the technology that they brought from the university and the (officially) established recommendations. The majority failed. Following these experiences, new graduates have learned to consult others and particularly the local farmers themselves. These (graduates) have had greater success [Ruano and Fumagalli, 1988, p. 50].

Such personal experiences probably were more influential in persuading the young professionals that they really needed the information and ideas of the local farmers than any lectures designed to make the same point.

As the first socioeconomic unit projects yielded interesting results, the administration encouraged the use of the SE methodologies by other units engaged in on-farm research. To encourage diffusion within ICTA, *sondeos,* in some cases, were carried out by interdisciplinary teams. For each pair of field interviewers, one would be an agronomist, the other a social scientist, thus establishing a base for them to learn from each other as well as from the farmers.

When Ramiro Ortiz became technical director for ICTA nationally, he gave strong backing to the adoption of the socioeconomic methodologies by the Technology Testing Teams.

Dissatisfied with the performance of the extension service, as early as 1974, leaders of ICTA began a project to carry on its own extension on an experimental basis in the village of San Martín Jilotepeque. Here ICTA was building on a program launched by Oxfam and World Neighbors in 1970 in that village.

By the time ICTA came in contact with them, farmers were already working in organized groups and experimenting with agricultural innovations. They had begun to increase yields through the use of soil and water management practices that the project had introduced.

ICTA negotiated an agreement with the project to put three informal farm leaders on ICTA's payroll to collaborate with an ICTA technician assigned to the project in managing agronomic trials throughout the community.

This arrangement extended the reach of ICTA very rapidly. ICTA dealt with farm leaders, and the farm leaders took responsibility for communicating information and managing experiments with organized groups in communities. Farm leaders in the San Martín project were able to manage approximately 60 field trials a year, compared with the average of 25 for the professional agronomists in the ICTA program. Of course, these trials were not so neat and scientific as ICTA's more controlled experimental work, but they provided data to the research program and were of high credibility to the participating farmers. The farmer paraprofessionals working with ICTA extended their work into 11 villages, providing one-on-one technical assistance and holding regular instruction and discussion meetings with the villagers. By 1979, the paraprofessionals were working actively with two large farmer cooperatives, thus further extending their outreach through linking up with indigenous organizations.

A follow-up study on ICTA (Ruano and Fumagalli, 1988) indicates that the changes instituted by ICTA up to this point had taken root and were being applied and practiced. The diagnostic agrosocioeconomic studies were being carried out in all areas of the country; 100% of the technology generated or adapted by ICTA had been or was being tested on farms; and small farmers had been actively participating and managing their own farm testing. The office found no cases where this on-farm testing was being run by ICTA professionals. Finally, with active small farmer participation, the technologies developed by ICTA had been diffusing widely.

The fact that the methods and findings of ICTA were being diffused among small farmers in areas where ICTA concentrated its work, without any involvement of DIGESA, the extension service, indicates serious deficiency in Guatemala's agricultural research and development program. In fact, this deficiency has not been peculiar to Guatemala. Up through the 1970s, it might be said that cases of lack of integration between research and extension were much more common in developing nations than cases where the two units worked together effectively. Nevertheless, the gulf between the two agricultural units seems to have been wider in Guatemala than in most other countries, which leads us to look for the causes of this lack of integration.

The two units built their programs on quite different models of the nature of peasants or small farmers. After some preliminary and less focused exploratory efforts, ICTA developed a model of the small farmer as a rational human being, capable of learning from experience and possessing information and ideas regarding farming that needed to be integrated with the information and ideas generated by the agricultural professionals so that solid assistance could be provided to small farmers. In other words, ICTA conceived the research and learning process as going in both directions: from farmers to the agricultural professionals as well as from them to the farmers. The action implications of this model, therefore, dictated that the small farmers should be active participants in the research and development process and not simply subjects to be directed by the professionals.

The DIGESA model of the small farmer reflected the then-conventional view that I have called the myth of the passive peasant.

Following this model, DIGESA and BANDESA arranged to work together so that the agricultural bank would concentrate its loans to small farmers upon those who worked out an annual plan, approved and supervised by an agricultural extension agent. This not only reinforced the dependence of small farmers upon the agricultural bureaucracy but also drastically limited the outreach efforts of extension agents. Working with the small farmer to develop and write his farm operations plan for the year, seeing that proposal through BANDESA for an agricultural loan, and then supervising the farming activity to make sure that the farmer was complying with the approved plan constituted such a heavy work load that extension agents were only able to work with about 50 small farmers during the course of a year.

In the 1970s, leaders of both ICTA and DIGESA became well aware of the weaknesses in the relationship between the two organizations and made several attempts to achieve a closer integration.

The failure of top-level agreements to produce results suggested to some of the leadership that a structural change was required. They would have to devise a program in which ICTA and DIGESA personnel worked together full-time on the projects.

This line of thinking gave birth in 1986 to a new organization, PRO-GETTAPS (Proyecto de Generación y Transferencia de Tecnología Agropecuaria y Producción de Semillas, or Project for the Generation and Transfer of Technology in Agriculture and Animal Husbandry and for the Production of Seeds). In the next chapter of this book, Ramiro Ortiz describes and interprets the development of PROGETTAPS and provides some preliminary indications of its success in bridging the gap between extension and research.

## References

HORTON, D. E. (1984) Social Scientists in Agricultural Research: Lessons from the Mantaro Valley Project, Peru. Ottawa, Canada: International Development Research Centre.

RUANO, S. and A. FUMAGALLI (1988) Guatemala: Organizacion y Manejo de la Investigacion en finca en el Instituto de Ciencia y Tecnología Agrícolas (ICTA). OFCOR Case Study #2. The Hague, the Netherlands: ISNAR.

WHYTE, W. F. (1982) "Social inventions for solving human problems." American Sociological Review 47 (1): 1-13.

WHYTE, W. F. and D. BOYNTON (1983) Higher Yielding Human Systems for Agriculture. Ithaca, NY: Cornell University Press.

*13*

# A Joint Venture in Technology Transfer to Increase Adoption Rates

## RAMIRO ORTIZ

In the last two decades, there has been an increasing effort within the agricultural sectors of Third World countries to design technological models and identify research methodologies to guide technological innovation institutions and programs in the development of production technologies appropriate for the needs and expectations of limited-resource and resource-poor farmers. This attitude has produced substantial changes in the work approach of national and international institutions in the world. They are coming rapidly closer to adopting research models based on on-farm activities to generate appropriate technology. International financing institutions and international centers have also been involved in this effort. They have played an important role in promoting this new attitude through the financing of projects with the new approach and in the training of large numbers of this new type of scientists.

Nevertheless, agricultural extension institutions have been left out of this effort, and the technology transfer programs have become secondary in importance. One reason for this is the belief that appropriate technologies are disseminated and adopted very easily. This may be the case, but only up to a point, and the adoption rates still remain relatively low when widespread, massive dissemination is expected. This has been true, more often than not, in areas where limited-resource farms are predominant and the number of farms is large. It would be necessary to identify other mechanisms, incorporate other institutions with wider coverage, and design the models through which a new technological infrastructure would reach a much larger number of farmers than those reached by on-farm research activities alone.

Since the last decade, Guatemala has begun an effort to create a larger impact in technology adoption by incorporating other technical institutions into the work conducted by on-farm researchers (ICTA). The best alternative was the agricultural extension institution (DIGESA), which has wide coverage and conducts activities through its agents at the community level. This strategy has worked very well in terms of the methodological approach of integrating both institutions, which overcame the philosophical and methodological conflicts with the mainstream approach of doing research and extension, but the impact was still not what was expected. Isolated successful cases in different parts of the country showed the potential of this joint venture in terms of reaching larger numbers of farmers with new technology, and this provided the higher authorities of the Agricultural Public Sector with the necessary evidence to establish a new project to integrate these institutions in the generation and transfer of agricultural technologies (Fumagalli and Ortiz et al., 1985; Ortiz and Ruano et al., 1989).

## Linking Research and Extension and Farmers

In the second half of 1986, a new technology generation and transfer project for crop-livestock technology and seed production (PROGETTAPS) was established to strengthen the research and extension (R-E) system of Guatemala (Ortiz, 1987). This project began activities in five regions (seven *departamentos*) of the country, where small limited-resource farmers constitute the largest part of the population. The overall goals were to increase production and productivity of the existing farming systems, which mainly produce staple food crops (basic grains).

Within this project, technology for crop production is generated and validated by the Institute of Agricultural Science and Technology (ICTA) and transferred by extension agents of the Directorate General of Agricultural Services (DIGESA). PROGETTAPS has also developed a new model for technology generation and transfer that has achieved outstanding results. The design of this technological model and its implementation is based in the Farming Systems Research and Extension (FSR/E) methodology, as there is a linkage between on-farm researchers and extension agents who jointly plan, conduct, and evaluate on-farm activities (farm trials, farmer-managed tests, and transfer plots) and promote active participation of farmers in technology testing, adaptation, integration, and transfer activities that are conducted on their own farms (Ortiz and Meneses, 1989).

Before this project, ICTA had developed a technological model with a strong emphasis on on-farm research. This was successful in developing appropriate technologies relevant to farmers' needs that integrate easily into their existing systems (Castillo and Juárez, 1985; Ortiz and Ruano et al., 1989). ICTA's technologies were well accepted and adopted, but this was limited to certain regions and to small farmers with more favorable conditions (e.g., those located in the south coast and valleys). There was still no impact among limited-resource and resource-poor farmers located in densely populated areas under less favorable conditions (mostly hillside farmers; Ortiz and Ruano et al., 1989). By incorporating DIGESA, with its wide coverage, the adoption rates could increase dramatically. These were some of the ideas on which great expectations were based, but this could only be true if ICTA and DIGESA could integrate their work within the new technological model.

## The New Model for Technology Transfer

In the design and execution of PROGETTAPS, the R-E authorities and field teams adopted a new attitude by orienting their joint effort toward the *active participation* of farmers in the different phases of the model rather than toward *educating* them. That is, for technology production in food crops, the extension effort to "educate" farmers in the use of new technologies was replaced, for technology transfer purposes, by joint participation of farmers, extension agents, and on-farm researchers in all the phases of the technology innovation process (Ortiz, 1987). A brief discussion of the outstanding features of the new transfer model follows (Ortiz, 1987):

*(1) Developing a strong and wide interface between research and extension.* Because this allows joint participation of both groups in the planning, execution, and evaluation of R-E activities, extension agents have the opportunity to participate in on-farm research activities and get to know firsthand the characteristics and management of the new technologies. In addition, on-farm researchers also have the opportunity to get involved in extension activities (transfer plots and transfer days) to get direct feedback from farmers on the performance of new technology and bring technical-scientific support to this effort (see Figure 13.1).

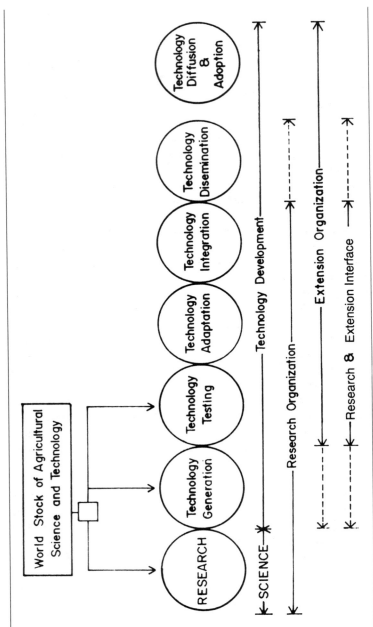

**Figure 13.1.** The Technology Innovation Process Within the Agricultural Research-Extension System of Guatemala

SOURCE: Adapted from the Farming Systems Support Project (1985).

*(2) Directly involving farmers throughout all phases of the technology innovation process* (TIP). This means active participation *rather than* education. This is probably the feature that has been most stressed in guiding the design and execution of the R-E work plan. In addition to participating in field trials and transfer plots, and being the main speakers on transfer days, farmers have been incorporated in the decision on what the annual R-E work plans will be. This is done through a methodology using Consultative Groups (*Grupos de Consulta*; Ortiz, 1988), which is a systematic procedure to obtain information from the rural population, thus promoting more participation from them in making decisions as to which R-E activities are relevant to their needs and problems.

*(3) Rural leaders participating to generate a "multiplier effect" in technology transfer.* Rural leaders have been recruited and hired by the Ministry of Agriculture to work part-time as *Representantes Agrícolas* (RAs), representing the institutions of the Agricultural Public Sector (APS) and serving as links between the rural committees and the APS. They have been formally selected by their communities to work as RAs based on their ability as farmers, their leadership quality, and their willingness to serve their communities, where they are well known and respected. In their work in support of PROGETTAPS, they have been a key element in the transfer process, conducting some of the transfer plots, maintaining farm records, and conducting transfer activities with groups of farmers that they have formed. They also have brought information to better guide the research programs by identifying new technologies for transfer and have helped in establishing a seed distribution system. Their participation has been a success in terms of the wider dissemination of new technology and increasing adoption rates. This success is based on (1) their ability to get the message across in clear and appropriate language, (2) a well-established credibility within their communities and groups, and (3) a great sense of responsibility in doing their work because they realize it contributes to community development.

*(4) Emphasizing the transfer and promotion of new technologies.* The purpose of this is to reach larger groups of farmers and increase the adoption rates. This wider scope is possible in this project, because, for staple food crops, the technologies selected for a transfer model involve only a few technological options, replacing the complicated technological packages and the intensive one-to-one relationship (extension agent-farmer) used in the previous technical assistance approach.

The decision to shift to a strong emphasis on transfer and promotion activities is based on the fact that the technology transfer approach allows an easier working strategy with the groups organized around the RAs, thus generating a large "multiplier effect" with wide coverage and dissemination.

*(5) Facilitating adoption of new technologies.* For a sharper increase in the adoption rates, DIGESA has begun to facilitate use of new technologies by developing, within and among small limited-resource farmers, a nonconventional seed production and distribution system for the improved varieties that have reached the transfer phase (Ortiz, 1989). This decision originated from the fact that new, improved food crop materials were being adapted well to farmers' circumstances; the seed was demanded by large groups of limited-resource farmers in the areas where PROGETTAPS was conducting R-E activities; and no seed industry existed to cover those demands. Here, the extension agents work closely with the farmers who have been chosen as seed producers based on their ability as farmers and their slightly better economic status, which allows them to invest a little more than what they must put into their subsistence crop. Through barter and monetary transactions, the better quality seed that they produce is reaching large numbers of farmers (Ortiz, 1989).

## *A Modular System for Technology Transfer*

Within this new project, ICTA and DIGESA are jointly responsible for the organization and operative methodology of a Modular System for Technology Transfer (MSTT). There is one of these in each of the five regions covered by the project, and its activities are coordinated by one representative from ICTA and one from DIGESA. In the case of ICTA, it is the leader of the Technology Testing and Transfer Team (on-farm researchers), and in the case of DIGESA, it is a university graduate with experience in extension. The MSTT has a total of four on-farm researchers (university graduates in agronomy), and to each one of these is assigned from a minimum of three to a maximum of seven extension agents (agronomists at the high school level), depending on the number of extension agencies within the area covered by the researcher. Each one of the extension teams is assigned an average of 10 to 15 RAs, and each one of these has at least one group of 20 farmers organized.

Technology generation and technology testing (validation) are ICTA's responsibility, but the extension agents get involved, beginning with diagnosis (*sondeo*), further in the farm trials (generation), and more intensively in the farmer-managed tests (validation). Here the extension agents get in contact with new technology as it develops, participate in the evaluation of its performance, and enthusiastically make it their own through their knowledge of how it performs and how it is managed. Then, in the next stage (technology transfer), DIGESA's extension agents and RAs conduct the transfer plots with ICTA's on-farm researchers also participating to get direct feedback from farmers, extension agents, and RAs and to technically and scientifically support those activities (transfer plots and transfer days).

## Technological Impact on Food Production

In the three-year effort beginning in the second half of 1986, the work of 72 agricultural extension teams, backed up by technical support of 20 on-farm researchers in 7 of the 22 *departamentos* of the country, has resulted in an estimated 80,000 limited-resource farmers adopting those new technologies selected for transfer. (These technologies were selected after it was established that they were relevant and adapted well to those farmers' circumstances.) There are an estimated 800,000 total family farms in Guatemala. In 1989, due to the success achieved, the new model was extended to 8 more *departamentos* to make a total of 15 (68% of the country) using the new approach, while the conduct of these on-farm activities has involved 149 extension teams and 40 on-farm researchers.

The established project goals for number of farmers adopting new technology in four years were reached and surpassed in just three years, with close to 200% of the expected number. This integrated R-E effort has taken place in regions that predominantly have subsistence agriculture systems (small family farms), where, until the arrival of the new approach, very little or no impact had been achieved in productivity. ICTA had Technology Testing Teams working in these regions previously and evaluated and identified relevant technologies (mostly improved varieties) for those systems. However, the number of on-farm activities was very limited, and this restricted dissemination of the new technologies.

It is estimated that, because of the adopted technologies (mostly new varieties), the 1989 harvest in those areas will show an increase of 16,200 metric tons of food (basic grains and potatoes) due to an increase in productivity. In terms of food security, this increase is enough to satisfy the annual food requirements of a little more than 26,000 additional typical rural families. By extending the new transfer model to the eight new geographical areas, it is expected that, in the 1990 harvest, food production increase will

**Table 13.1** Activities of the Research and Extension Integrated Effort in Guatemala: PROGETTAPS, 1986-1988

| | *Number of Each Type of Activity by Year* | | | | |
|---|---|---|---|---|---|
| *Type of Activity* | *1986* | *1987* | *1988* | *Total for 1986-1988*[a] | *1989*[b] |
| 1. Farm trials | 193 | 99 | 242 | 534 | 422 |
| 2. Farmer-managed tests | 274 | 724 | 248 | 1,246 | 368 |
| 3. Transfer plots | 506 | 2,876 | 2,547 | 5,929 | 4,630 |
| 4. Seed plots | — | 11 | 719 | 730 | 1,722 |
| 5. Communal gardens (vegetables) | — | — | 445 | 445 | 898 |
| 6. Transfer days[c] | 23 | 122 | 678 | 823 | 1,241 |
| 7. Farmers' tours[d] | 11 | 76 | 275 | 362 | 415 |
| 8. Agricultural encounters[e] | 13 | 63 | 267 | 343 | 342 |
| 9. Farm records[f] | 367 | 4,580 | 2,735 | 7,315 | 12,500 |

a. From 1986 to 1988, only 7 *departamentos* were covered by PROGETTAPS. There are 21 *departamentos* where DIGESA has activities, out of a total of 22 in the country.

b. In 1989, PROGETTAPS activities were extended to a total of 15 *departamentos*, as shown in Figure 13.4

c. Transfer day is a field day to show the new technology performance. Here, R-E work is shown to large visiting groups by agricultural representatives (RAs) and by farmers conducting farmer-managed tests and transfer plots.

d. Farmers' tours consist of groups of farmers moving through the region with the extension teams to see new technologies being performed in different environments.

e. The agricultural encounter consists of groups of farmers being invited to discuss a problem or outstanding performance of a new technology in the field, with the R-E team (or problem analysis in the field).

f. The farm record is a data gathering process on a daily basis to track production management and costs.

be almost three times the 1989 increase (45,000 metric tons) on the basis of the higher productivity produced by the adoption of the new technologies. This increase in production only calls for a small increase in cost and does not require credit because it is mostly associated with more labor required for harvest, which is usually already available on these family farms. The total amounts resulting from the diverse R-E activities conducted from 1986 to 1989 are shown in Table 13.1 (Ortiz and Meneses, 1989).

## *In Support of the New Model:*
## *Key Strategies and Mechanisms*

Designing the new project with its innovative research-extension integration was relatively easy when compared with implementing it. Some strategies were adopted and mechanisms identified to support the implementation and consolidation of the new transfer model.

(1) Researchers and extension agents learning to understand the new model was the first and possibly most important activity in support of PROGETTAPS. This was done through a training program focused on introducing the extension agents to, and strengthening the knowledge of the on-farm researchers of, the conceptualization and working methodologies of the Farming Systems Research and Extension (FSR/E) methodology and the characteristics, stages, and role for each institution in the new technology transfer model. In a series of short, intensive courses, these people were also trained in the methodology used, the characterization of rural population living and production systems, the methodology for the analysis and interpretation of on-farm research and transfer activities, and the methodology used to define recommendation and diffusion domains.

All this training proved to be more beneficial to the extension agents, who did not have previous experience in those topics, and it allowed them finally to understand the process through which each technology had passed before being selected for transfer, thus establishing credibility for the process and for the technologies selected. In addition, a better understanding of the new model, and their contribution within its implementation, was grasped, and the extension agents were able to begin an all-out effort in the technology transfer. Through this training, the R-E teams began to work, sharing the same philosophy and methodology, and realized that they shared the same objectives. This established the foundation for successful collaboration.

(2) The *transfer plot* was designed as the physical field unit to replace the demonstration plot and to be the center for technology diffusion. Its most significant characteristic is that it is conducted by a cooperating farmer who invests in the new technology, and it is he himself and the RAs who conduct the transfer activities as the main advocates for the new technology. This is a farmer-managed plot that provides the opportunity of *multiplying* the number of field units that function as dissemination centers of new technology.

(3) An organizational framework was established within the extension institution to support the new project and its transfer model. This promoted key changes in the institutional structure and organization to facilitate project activities. The functions and role of the regional coordinators for PROGETTAPS

within DIGESA were defined to ensure them enough freedom to work with ICTA and to make decisions on how the budget would be used. It was determined how these regional coordinators would be technically responsible and how they would support the extension teams and also what type of relationship would exist with the different levels in the chain of command within the region (regional director, subregional leaders, and supervisors). And it was also clearly defined that extension agents would dedicate most of their time and effort to transfer activities.

(4) Since 1987, PROGETTAPS has sought to involve farmers more and more in the R-E activities. It has been stressed that technology transfer, to be dynamic, requires *participation* rather than *education*. Farmer participation is needed for the design and execution of the R-E work plans. In addition to farmers participating in field trials, farmer-managed tests, and transfer plots, they have been the main speakers for the new technology on transfer days and have been invited to participate in the planning of R-E activities for the next cycle. This has been done through the Consultative Groups in a systematic procedure to obtain feedback from the rural population on an R-E proposal for a work plan. This activity promotes more farmer participation because they are able to realize the importance of determining what R-E activities are relevant to their needs and problems.

The Consultative Groups consist of the RAs assigned to one extension team and at least one member from each of the groups formed by the RAs. This makes a total of around 30 persons from the community to whom the R-E team presents its tentative work plan for the coming season. The group gives its approval or makes suggestions to change or modify the plan in terms of including things important to them that might have been left out.

### Summary

The involvement of the national agricultural extension institution (DIGESA) to support on-farm research conducted by ICTA has achieved a massive dissemination of new technologies. It has also provided the Agricultural Public Sector of Guatemala with the necessary evidence to establish, in two-thirds of the country, an integrated R-E effort to reach higher production levels for food crops as a direct result of higher adoption rates of new technology. A new technology transfer model, where research and extension interface, has been established, and it has gained in effectiveness by incorporating rural leaders (RAs) and the groups of farmers they have organized as active participants in all the phases of the technology innovation process.

# References

CASTILLO, L. M. and H. JUÁREZ (1985) Investigación en Sistemas de Producción y su Contribución al Desarrollo Rural en América Latina. Guatemala City, Guatemala: Instituto de Ciéncia y Tecnología Agricolas (ICTA).

Farming Systems Support Project (1985) Research and Extension (Emphasizing Farming Systems Research and Extension). Working draft no. 3, February. Gainesville: University of Florida.

FUMAGALLI, A. and R. ORTIZ et al. (1985) "A new model for technology transference within farming systems research and extension (FSR/E)," in FSR/E Symposium Proceedings: Manhattan: Kansas State University.

ORTIZ, R. (1987) "Transferencia de Tecnologia en Guatemala," in Proceedings of the Programa Cooperativo Centroamericano para el Mejoramiento de Cultivos y Animales (PCCMCA). Guatemala City, Guatemala: PCCMCA.

ORTIZ, R. (1988) Los Grupos de Consulta: Una Estrategia para Incorporar Agricultores al Proceso de Innovación Tecnológica. Guatemala City, Guatemala: Dirección General de Servicios Agricolas (DIGESA).

ORTIZ, R. (1989) "Developing a non-conventional seed production and distribution system for limited-resource farmers in Guatemala," in Farming Systems Research and Extension (FSR/E) Symposium Proceedings. Fayetteville: University of Arkansas.

ORTIZ, R. and A. MENESES (1989) "Increasing the adoption rates of new technologies with a new technology transfer model," in Farming Systems Research and Extension (FSR/E) Symposium Proceedings. Fayetteville: University of Arkansas.

ORTIZ, R. and S. RUANO et al. (1989) Closing the Gap Between Research and Limited-Resource Farmers. The Hague, the Netherlands: International Service for National Agricultural Research (ISNAR).

## 14

# Participatory Action Research in Togo

## An Inquiry into Maize Storage Systems

RICHARD MACLURE
MICHAEL BASSEY

In much of the Third World, participatory action research (PAR) has emerged as part of the search to render development assistance more responsive to the needs and opinions of local people. Although conventional research is generally characterized by a high degree of doctrinaire professionalism, with the prescribed standards of design, rigor, and disengaged "objectivity" unique to each scientific discipline, PAR is defined by an approach that aims to democratize science, to engage the subjects of research as active participants in what is often an interdisciplinary enterprise. When the participants include groups of people with little or no formal education, and with experiences and perceptions vastly different from those of the professional scientists, the implications for research and development are far reaching.

Three particular attributes distinguish PAR from established research strategies. First, PAR postulates *shared ownership* of the research enterprise. By involving community groups in most or all aspects of the research process, PAR functions as a partnership, with decision making and control shared among all those having a stake in the outcome of research (Ashby, 1984; Blackie, 1984). Second, PAR is a method of *community-based learning*. Through collaborative investigation or experimentation, accompanied by reflective dialogue, participating groups ideally can learn to critically analyze their own particular situations and problems and so be able to devise solutions (Grossi et al., 1983; Korten, 1983). Likewise, PAR enables professional

190

researchers to gain insights that allow for reformulation of research questions and more realistic interpretations of data. Through research, therefore, the roles of educator and learner become interchangeable (Ashby, 1984). And, third, PAR aims to stimulate *community-initiated action*. By instilling among participants a sense of immediacy and personal identification with the discovery enterprise, PAR ideally induces them to apply what they have learned.

By reaching beyond the formal orthodoxies of established scientific disciplines, PAR undoubtedly offers an opportunity in the developing world to enhance the appropriateness of much so-called applied research. Yet, precisely because it compels researchers to move away from the certainties of positivist inquiry into the less easily charted territory of community development work, PAR is also subject to complexities and limitations that can attenuate its value as an alternative approach to development assistance. This is particularly true in many parts of sub-Saharan Africa, where research environments have been seriously impaired by deteriorating infrastructure and dwindling financial and material resources, and where the research agendas of national scientists are now usually determined by government ministries and the major aid agencies. In such circumstances, any independent research project, let alone one oriented toward local participation and action, is a difficult undertaking.

Nonetheless, given a fortuitous coalescence of dynamic personnel, assured sources of funding, and a supportive institutional climate, participatory action research does remain a viable method of development assistance in Africa. This has been demonstrated recently in Togo, where scientists at the University of Benin have collaborated with peasant farmers in conducting a research project aimed at improving traditional maize storage systems. By incorporating into the research process the three attributes of shared ownership, community-based learning, and an orientation toward community action, this project has proven to be a useful formative experience for its participants. In a region where PAR is still relatively novel, it has also led to a greater understanding of the conditions that are essential for the successful implementation of PAR in an African context.

This chapter presents a brief descriptive summary of the project—its objectives, methodology, and results—as well as a number of observations concerning both the benefits and the difficulties arising from the project's participatory action approach. The chapter concludes with a more general discussion about conditions that facilitate PAR in sub-Saharan Africa.

## The Maize Storage Project

### Background and Initial Project Objectives[1]

Maize is one of the most important staple foodstuffs in the southern region of Togo. About 90% of the country's annual maize yield (approximately 140,000 metric tons) is produced by small-scale farmers. Once harvested, maize is stored in traditional household silos, circular or rectangular structures constructed with wood poles, twining, and woven straw. In the months succeeding harvest, a portion of the maize crop is sold in the open market. The rest is consumed domestically. Unfortunately, it is during this postproduction period that farmers suffer considerable losses of stored maize—anywhere from 20% to 60% of their total harvest each year. The consequences of these losses can be devastating. Not only do they lead to shortfalls in food consumption, especially during the rainy season when farmers are cultivating the next year's crop, but the anticipation of annual storage loss invariably pushes farmers to sell their market portion of maize soon after harvest when prices are at their lowest. This results in persistent undernutrition and low income.

For researchers in the École Supérieure d'Agronomie (ESA) at the University of Benin, a likely explanation for such losses appeared to lie in the continued use of traditional storage methods. A cursory survey conducted by ESA in the early 1980s had shown that, regardless of variation in shape, size, and household locale, traditional silos offered minimal protection against the effects of humidity, insects, rodents, and crop mold. It appeared logical, therefore, that new models with a better conservation capacity should be devised and introduced to village farmers. Yet more in-depth research into the characteristics and performance of traditional structures was needed before new models were developed.

It was to this end that in 1983 the researchers at ESA approached the International Development Research Centre (IDRC)[2] with a request for funding. Their proposed project consisted of four objectives: to examine traditional storage systems with a view to identifying particular features associated with crop losses, to develop modified silo facilities to help to reduce crop damage and loss, to test the effectiveness of the improved facilities through on-farm field tests, and to disseminate the results of the study.

As initially designed, the proposed Maize Storage Project was not particularly unique. Other studies in West and Central Africa had also examined problems of cereal conservation and had developed and tested alternative grain storage methods. Yet, for program staff at IDRC's office in Dakar, virtually all such studies were highlighted by two fundamental weaknesses. First, given the paucity of documentation concerning the characteristics and performance of traditional storage methods in natural village settings, the underlying assumption of previous research—that major changes in traditional storage methods were required to improve grain conservation—had not been fully verified. And, second, despite the evidence of reliable testing procedures and valid results, recommendations ensuing from earlier studies had generally been ignored by farmers. From the IDRC perspective, neither the validation of initial assumptions nor the implementation of final recommendations could be realized without the active involvement of the users of village grain storage systems in a related research project. Consequently, while favoring the ESA proposal, IDRC program staff suggested that a participatory action approach would likely enrich the process of inquiry and facilitate the subsequent application of results. Although none of the ESA researchers had had any familiarity with PAR, after some deliberation, they readily accepted this advice. As it turned out, the adoption of a participatory action approach had a salutary effect on the entire focus and direction of the research.

## The Stages of Research[3]

The Maize Storage Project began in early 1984 and proceeded in three stages.

### Stage 1: Baseline Studies and the Adjustment of Research Parameters

For field study purposes, the ESA research team selected 22 villages across the four geographical zones of southern Togo.[4] After receiving the permission of village leaders, the researchers began a baseline inquiry into household production and storage systems. The aim of this first stage of research was to validate initial assumptions concerning the inadequacy of village silos. Once these were ascertained, the parameters of further investigation were to be delineated.

Three methods of data collection were adopted. A six-month survey centering on 44 household silos (2 per village) accumulated information on the structural composition of silos, on their relative effectiveness in conserving grain, on the comparative duration of storage, and on corresponding levels of maize damage and loss. Although the silos continued to be managed by their owners in customary fashion, all stored maize was bought by the project at prices normally paid to farmers during periods of scarcity. The researchers also arranged a series of structured interviews with 64 respondents, among whom were all the owners of the monitored silos. Although conducted as informal discussions, often intermittently over several days, the focus of these purposive exchanges was on all aspects of maize production and storage and on the factors affecting domestic grain conservation. A third data gathering technique involved anecdotal observations of the maize production and management practices of those households not participating in the more detailed silo survey.

Following baseline fieldwork, the researchers spent a short interval at the university analyzing their data. A seminar was then organized at the university for purposes of presenting initial findings to the 44 farmers involved in the survey (of whom 6 were women). Throughout the proceedings, which were presided over by the ESA director, the visiting farmers were encouraged to respond openly and critically to baseline study findings and to share in identifying those factors affecting grain storage that were to be the subject of more detailed investigation in the next project phase.

As a result of these activities—measurements, observations, and most especially dialogue with village farmers—the design and focus of the research underwent a notable shift by the end of the first project stage. Rather than centering all attention on the relation between silo structures and maize damage and loss, the consensus among researchers and farmers was to broaden the parameters of research. Investigation in the second stage was to focus on the possible effects of a range of production- and storage-related practices. These included

- planting and harvesting times
- comparative effects of planting hybrid seeds as opposed to local varieties
- use of chemical fertilizers in maize fields
- numbers of times fields are cultivated
- the relative maturity of maize at the time of harvest
- the effects of different substances used to preserve stored grain

The inclusion of these additional points of inquiry signaled a departure from the original project objectives, for the assumption now was that factors *other* than traditional storage structures might also account for the problem of maize loss. This enlargement of focus was a direct consequence of collaborative fieldwork and prolonged consultations with village farmers.

## Stage 2: Testing of Factors Affecting Maize Conservation Prior to and During Storage

The second stage of the project consisted of two levels of inquiry. At one level, extensive examinations of prestorage and storage factors were undertaken in the same selected villages by the university researchers and peasant farmers. This time, only one household granary per village was appropriated for the purpose. To facilitate mutual understanding of what was now a formal collaborative enterprise, and to ensure that it was maintained, contractual agreements were made with each household head. As in the previous stage, each of the 22 participating households was paid the highest estimated seasonal value of one fully stocked maize silo. The farmers thereupon agreed to manage the selected silos in the same way as they did their other granaries—stocking similar varieties of grain and using traditional preservatives and insect controls. For their part, researchers had complete monitoring access to the granaries and their contents. During a subsequent period of approximately six months (slightly longer than the average storage season), researchers visited each village once every 14 days to collect samples of stored maize for further analysis at ESA, to speak with farmers about their ongoing storage management procedures, and to carry out a battery of field measurements (related to temperature and humidity, mold formations, and levels of insect and rodent infestation).

The second level of inquiry during this stage of the project consisted of the construction and testing of 52 silos on ESA's experimental farm. Each unit was modeled after one of four standard traditional village structures.[5] These were then stored with assorted varieties of maize and treated with different quantities and combinations of preservative substances. In addition to seeking to ascertain the optimum conservation capacities of traditional silos, an additional purpose of these tests was to assess what structural improvements could be made.

Following these two concurrent levels of testing and analysis, a second seminar was held at the university. This was a grander affair than its predecessor, for, in addition to the presence of ESA personnel and two representatives from each of the village sites, others in attendance included the university rector, members of the other university faculties, and the staff of two government extension services.[6] Proceedings were recorded by print journalists and radio and television crews. As in the previous seminar, the findings of the second research stage were presented and discussed. The meeting concluded with a consensus to field test several proposed alterations in maize production and storage systems.

### Stage 3: Field Testing of Recommended
### Production and Storage Alterations

During the final year of the project, comparative tests of alternative production and storage methods were conducted in 16 of the original 22 study villages. One household in each village participated in this stage of the inquiry, again on the basis of mutually determined contractual agreements. Following from the second-stage findings, each household cultivated a portion of its fields in one of four ways (using either local maize grown with or without chemical fertilizer or planting one of two hybrid varieties with fertilizer). The harvested experimental crop was then divided into two equal parts. One part was stored in a traditional silo and was subjected to the same treatment as the rest of the farmer's crop. The second part was stored in a modified traditional structure modeled after a prototype developed at ESA the year before. For comparative purposes, recommended preservative procedures were applied to grain stored in the new silos. During the following months, participant farmers and research assistants conducted regular monitoring and measurement, while further tests on drying and temperature fluctuations in the interiors of traditional silos were continued at ESA's experimental farm. Both types of activities were filmed by national television crews.

At the end of the third project stage, five public seminars were organized in different localities of the southern region. These were attended by representatives of neighboring communities and by local government officials, extension agents, and journalists. At each meeting, after presenting oral summaries of their research, the scientists and participant farmers concluded by expounding two sets of recommendations. The first centered on structural alterations of traditional granaries. These included

— the construction of conical as opposed to uniformly level platforms in areas where the stability of silos is a problem
— the use of cords or creepers, spaced at regular intervals, to reinforce the circumference of silo structures
— the fabrication of conical straw roofing
— the insertion of plastic coverings below the roofing and about the circumference of each structure for purposes of reducing air circulation (on condition that the grain is sufficiently dry)

The second set of recommendations centered on production and storage procedures. The most notable included

— row planting of hybrid maize or local maize using fertilizer

— early harvesting to avoid insect infestation in the fields (except in humid mountainous regions where a later harvest is recommended due to problems related to mold formation)

— suggestions as to silo placement and differential storage heights

— the use of macerated neem leaves for interior binding, of ash to protect against insects and rodents, and of smoke to reduce the incidence of mold

— the sorting of maize, and elimination of spoiled cobs, before storage

— general avoidance of chemical insecticides in view of the risks of toxicity and peasants' lack of familiarity with their use

— the planting of rodent traps and the assurance of tidy surface areas surrounding household silos

Except for the suggested use of plastic coverings, what is immediately striking about the recommendations advanced in the final project seminars is that they were founded on evidence of the most effective *existing local practices*. This represented a major departure from earlier studies, for the end result of the Maize Storage Project was that *very little new* was being proposed. Instead, having worked together, the ESA researchers and participant farmers were able to recommend a particular set of procedures that, for the most part, were rooted in the accumulated knowledge and experience of the local populace. When combined systematically, these methods could substantially reduce prevailing levels of maize damage and loss.

Although the final regional seminars served to publicize the methodology and findings of the Maize Storage Project, it became clear that subsequent community-based action—that is, the widespread adoption of project recommendations—was anything but certain. For improved practices to be widely disseminated and accepted by farming households at large, more time and resources would be needed.

### Project Follow-Up

At the time of writing, the project has moved into a second round of activities, again supported by IDRC. The specific purpose of this follow-up phase is to disseminate the results and recommendations of the first phase and simultaneously to assess the effectiveness and impact of the dissemination process. Although the ongoing collaborative relationship between ESA researchers and representative village farmers has been retained, the dissemination phase now directly involves a team from the national television service as well as staff from government and nongovernment extension agencies.[7] On a broader dimension, the project has become an integral part of a regional PAR network that focuses on specific issues of postproduction agronomy in West Africa. Developed and sponsored by IDRC, the network serves as a means of extending collaborative interdisciplinary linkages among farming systems researchers and small farm households.[8]

## Benefits and Difficulties of the
## Maize Storage Participatory Method

Apart from having produced useful technical results, the Maize Storage Project proved to be an invaluable learning exercise for all those involved. While its participatory approach lent a penetrating dimension to the research, there emerged too a recognition that participatory practices were not devoid of problems.

### The Farmers' Perspective

In marked contrast to the all too common disinterest of village farmers toward agricultural research (Chambers, 1986), the involvement of farmers in the Maize Storage Project, from reformulating the parameters of inquiry to initially disseminating project results, had a remarkably salutary effect on their attitudes to farm research. Knowing that the university scientists wanted to hear and act upon their views, and that their collective input would help to direct the exercise, participant farmers proved to be highly cooperative. They complied with the terms of their contractual agreements, a crucial factor for ensuring the reliability of field measurements, and they readily divulged information about production and prestorage practices that otherwise would have been difficult for researchers to obtain. Their confidence reinforced, participant farmers also offered critical opinions about the comparative feasibility of alternative production methods and modified silo structures.

That such a high level of commitment was achieved was fortunate, for participant farmers were required to spend extensive periods of time erecting new model granaries, learning and carrying out basic monitoring procedures, and attending project-related meetings. Ordinarily, while agricultural activity slackens during the dry season, peasant farmers use this period to carry out important social obligations and other income-earning activities. Time is not a luxury and, for many of them, the days consigned to the participatory research exercise meant a calculated relinquishment of some personal and more profitable concerns. While they bore allocations of time to the project with no complaint, it was notable that those who did participate generally had larger landholdings than most of their neighbors. A concern must be, therefore, that although the research-cum-learning process of PAR has undoubted attractions for small farmers, the personal opportunity costs for many—particularly the poorest—may prohibit their genuine involvement in village research.

**The Researchers' Perspective**

The Maize Storage Project was originally proposed by an entomologist (who became the team leader) and an engineering physicist. Following IDRC's suggestion to revise research methodology, the team expanded to include an agricultural engineer, an agronomist, a rural sociologist, and two extension workers. As noted earlier, none of the team had had previous training or experience in participatory, interdisciplinary research. The Maize Storage Project was thus very much a "learning by doing" experience for the researchers, just as it was for the farmers.

In positive terms, although the active participation of farmers in the research project deviated from the norms of conventional research at the University of Benin, and was thus viewed at the outset with some skepticism, the general attitude of the researchers toward the participatory approach improved once it became apparent that farmers had, in fact, much to contribute. This was exemplified by the enlargement of the parameters of research at the end of the first stage, a direct outcome of early collaboration. Not only were the opinions of farmers instrumental in altering the perceptions of the university researchers, the modification of the research design to suit farmers' preferences undoubtedly averted much wasted time and effort. Likewise, in approaching the problem of maize storage and loss from an interdisciplinary systems perspective, the researchers were better able to appreciate the myriad factors affecting maize conservation in household silos and to recognize that village-level problems are often not amenable to investigative methods that require key variables to be held constant. By ensuring ongoing dialogue and critical feedback from farmers, and by attempting to integrate aspects of entomology, agricultural engineering, and social science into the overall inquiry, the university researchers widened the scope of their own learning.

As with farmers, however, the participatory process proved to be more time-consuming than the researchers had initially anticipated. Given the almost total absence of telecommunication systems in the rural areas, and with no reduction in their teaching and other university duties, team members were obliged to devote numerous weekends traveling to and from village sites to monitor fieldwork and to meet with farmers. An estimated 16,000 kilometers were covered by university personnel each year, often on poor roads. Such arduous travel entailed regular maintenance and frequent purchases of vehicle and moped parts. Considerable time too had to be devoted to other administrative issues: the drafting and signing of contracts with each participating household; the coordination of travel and meetings; the provision of hybrid grain, fertilizers, and other matériel to community sites; assistance with the construction of prototype silos in the selected villages; and arrangements for farmers' attendance at project seminars. Occasionally, the need to respect the domestic contingencies of individual farmers and other formal community activities caused delays and the necessary rescheduling of activities. Because projected deadlines were frequently related to other professional activities, these delays added to the stress of the university team.

One possible way of alleviating the work load of the core group of researchers might have been to invite the participation of additional university staff. The idea was rejected, however, because, in addition to adding to the project's administrative overhead, it was felt that the inclusion of less sensitive, less committed personnel might undermine what was so crucial to the project—the retention of farmers' trust and confidence. Far better, it was decided, in view of the rigors of accommodating both village-level and interdisciplinary teamwork, a small group of dedicated individuals should remain as the professional core.

## Institutional Linkages and Dissemination Channels

A common criticism of PAR is that it is case specific, at best benefiting those immediately involved in the process but having little impact beyond the restricted bounds of those groups and communities that are the focus of each study. In the case of the Maize Storage Project, there is no doubt that its impact among regional communities has so far been marginal. Given its context and initial time frame, this was to be expected. Anticipating these limitations, however, the ESA researchers took advantage of the Togolese government's outspoken concern for the improvement of agricultural production and food security by arranging for media coverage of the project.

This involvement of the popular press, while falling short of galvanizing communities to action, has proven beneficial for other reasons. As in many developing countries, the media in Togo are largely funded and controlled by the state. Consequently, the interest of print journalists and television crews in the Maize Storage Project served not only as a useful means of disseminating the research findings and promoting a participatory approach among other researchers and extension agents but it also signaled a measure of government interest and support. The legitimacy of the project, particularly its emphasis on farmers' participation in the research process, was thus enhanced—as was the public profile of the project leaders. This has not been lost on members of Togo's scientific community, many of whom are also financially sustained by the state.

As noted, the current second phase of the project includes the preparation of audiovisual materials by state television. The inclusion of this key communication institution, from invited observer to full participant, is a useful step in publicizing PAR and signals ways in which popular media in Africa can contribute to applied research.

The involvement of extension agencies has likewise contributed to a heightened understanding of certain technical factors underlying low farmer income and food loss. Also enhanced has been the credibility of university-based research as a potentially useful resource for rural development purposes. All too often, and with some justification, development organizations—government and nongovernment alike—have looked askance at university research as being far removed from the issues of daily rural life. The Maize Storage Project, however, by moving beyond the conventional boundaries of most agricultural research in Africa, has enabled researchers and extension agents to breach the walls of their dual perspectives. The link between research and community development work has enhanced mutual appreciation of the complexities of fostering community-level change and of the value of collecting and analyzing scientific data.

## Conditions for the Facilitation of PAR in Sub-Saharan Africa

As one instance of participatory action research conducted in one selected region, it would be presumptuous to regard the Maize Storage Project in Togo as a prototype for PAR in sub-Saharan Africa. Neither the enormous heterogeneity of the continent nor the singular nature of each participatory exercise can allow for such a claim. Nonetheless, in line with other studies—particularly those that have examined rural nonformal education in African communities—the experiences of the Maize Storage Project do suggest a number of conditions that facilitate PAR and may even be necessary for its successful implementation in rural Africa.

## The Researcher as Ethnographer and
## Community Development Worker

In an ideal world, PAR would always be initiated by groups for whom the research is meant to benefit. Rarely is this the case, however, and, in much of sub-Saharan Africa, it is simply not possible. Having limited or no access to formal education of any kind, the great majority of the rural populace remains illiterate. Although possessing complex bodies of informally learned skills and practices, village people generally have a limited capacity to evaluate techniques that are most often derived from acquired beliefs and immediate observations (Brokensha and Werner, 1980; Fernandez, 1986).

A major thrust of development assistance programs, of course, has been to alter many village practices through the introduction of new technologies and methods. Yet the history of such efforts has been characterized by an almost total lack of genuine consultation with village farmers. Customarily, professional researchers develop a technology in controlled circumstances according to their own perceptions of a specific need. Once the technology is satisfactorily tested, it is handed over to extension agents, who become responsible for introducing it to farmers and promoting its widespread adaptation. Time and again, however, having had no responsibility in the development of new technologies and processes, village farmers have borne the brunt of unanticipated problems and negative effects. Invariably, they have become impervious—even resistant to—externally introduced change (Chambers, 1986).

A further hindrance to PAR derives from the cultural ambiguity of participation (Cao Tri, 1986). From a Western perspective, participation involves the open exchange of arguments and ideas, it sanctions the right to question, and it legitimates the prerogative to be different, to conduct experiments, and to make mistakes. In many rural regions of sub-Saharan Africa, however, direct questioning and open dialogue among different subgroups are shunned, and, in subsistence economies, experimentation and mistakes are often regarded as conveying unacceptable risk (Fernandez, 1986). If it is not rooted in existing cultural mores, participation is likely to be a meaningless exercise—at least in a form that a professional researcher might expect or hope for. In addition, where disadvantaged village people have been manipulated by other more powerful social forces—a historically common occurrence across the continent—intervention by outside researchers, even those espousing principles of dialogue and participation, is likely to generate suspicions or deep caution (Chambers, 1986).

As it is, few professional researchers are aware of, let alone versed in, PAR. Because of the increasingly specialized nature of scientific disciplines, most professionals are trained to examine certain problems and use particular methods within the relatively circumscribed epistemological frameworks of their own disciplines. They tend to be specialists, concerned with explaining and solving problems either in controlled laboratory environments or by using replicable survey techniques. Their task invariably culminates in written reports and conference presentations, which in form and content adhere to the prevailing standards of their respective disciplines. In this way, researchers further develop their specialist skills and concomitantly advance their scientific careers. For such specialists, collaboration with illiterate and semiliterate peasant farmers, coupled with the adoption of a multidisciplinary systems approach to research, is usually beyond the realms of their own past training and experience. Yet the nature of village-level problems in sub-Saharan Africa, encompassing as they do a range of economic, political, sociocultural, and ecological factors, often necessitates just such a broad perspective (Bassey, 1989).

For professional researchers, therefore, participatory action research in rural African communities poses an enormous challenge. To draw communities and groups into the novel exercise of PAR, and for project-related learning and participation to be sustained, professional researchers must strive to assume some of the skills normally related to ethnography and community development work. They must be able not only to identify those individuals with whom collaborative work will be most effective but to determine as well the forms of relationships that can simultaneously accommodate prevailing sociocultural norms and the objectives of participatory involvement in applied research. They must be as well versed in communication and teaching skills as they are in the techniques of scientific inquiry, able to transmit information clearly and simply, and to encourage participants to respond critically. As catalysts of a novel exercise, professional researchers must also know when to accede to the suggestions of villagers where these are feasible and appropriate—and, if they are not, to explain what they see are the attendant difficulties and shortcomings, and then negotiate alternatives. In short, professional researchers must be able to establish relations with village people wherein both sides interact by learning and teaching together on an equal footing (Ashby, 1984; Cao Tri, 1986).

Ethnographic and community development skills are, of course, not easily acquired; neither should it be assumed that those proposing to carry out PAR possess them. Indeed, techniques for working with community groups, and coping with sociocultural distances that may separate professional researchers from non-professional participants, are ones that traditional scientific training has up to now done little to provide most researchers. That in itself is one of the major challenges of PAR in sub-Saharan Africa. Yet, as became apparent in the Maize Storage Project, with some guidance and trial experience, such capacity is within reach of committed researchers.

### The Need for Institutional Support

The Maize Storage Project has revealed the utility of PAR as a method of learning and of incremental technical change in village communities. It has also demonstrated the significance of support from predominant social and political institutions. Indeed, retrospective observations of the project tend to confirm a common, seemingly paradoxical finding of earlier studies; namely, that in many parts of sub-Saharan Africa, overt assistance from national institutions is a necessary condition for participatory community-based change (Moulton, 1977; Easton, 1983). Intimations of contradiction arise when community activities aiming at self-reliance are dependent on nonvillage institutional support. Yet the phenomenon of rural dependency in Africa has deep historical roots.

During the last 100 years, the lives of peasant people have been profoundly affected by the emergence of centrist political economies, managed first by colonial powers and later by national elites.[9] Generations of African peasants have had to comply with the dictates of urban-based authorities while opportunities for formulating and asserting a collective voice have been exceedingly rare. Institutional structures and processes—including those of national education systems—have thus led to widespread popular perceptions regarding associations of knowledge and power (the latter serving to legitimate the former) and of change as a process that is necessarily initiated and sustained "from above." Such perceptions are not only deeply ingrained among village people, they are quite rational responses to the current realities of Africa's political and economic landscape. In a world where ecological and socioeconomic transformation is largely effected by the vicissitudes of transnational forces, villagers are clearly aware of their inability to fully determine their own destinies or to prosper solely by relying on their own innate and learned capacities (Maclure, 1988).

For those who intervene from outside for purposes of augmenting rural social welfare, it is, therefore, illusory to expect villagers to respond to short-lived prescriptions for technical and behavioral change or to heed cursory blandishments about the need for greater community self-reliance. Individual projects aiming to enhance village participation cannot by themselves achieve more than transitory success. Only through linkages with other regional or national political, financial, and administrative institutions can the potential of participatory interventions be fully realized.

It is this notion of linkages, and what Bock and Papagiannis (1983, p. 344) have indicated is the dependence of participatory models of community development on "charismatic leadership," that became manifest in the Maize Storage Project. The ESA director's support for the project, the attendance of the university rector at the second seminar, the involvement of state media and other rural development organizations, and the financial and technical input from a major research funding agency all helped to sanction the project's participatory approach and to legitimize the contribution of farmers to applied research. As the Maize Storage Project would seem to indicate, for the ends of PAR to be achieved in a rural African context, the participation of villagers must be reinforced by tangible ongoing support from external national and international institutions—in short, by structural conditions that render community-based participation a meaningful exercise.

### Flexible and Accommodating Sources of Funding

In view of the severe financial constraints confronting African states, international donor agencies now fund most research undertaken in sub-Saharan Africa. The yardsticks by which conventional research projects are normally selected for funding (and for which agency personnel are usually trained to adjudicate) are the general relevance of topics, the clarity of project objectives, the rigor of design and methodology, and the expertise of the researchers. For PAR, however, selection criteria are not so clear-cut. Although the tenets of clarity and rigor should be retained, standards used to assess conventional research proposals are not likely to illuminate all the relative merits of prospective PAR projects.

In this regard, the role of IDRC in supporting the Maize Storage Project is instructive. In addition to ensuring the necessary funding, IDRC program staff provided key input on issues of research design and methodology. In effect, by promoting the adoption of a participatory approach, they were arguing for a more direct iterative connection between science and community development. For IDRC and other donor agencies, this view of science has far-reaching ramifications. If funding agencies are to substantially increase support for initiatives that involve local people as participants in the research process, rather than simply as beneficiaries of end results, then new criteria for project selection are required. In all such cases, donor agencies must estimate the needs and capacities of prospective nonprofessional participants as much as the qualifications and intentions of professional researchers. To this end, critical reviews of project proposals labeled participatory or action research should heed the following:

— who the participants are and how they have been (or are to be) engaged
— how specific research questions have been identified
— how the framework and methodology of inquiry have been (or will be) designed
— how participation is to be operationalized
— the extent of researchers' commitment to the improved well-being of participating communities

Modifications in monitoring procedures are likewise essential. Funding agencies are bureaucracies that operate according to stipulated time frames, annual budgets, and stringent accounting procedures. It follows that they tend to treat conventional research projects as discrete activities subject to similar regulatory standards. Yet PAR does not fit readily into the discrete project mold. Its attendant aspects of shared ownership and community-based learning and action make it difficult to separate its inevitable "project" status from extensive ongoing social processes. Attempts to monitor and assess PAR in a limited time frame through standard financial and technical reporting are thus almost always inadequate.

In light of the example of the Maize Storage Project in Togo, for which IDRC moved beyond the established pattern of bankrolling and periodic monitoring, agencies must be prepared to actively assist in the development of PAR proposals, to devote resources to field training, and to provide judicious support for recommended actions emerging from research findings. Sufficient resources and time should be allotted so that professional researchers and prospective participants can establish structures and methods of collaboration and ensure that systems of genuinely shared control are in place. In brief, as funding agencies increasingly espouse rhetoric about including disadvantaged (and thus less formally educated) people as full-fledged participants in the development process, and if research is indeed to extend beyond its proverbial ivory tower and policy-level confines, then agencies must adopt approaches more suitable to the complexities of community participation—as opposed to insisting that modes of participation suit the agencies' existing policies.

Such a reorientation of funding agency procedures is not without risk. The prospect of concrete results emanating from PAR is usually less certain than with conventional research. Returns on research investment may be less quantifiable. In addition, there remains the persistent hazard of exacerbating the dependent linkages that are too often characteristic of African development assistance. While encouraging and responding favorably to the emergence of participatory action research as a potentially effective means of addressing community problems, agencies should avoid "shopping around" for PAR projects in order to fulfill their own mandates. It is a fine line to tread, of course, for as the example of IDRC's role in supporting the Maize Storage Project has demonstrated, there is considerable merit in fostering participatory action research approaches *where these are appropriate*. But, in regions that have long been besieged by innovations of all kinds, PAR should be advanced with prudence. Increasingly, the dynamic for exploring and adopting PAR should emanate from indigenous research communities, not from the donor agencies.

Finally, while assessments of the processes and results of PAR projects must remain an essential function of funding agencies, project appraisals should include more qualitative factors than are typically used in conventional evaluations. In addition to the customary assessments of methodological reliability and the validity of research findings, agencies must also consider the extent to which shared ownership, learning, and action—the fundamental objectives of PAR—are achieved. This ultimately requires more subjective, even participatory, methods of monitoring and the acquisition of reports that refer as much to the facets of participation as they do to research methods and results.

## Notes

1. Information on the project background and design is drawn from IDRC (1983).
2. Financed by the Canadian government, IDRC supports development-related research in developing countries. The Maize Storage Project was submitted to IDRC's Post-Production Systems Programme at the centre's West African regional office in Dakar. Staff in the program are experienced agricultural researchers in their own right. Given their positions in an international agency, they are able to have an overview not only of ongoing agricultural research in West Africa but of current research trends in other parts of the world.
3. More detailed information on the research is provided by Kpakote et al. (1988) and Smith (1989).
4. In Togo, these zones are designated as the Maritimes, the Plains, the Plateau area, and the Mountain region.
5. Traditional granaries of southern Togo can be classified into four types. Two are circular structures, framed by four poles and enclosed by careful emplacement of bound maize cobs.

They differ only in the elevation of the base from the ground. A third type, also circular, has woven straw matting as material for the walled enclosure. The fourth type is a rectangular crib usually constructed of bamboo stalks.

6. l'Institut de Recherches Agronomiques Tropicales and le Service de la Protection des Végétaux.

7. Personnel from CUSO (a Canadian NGO) and INADES-Formation (a regional extension training service) are currently pursuing a similar participatory approach, monitoring, and testing various aspects of maize production and storage systems with farmers.

8. Similar research networks in the social and health sciences have also emerged in West Africa.

9. It can be argued that, in recent years, as the African continent has become overwhelmed by social and economic crises, state institutions now largely serve as conduits for the policies of bilateral and multilateral aid agencies. Yet this does not alter the long-standing pattern of structural disparity that has so marked recent African history.

## *References*

ASHBY, J. A. (1984) Participation of Small Farmers in Technology Assessment. Muscle Shoals, AL: International Fertilizer Development Center.

BASSEY, M. W. (1989) "Besoins en séchage: le point de vue des fermiers de Sierra Leone," pp. 57-69 in M. Parmentier and K. Fouabi (eds.) Céréales en régions chaudes: Transformation et conservation. Paris: John Libbey Eurotext.

BENOIT-CATTIN, M. (1984) "Farmer-researcher dialogue: reflections and experience," pp. 41-44 in P. Matlon et al. (eds.) Coming Full Circle: Farmers Participation in the Development of Technology. Ottawa: International Development Research Centre.

BLACKIE, M. J. (1984) "Research design and implementation in the Sebungwe Region of Zimbabwe," pp. 51-62 in Matlon et al. (eds.) Coming Full Circle: Farmers' Participation in the Development of Technology. Ottawa: International Development Research Centre.

BOCK, J. C. and G. J. PAPAGIANNIS (1983) "The paradoxes of nonformal education and the unplanned emergence of strong participation," pp. 337-348 in J. C. Bock and G. J. Papagiannis (eds.) Nonformal Education and National Development: A Critical Assessment of Policy, Research, and Practice. New York: Praeger.

BROKENSHA, D.M.W. and O. WERNER (1980) Indigenous Knowledge Systems and Development. Washington, DC: University Press of America.

CAO TRI, H. (1986) "La participation des populations au développement: problematique, conditions de mise en oeuvre et domains de compétence de l'Unesco," pp. 41-66 in Participer au Développement. Paris: UNESCO.

CHAMBERS, R. (1986) Normal Professionalism, New Paradigms and Development. Sussex, England: Sussex University, Institute of Development Studies.

EASTON, P. A. (1983) "Functional literacy in the West African Sahel: the Operation Arachide Project in Mali," pp. 63-86 in J. C. Bock and G. J. Papagiannis (eds.) Nonformal Education and National Development: A Critical Assessment of Policy, Research, and Practice. New York: Praeger.

FERNANDEZ, M. E. (1986) Participatory-Action-Research and the Farming Systems Approach with Highland Peasants. Columbia: University of Missouri, Department of Sociology.

GROSSI, F. V., S MARTINIC, G. TAPIA, and I. PASCAL (1983) Participatory Research: Theoretical Frames, Methods and Techniques. Ottawa: International Council for Adult Education.

INTERNATIONAL DEVELOPMENT RESEARCH CENTRE (IDRC) (1983) Maize Storage (Togo): Project Summary (No. 3-P-83-0272). Ottawa: Author.

KORTEN, D. C. (1983) ''Social development: putting people first,'' pp. 201-221 in D. C. Korten and F. B. Alfonso (eds.) Bureaucracy and the Poor: Closing the Gap. West Hartford, CT: Kumarian.

KPAKOTE, K. G., H. SMITH, and P. SMITH (1988) "Etudes togolaises de stockage de mais en milieu rural," pp. 201-237 in A. M. Adjangba (ed.) La production alimentaire et l'agriculture en Afrique. Athens: Foundation Publishing.

MACLURE, R. (1988) Intervention and Dependency: A Case Study of Animation Rurale Programmes in Burkina Faso. Ph.D. dissertation, Stanford University.

MOULTON, J. M. (1977) Animation Rurale: Education for Rural Development. Amherst: University of Massachusetts, Center for International Education.

SMITH, P. (1989) A Study of the Drying Mechanism of Traditional Maize Storage Structures Used in Southern Togo: Final Report (CIDA Awards for Canadians Programme). Lomé: University of Benin.

## 15

# The Role of the
# Social Scientist in
# Participatory Action Research

### SERGIO RUANO

This chapter presents my interpretation of the role of social scientists within agricultural research programs. It is based on 16 years of experience that began in Central America and on what I have learned from many friends, colleagues, and farmers.

I had the privilege of becoming an active participant in one of the first national teams organized to develop what later became known as farming systems research (FSR). That occurred in 1974, within the Instituto de Ciencia y Tecnología Agrícolas (ICTA) in Guatemala. The early days of this learning process were for me full of enthusiasm and devoid of knowledge, but this void began to be filled by experienced professionals such as Peter Hildebrand, Carlos Reiche, Amalia Corisco, Bruno Busto Brol (teammates), Astolfo Fumagalli, and many farmers of the southeast of my country.

Social scientist participation within agricultural research is increasing at a rapid pace, not just in field research but also at other levels like planning, evaluation, policy-making, and institutional analysis. The pioneer discipline was agricultural economics, which has developed a well-known and respected set of methodologies. Here I will be referring to the role of non-economist social scientists, especially anthropologists and rural sociologists, whose involvement came later.

I will focus on what I believe the role of the above social scientists should be, within an agricultural research institution using a system perspective with a participatory approach. I will be referring to a social scientist who, as a part of a team, will be carrying out applied work to help and support biological scientists to generate, adapt, validate, and transfer technology that is more meaningful, more useful, and more adoptable by farmers.

## A Brief Background

Agricultural economics (AE) first gained general recognition within social science research (Ruttan, 1978). AE products are normally concrete and tangible. In terms of research results, one of the AE contributions has been the quantifying of production functions for already generated technologies. Currently, it participates within a much more complex framework. AE analyzes different aspects of economic activity, integrating all the production factors under different circumstances from the beginning or even before the biological process starts. AE methods and techniques are now being applied throughout the entire agricultural research process so that even results and field-level impact are evaluated. AE has been the least controversial of the social science disciplines and the most widely accepted by biological scientists.

Fields such as anthropology and rural sociology have been introduced very recently. As a result, they have been less well defined, less understood, and less recognized by natural science-based people. Their products within agricultural research have been less concrete and less tangible, sometimes with little or no applicability or usefulness for the biological programs.

In many cases, an agricultural economist has a strong background in biology, having graduated from an agriculture school and specializing in one of the various related fields. On the other hand, most of the noneconomist social scientists (SS) have never been in touch with either biological theory or agricultural field experience. Their agricultural knowledge is just in terms of agricultural products through their daily gastronomic experiences at home.

## Some Potential Contributions

The participatory action research approach has developed a widely accepted general methodology that follows sequential stages: (1) diagnosis, (2) technology generation and/or adaptation, (3) technology testing, (4) technology validation, and (5) technology transfer or technology communication. The following are some specific tasks that a social scientist should perform in this sequential framework.

(1) In diagnosis, the team will identify production problems and constraints and will also know, define, and characterize the clients. The diagnosis should be the main base for most of the work that follows.

From this stage on, the SS should be the bridge between farmers and natural scientists. The SS should be able to interpret and understand both parties' conceptualizations of the world. Among other things, he or she would have the responsibility to lead the organization of the diagnostic study. That means technical leadership in terms of methodology, monitoring, and evaluating the results. He or she would train the others for sampling, surveying, and communication techniques (to teach the others about local culture and language). Other key contributions would be developing ways of incorporating farmer participation; the definition of "recommendation domains"; and the selection of collaborating farmers (to make sure that those farmers belong to the recommendation domains defined for participation). An appropriate interpretation of social structure and social interrelationships is extremely valuable.

(2) In the second stage, when appropriate, applied research will be carried out, mainly at the laboratory and research station levels. Eventually, some researcher-managed research will be accomplished on some selected farms.

Before field research is possible, potential solutions must be discussed with the farmers to ensure that those potential solutions fit with and make sense in terms of farmers' expectations and constraints. Methods to apply in this encounter with farmers would also be the responsibility of the SS.

The organization of any field day at this stage and later on would be a primary task of the SS. Other activities such as farmers' participation in germplasm selection should be organized, institutionalized, and recorded by the SS.

(3) The testing stage will generally be performed as on-farm adaptive research. Some technologies need to be screened first through researcher-managed trials to pass on later under the farmer's management. Simple experimental designs are used.

Farmers' understanding of what institutionalized research is all about, and what is occurring on their farms, is a key issue. To ensure farmers' full participation and to record farmers' reactions to new technology are other duties of the SS.

(4) Technology validation, if it is needed, is under the farmer's management, risk, and financing. Promising technology with a high probability of being widely adopted is tried. There are no experimental designs at this stage.

Again, farmers' participation must be kept up and their reactions in terms of acceptance or rejection of the new technology should be recorded, evaluated, and reported. Neighboring farmers' reactions as well as the social or natural diffusion and local adaptation or modification of the new technology are also crucial to document.

(5) Experience has shown that the most effective transfer mechanisms are the ones in which farmers have the main responsibility. Those carried out by the farmers themselves, with only limited institutional backup, have proved to have higher probabilities of success. The SS would have the most appropriate training to lead the development of those mechanisms and to maintain an efficient feedback system.

My personal experience has been that most extension professionals (mainly general agronomists) do not have training in or understanding of the participatory approach. Formal extension training under this paradigm is still either very weak or nonexistent.

### Some Potential and Real Problems

The following personal assumptions do not include all noneconomist social scientists but certainly do include many of us.

A very common mistake that blocks effective participation and contribution by social scientists working in agricultural research programs is that many SS try to convert agricultural research programs into social science research programs. Some SS try to make agricultural research something to be regulated under social science methods and techniques. Worse still is a type of research based on the particular ideology and theory held by the anthropologist or sociologist.

Although the final objective of agricultural research is social and economic, this research is and will be a domain of the biology field. With or without SS participation, agricultural research has existed and will continue to exist. SS participation should be a means of support and cooperation to make agricultural research more appropriate to certain circumstances— especially to those faced by most of the world's poor farmers.

It is not possible to turn agricultural research into social science research; neither is it possible to turn biological scientists into SS under the assumption that this is the only way to set an adequate strategy for participatory research.

I have many times come into contact with colleagues who presume to be applying a participatory approach. However, rather than using a team effort, these people are carrying out individual work using orthodox social science methods, which in turn does not create any interest on the part of the biological scientists. In other words, there is a total divorce between the SS and his or her work and the rest of the team. Normally, the SS excuses him- or herself, saying that he or she prefers not to deal with such closed-minded people (the biological scientists); they do not understand the importance of social science variables, so it is more profitable to work alone and to prove to the others that he or she is working on something worthwhile. Most of the time this isolated work does not lead to any contribution to project objectives.

What seems to be the problem? Some years of shared experience and a little meditating suggest that the main problem is the SS him- or herself, either his or her personality, his or her training, or both. Usually this SS wants to work within the project but makes no efforts to differentiate agricultural research from a pure social science type of research. This SS may bring a strong academic background to the team, and at times some field experience, but be strongly biased toward very specialized disciplinary work. When he or she joins the multidisciplinary team (where most of the scientists are biology majors), then a negative minority reaction feeling takes place. From the beginning, he or she overestimates the real value of his or her discipline but provides insufficient explanation of it. As a consequence, communication is distorted.

The contribution of the social sciences does not generally offer tangible products like a crop variety. Instead, it offers concepts, methods, techniques, points of view, and strategies, which can be useful and applicable to the objectives of the project to the extent that they can be adapted under the conceptual and methodological framework of the biological sciences. The project's primary objectives are agricultural, therefore, the criteria, the approach, and the general methodology should remain under natural science leadership in spite of its socioeconomic goals.

The above situation sooner or later ends up being very complicated. On the one hand, biologists do not highly value socioeconomic criteria; moreover, usually they overlook them. On the other hand, the SS does not understand a natural science-based discipline and does not try to understand at least some of its main principles. Due to the nature of the project (agricultural), it is the SS who is supposed to look for better ways of communication with the biologists, not necessarily the other way around. To accomplish this, the SS must understand some general aspects of the natural science-based disciplines, methods, and techniques being applied within the project. Moreover, the SS must also understand some information regarding the nature and implications of the main biological variables.

Experience has shown me that it is not sensible for the SS to promote the advantages of his or her field until he or she has learned vital information pertaining to the agricultural part of the project. He or she should come into the team very cautiously. (We have to remember that the SS is the stranger to the group.) Then he or she should take some time to analyze project objectives, the institutional framework, the social and cultural working environment, and the background (especially previous experiences with social scientists in the project). After this process, the SS may be in a position to move toward training others in various social science tasks. If the SS's background does not include some biological knowledge related to the project, then he or she must immediately start a kind of self-training program, beginning with some general topics that are directly related to the project. (The natural science-based people can be of great help.) The main objective of this self-training would be to understand general principles of the most relevant natural science-based disciplines of the project.

If the first part of the project is a diagnostic study, it would be a mistake to implement an orthodox social science methodology and even worse to make the analysis based on social science techniques and jargon. This type of agricultural and socioeconomic study, as the basis of the project, normally needs the collection of firsthand information, and the most important informants are the farmers themselves. If the SS is an anthropologist, he or she could be very useful in improving communication between the team and the rural population. He or she would be better trained in communication and interviewing techniques. The anthropologist could also be of great value in interpreting farmers' views of their world and then translating it to teammates using the biologist's perspective. However, to do this, the SS would need some knowledge of agricultural production.

If the SS is a rural sociologist, then one contribution could be in survey planning (structure and organization of the questionnaire, coding, and so on). However, the ones that know best which biological variables to include are the biologists themselves. Both sociologists and anthropologists could also be very important in helping others to understand the social, cultural, and economic structure of the rural population. They also have more formal training in analysis (according to different criteria) to better define and communicate to others about the relationship among different types of farming systems and the social strata and the rationality of those systems.

To define what could be the main contributions of an SS is not a simple task, especially when their biologist counterparts do not have a clear idea about it. When the SS role remains unclear and no extra efforts are made to better define it, the SS disciplinary perspective takes over and the SS is isolated. A considerable amount of information is available, but most of it with little or no application and utility for biologists involved in the project. Then a pile of papers becomes part of a library's resources to be eventually looked at by a student.

A final comment is necessary regarding political ideology. There is a much stronger normative orientation in the social science than in natural science based disciplines. In other words, an SS has a stronger commitment to social reform. This situation has been a primary source of tension that seems almost unresolvable. First of all, in the social sciences, there are many more theories focused on a single phenomenon. There is a simple explanation for that: Natural science-based disciplines can be experimented on relatively easily, so many of their laws have become universal. On the other hand, in the social sciences, an understanding of a social, economic, or cultural phenomenon depends on many different factors, some of them depending on strongly biased personal interpretation.

Many times I have worked with an SS who takes an inflexible ideological position, for example, regarding project objectives. Here he or she argues for working completely according to the "manual," under unrealistic situations. The project then becomes seriously affected by the resulting conflict.

In several Latin American countries, an agricultural project is often part of a national development plan. It would be crucial to understand that that project under that framework is contributing something or will be able to make a contribution as part of a larger system. In other words, the project by itself would not change, overnight, a problematic rural situation that has lasted for hundreds of years. As part of the project, technological problems can be solved in a short time. It would be expected that those partial solutions could have direct or/and indirect positive effects on other problems in the long run, which in turn will affect rural well-being. In other words, the hope seems to be to make quantitative changes first in order to be able to make qualitative ones later on.

When the above analysis is not very clear, we social scientists are in great danger of becoming isolated and frustrated, and no participation takes place at all. The main tasks that were expected to be performed by the SS are not accomplished or are carried out in a defective manner. As a result, instead of having a much more integral approach, the project runs a risk of taking on a traditional approach, focused on just biological and agronomic variables and without farmers' participation.

## Some Conclusions

An SS who becomes involved in participatory action research must be very clear about the strengths, weaknesses, and constraints of the project. If he or she can do that, but does not have any background in biology, that knowledge should be obtained at least at the basic level. One way that I personally have used is to become involved in all the research tasks that the natural science-based people carry out as part of the project and also become involved with neighboring farmers in their daily farming duties. In other words, in-service training is necessary in order to comprehend the agricultural process. It can be complemented with some selected readings.

The in-service training should include the entire agricultural process and all the steps related to agricultural research, from planning to analysis. It does not mean that the SS must become an experimental design expert, but certainly he or she should know what it is about. This type of training is difficult, and perhaps some would consider it useless for an SS. My opinion is that it is the only way to really become a team member and contribute to the project. On one hand, the SS should understand the language and dynamics of the agricultural process from the farmers' perspective, and, on the other hand, it is also necessary to understand language and methods from the biologists' perspective. If the SS is willing to learn, then he or she is in a position to make important contributions.

## Reference

RUTTAN, V. (1978) Agricultural Research Policy. Minneapolis: University of Minnesota Press.

*16*

# Social Scientists in International Agricultural Research

## Ensuring Relevance and Contributing to the Knowledge Base

### DOUGLAS E. HORTON

The first social scientist—economist Michael Twomey—joined the International Potato Center, known in Spanish as the Centro Internacional de la Papa (CIP), in late 1973. Soon after he arrived, he requested transportation to the Peruvian highlands to plant a potato trial on the farm of a peasant family. He saw this as a logical way to begin learning about Andean potato farming, production problems, and possible avenues for technological change.

CIP's director of research, a mycologist by training, denied the request for three reasons: First, economists should concentrate on economics and leave experimental work to biologists, who have the required training and experience. Second, research should be done on the experiment station, where nonexperimental variables can be controlled, not on farms. Third, extension-type on-farm work was beyond CIP's mandate and should be left to Peru's National Potato Program. Undaunted by the veto, CIP's young economist arranged for his own transportation to the highlands and planted the trial anyway.

So began on-farm research at CIP: as a focal point for clashing perspectives about agricultural research and development (R & D) and about the role of social scientists in CIP (Rhoades et al., 1986). Gradually, a fruitful dialogue was established between social and biological scientists, which contributed to the center's understanding of farmers' needs and to its responsiveness to them.

However, as CIP's programs and social scientists' activities evolved, perspectives have clashed again and again. This constructive conflict has helped CIP develop more effective strategies to understand and respond to the needs of people in developing countries. It has also led to greater understanding of the role of social scientists in international agricultural research.

Much of the work of CIP's social scientists over the years fits the broad definition of participatory action research (PAR). Social scientists have worked to improve CIP's organizational performance, the quality of work life, and the center's responsiveness to client needs. They have contributed also to applied social science in a broader sense.

The work has been participatory in several respects. Social scientists have participated on interdisciplinary teams working on technical problems, like pest management and seed storage. They have also worked with biological scientists on teams charged with carrying out socioeconomic studies, like impact assessments. In both instances, attempts have been made to enlist the participation of CIP's clients—researchers and farmers from developing countries—in the applied research process.

The work has also been action oriented. CIP is an applied research center. CIP's programs are aimed at solving problems limiting potato and sweet potato production and use in developing countries, and the center's social science work forms part of this effort. Neither the problems nor their solutions are obvious. Hence social scientists work with their biologist colleagues to determine which problems the center should emphasize. (This is often referred to as "needs assessment.") Another important area of applied interdisciplinary research is the development of effective strategies for carrying out research and disseminating results. (This is often referred to as "research on research.")

Much of the action takes place in the field. Approximately half the center's resources go to regional programs that work directly with national crop involvement efforts. CIP's social scientists work as full partners in this task.

In most discussions of PAR, it is assumed that the professional researcher is a specialist in organizational behavior who comes from outside the organization in question. This chapter presents a case in which "the researchers" are members of an agricultural research organization. Two examples illustrate the work of CIP social scientists.

The first example is drawn from on-farm research in the Mantaro Valley of Peru's central highlands. This was the first time at CIP, and one of the first anywhere, that social and biological scientists formed interdisciplinary teams and carried out research with farmers on farmers' fields. Whereas an original goal was to improve methods to "transfer" improved technology to small farmers, we found that there was little appropriate technology to transfer. We also learned that Andean farmers were active researchers and developers in their right and that we could learn a great deal from them.

The Mantaro Valley project provided the motivation and the legitimacy for many researchers at CIP headquarters and especially in regional and national programs to begin working with farmers. It also resulted in the development of a new approach to agricultural research and development, called the farmer-back-to-farmer model. This approach has been extensively applied not only by CIP but by R & D programs throughout the world. The result has been to improve the effectiveness of R & D by focusing it on important problems of farmers and ensuring that solutions fit their own conditions.

The second example illustrates a rapidly different activity: the assessment of CIP's achievements and impact. Here, social scientists participated with biologists in evaluation terms that evaluated the center's work. Although the assessment could be faulted for "external objectivity," it sensitized staff members to the importance of achieving practical goals. It helped build a consensus within CIP on the relative performance of programs. It also provided valuable information for increasing public awareness of the value of CIP's work.

To set the stage for this chapter's two examples, we begin with a brief description of the conventional paradigm of agricultural R & D.

### *The Transfer of Technology Model*

The dominant paradigm for agricultural R & D—at both the national and the international levels—has long been the transfer of technology model (Chambers and Ghildyal, 1985; Rhoades and Booth, 1982; Lionberger, 1986). In this model, universities and research institutes are seen as the principal sources of new ideas and technologies, which are later transferred by extension agencies to passive farmer-adopters. This approach often results from attempts to apply some features of the U.S. land grant colleges in developing countries, where the setting and needs are radically different.

The core of the model is a one-way flow of improved technologies from researchers through extension to farmers. The numerous graphic representations of the model highlight the downward or outward flow of technologies from centers of excellence to passive beneficiaries or clients—from rich countries to poor ones or from basic researchers to applied research institutes, to extension agencies, and finally on to farmers (Figure 16.1), following with basic, registered, and certified seed, and ending up with farmers' common seed.

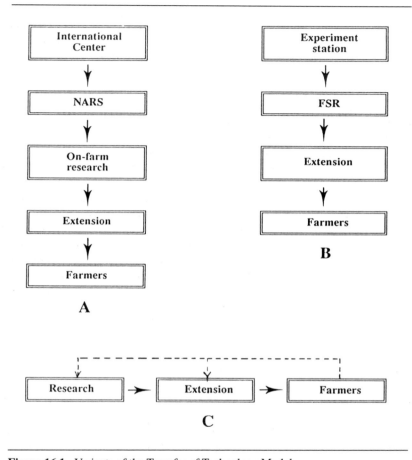

**Figure 16.1.** Variants of the Transfer of Technology Model

SOURCE: Reprinted with permission from the Quarterly Journal of International Agriculture (vol. 28, no. 3/4, December 1989).

Belief in the efficacy of technology transfer was one of the ideological cornerstones of the Consultative Group on International Agricultural Research (CGIAR). For example, a special issue of *Scientific American* (1976) dedicated to food and agriculture stated:

By conservative estimates, presently demonstrated agricultural technology, if applied to all land now in cultivation could support a world population of 45 billion. . . .

The transfer of modern agricultural technology from developed to under-developed countries is gathering perceptible momentum.

Many of the founders of CGIAR believed in the strategy of basing a group of competent scientists in a developing country, providing them with excellent facilities, and isolating them from political pressures for several years. Under these conditions, they were expected to develop valuable new technologies that could then be transferred to national programs and to farmers throughout the developing world.

This paraphrasing of conventional wisdom around 1970 was provided by R. L. Sawyer, CIP's founding director general, who was establishing the center at the time. Sawyer took quite a different approach and implemented many strategies at CIP to ensure that staff were exposed to real-life situations in developing countries.

At CIP, as at virtually all agricultural research centers in the early 1970s (and at many today), biological scientists generally assumed that they understood the problems of crop production and the ideal solutions for developing countries. In their view, economists and other social scientists had a secondary role (if any) to play in the R & D process. It was to facilitate the transfer of improved technology by helping determine optimal input levels and by training farmers and convincing them to follow recommendations.

In the 1970s, on-farm research came to be seen as a useful intermediate step between experiment station research and extension that could help validate improved technologies, establish "appropriate" input levels, and develop packages of recommended practice for extension to farmers. As in the case of feedback, the precise meanings of *validate, appropriate,* and *package* were unclear, as were the most appropriate methods for carrying out on-farm research.

### Example 1: On-Farm Research

In early 1975, Michael Twomey became frustrated and resigned from CIP. Before doing so, he had secured funding from the Inter-American Development Bank and from the Rockefeller Foundation to hire two young social scientists with ample field experience: I joined the staff in June 1975; Robert Werge, an anthropologist, arrived in September. Werge had a background in tropical agriculture and anthropology from the University of Florida, he had served in the Peace Corps in Ethiopia, and he had done extensive fieldwork on agricultural systems in the Dominican Republic.

He was the first anthropologist posted with an international agricultural research center under a new postdoctoral fellowship program of the Rockefeller Foundation. I had studied agricultural economics at the University of Illinois and economic development at Cornell, where I met and studied with W. F. Whyte. Whyte encouraged me to do the research for my Ph.D. dissertation in Peru, and, between 1970 and 1974, I spent three years living there studying agricultural organization and the land reform process. My position was included in a special project for research and training in Andean countries funded by the Inter-American Development Bank.

When Werge and I came to CIP, we went through a period of culture shock that was no less traumatic than anything we had experienced previously. We were both expected to have quick answers to "socioeconomic" questions: I was asked the optimal price of improved seed potatoes; Werge was asked how to convince farmers to use the new seed. Not only did we not have the answers, our previous experience living and working with small farmers made us suspicious of people who thought they had the answers. Werge and I felt, as Twomey before us, that any worthwhile improvements in technology needed to be based on a solid understanding of farmers' current practices and their rationale for the practices. We needed to get to the field.

Our initial opportunity to begin in-depth fieldwork was provided by a special grant from the Social Science Division of the International Development Research Centre (IDRC) of Canada. When we learned that IDRC was supporting interdisciplinary, on-farm research on constraints to rice yields at the International Rice Research (IRRI) in Asia, we quickly developed and sent a proposal to support on-farm research in the Mantaro Valley of highland Peru. The grant from a prestigious donor organization provided not only the resources but the legitimacy for CIP to begin interdisciplinary on-farm research.

## The Mantaro Valley Project

The Mantaro Valley Project had three main goals (Horton, 1984):

— to sensitize CIP and national program scientists to the value of on-farm research
— to develop and field test procedures for on-farm research with potatoes
— to train national program personnel in the use of on-farm research techniques

CIP's social science unit took the lead in this first experience with on-farm research, but biological scientists were involved from the outset. Three relatively independent on-farm research teams were formed that corresponded to three of CIP's major research thrusts. One focused on seed quality, one on seed storage, and the third on the broader area of agronomic problems. In each case, a social scientist teamed up with a biological scientist who was an expert in the technical area.

The project included a sequence of interdisciplinary research activities similar to those found in many other FSR projects, in how-to-do-it manuals, and in other international centers' approaches. These activities included a review of the literature on Andean agriculture, a baseline survey of agro-ecology and land use, single- and multiple-visit surveys, and on-farm trials designed to test the agro-economic performance of "improved" technological packages composed of recommended seed, fertilizers, and insect control measures.

At the outset, agricultural researchers generally assumed that a large stock of appropriate technology was available off the shelf. The main functions of on-farm research were believed to be testing, validation, and refinement of technologies prior to diffusion to farmers through the extension service. It was also assumed that a valid project goal was to develop a universally applicable, logical sequence of FSR steps. As we progressed through the planned sequence of activities, we gradually realized that these two assumptions were false.

Concerning the stock of technology, results of the on-farm trials and subsequent evaluations of farmer adoption revealed that, in fact, little technology was available "off the shelf," ready for transfer. Three critical problems were encountered with the technological packages. The first was that results of the on-farm trials varied greatly among sites, and, on average, the technological packages performed poorly. Prior to the trials, we had expected the recommended package of practices to outyield farmers' technology by 100% or more. But, on average, it increased yields only by about 50%. Results of the package trials also varied dramatically from farm to farm, indicating that farmers needed different packages in different places, not a single package. Efforts to establish valid "recommendation domains" for the technological packages were fruitless in this ecologically diverse mountainous environment.

The second problem with the technological package was that what was originally considered to be the most important component—improved seed potatoes—turned out to be a failure. When the project began, researchers believed that poor quality seed potatoes, caused by viral infection, were the principal constraint to Andean farmers' potato yields. They also thought that use of improved seed would greatly increase farmers' yields and economic returns. To our surprise, on-farm trials indicated that use of improved seed, in fact, reduced farmers' returns in many cases. Not only was "improved" seed more costly than common seed, its quality was highly variable and often rather poor. Additionally, farmers' common seed was often of much higher quality than previously assumed. This was because the Andean farmers were acutely aware of the importance of seed quality, and they employed many strategies to obtain and maintain quality seed potato stocks. Belief in the inherent superiority of modern science was so strong that most potato specialists, even those born in the Andes, had not considered this possibility. As one of CIP's directors pointed out,

> You simply cannot say that those farmers' seed potatoes are as good as our "improved" seed potatoes. It is a contradiction in terms!

The third problem was that farmers would not adopt complex combinations of unknown practices. Rather, they experimented with, adapted, and incorporated individual elements into their farming systems one at a time. Surveys conducted two years after the on-farm trials revealed that farmers had changed many of their practices but that none had adopted the complete packages tested on their farms. Most farmers who were using new practices had modified and adapted them to fit their specific needs and resources.

A striking illustration is provided by farmer adoption and adaptation of diffused-light seed storage (DLS) principles. DLS involves storing seed potatoes in the light to retard sprout growth, to reduce storage losses, and to maintain seed vigor for a longer storage period. Prototype storage structures were tested on a number of farms. The farmers involved showed great interest in the experiments but did not copy the model structures. Instead, they began to apply the principle of DLS in a wide variety of innovative ways. Hence farmers did not adopt the technology as a tangible entity or precise recommendation. They perceived and applied the principles behind the prototype structures. Rather than building elaborate new storage structures, farmers generally remodeled storage areas in their houses or outbuildings (Rhoades, 1984; IDRC, 1986). Concerning the proposed methods for on-farm research, we learned that there were no universally applicable formulas. Soon after beginning the project, in keeping with one of its major objectives (and with the rigid three-year project timetable), we began training researchers and extensionists from national potato programs. Simultaneously, in 1978, CIP began to implement on-farm research in regional programs around the world. It soon became apparent that different research institutions have radically different human, physical, and financial resources as well as different goals, interests, needs, institutional histories, and arrangements. For this reason, it is no more appropriate to recommend a single set of research methods to different institutions than it is to recommend a single package of agronomic practices to different farmers.

The predetermined sequence of steps that we included in our funding proposal to IDRC, which provided our funding, proved to be unrealistic when it came to implementation. In a project proposal, clarity of goals, foresight, and rigorous deductive reasoning are prized. However, in the day-to-day business of agricultural R & D, flexibility, corner-cutting, and responsiveness to changing conditions are the hallmarks of success. For this reason, R & D organizations, like farmers, need relevant principles, flexible problem-solving approaches, and useful tools—not complex, rigid methodologies.

### The Farmer-Back-to-Farmer Model

Our experiences in the Mantaro Valley led to a reexamination of the basic transfer of technology model. Based on the storage work, CIP's postharvest team—composed of two anthropologists (Werge and Robert Rhoades), a plant pathologist (Robert Booth), and a physiologist (Roy Shaw)—formulated an alternative approach, which became known as the farmer-back-to-farmer model (Rhoades and Booth, 1982). This model of applied agricultural R & D focuses on the identification and solution of farmers' problems and requires interdisciplinary teamwork and consultations with farmers in all phases of a continuous research/diffusion process.

The model consists of four stages linked in a circular fashion (Figure 16.2). The model stresses careful diagnosis of problems, but it does not impose a rigid sequence of steps. Work may begin at any point on the circle, and stages may be skipped.

The decision to work on a particular problem (Activity 1) is crucial for the success of R & D. Initially, this may require that social and biological scientists make independent observations and studies. Subsequently, through a process of interdisciplinary dialogue and interaction with farmers, often marked by conflict, the different diagnoses are brought together to arrive at a common definition of the problem. During this phase, team members begin research (Activity 2) to develop potential solutions to the problem. Armed with one or more potential solutions, the team proceeds to testing and adaptation (Activity 3). In cooperation with farmers, potential solutions are compared with existing farming practices. In some cases, it may be desirable to move to farm-level testing and adaptation with little or no on-station research. In other cases, it may be necessary to repeat the research, testing, and adaptation sequence several times before reaching what appears to be a promising solution.

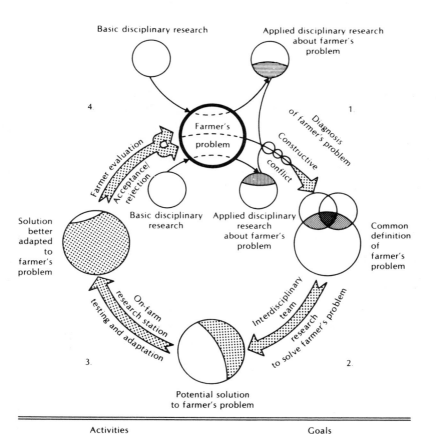

| Activities | Goals |
|---|---|
| 1. Diagnosis of farmer's problem | Common definition of problem by farmers and scientists |
| 2. Interdisciplinary team research to solve farmer's problem | Identify and develop a potential solution to the problem |
| 3. On-farm testing and adaptation | Better adapt the proposed solution to farmer's conditions |
| 4. Farmer evaluation | Understanding farmer acceptance or rejection of solution |

**Figure 16.2.** Farmer-Back-to-Farmer

SOURCE: Adapted from Rhoades and Booth (1982).

Farmers, of course, make the final evaluation (Activity 4) and either use or discard the new ideas. If the ideas are rejected, further research may indicate why, allowing researchers to improve future efforts. If the ideas are accepted and used by farmers, scientists may benefit from monitoring farmers' modifications of prototype technologies, because these may suggest improvements that could make demonstrations more effective in other locations. Impact assessments, which indicate how new technologies were developed and the extent and consequences of technological change, can provide useful information for justifying continued funding for agricultural R & D. They can also provide the organizational learning that is essential for improving future programs.

Encouraged by the early successes in improving seed storage, many CIP scientists and their colleagues in national programs embraced the farmer-back-to-farmer approach and began on-farm research. At headquarters, several interdisciplinary research projects were formulated to address problems related to seed multiplication and distribution, pest management, and consumer potato storage and processing. On-farm research also quickly became an important component of CIP's regional and national programs, which had short-term development goals and offered many opportunities for researchers to interact with extension agents, development workers, and farmers.

Not all the on-farm work has led to successful development and dissemination of better production methods. In some cases, like the attempt to develop low-cost potato processing methods for Andean farmers, what originally looked like promising avenues later turned out to be blind alleys. However, on-farm research has helped researchers to focus on important problems and develop practical solutions.

An important shortcoming of the on-farm work in many regional and national programs has been the lack of participation of a behavioral scientist. When an agronomist carries out a trial on a farm, he tends to concentrate on the trial—design, care, and the analysis of its results—and may never discuss the trial with the farmer. When an economist participates, he may organize a survey and do an economic analysis of the trial's results, but he may also show little interest in the farmer's view of the trial. A behavioral scientist can bring something quite different to the enterprise. By observing farmers and talking to them, he can often judge farmers' interest and their likely use of new practices better than his economist or agronomist colleagues, who use more "scientific" methods. A behavioral scientist is also more likely than a "hard scientist" to enlist the active participation of farmers in on-farm research. The active participation of farmers is a key ingredient, and, without it, on-farm research adds little to the R & D process except for additional testing sites that may be more representative of farmers' conditions than most experiment stations.

## *Example 2: Impact Assessment*

This case illustrates how social scientists participated in the evaluation of CIP's strategies, achievements, and impact. This work was done in 1984 and in 1989. On both occasions, the initial stimulus was external, but the impact assessment process became internalized. Management and scientists representing all branches of the center participated in the evaluations. Results included both products of use to CIP as an institution (reports and organizational learning) and contributions to the broader understanding of impact assessment.

### The 1984 Study

In 1983, CGIAR initiated a study of its impact. Baseline documents on the conceptual framework and methodology of the study were prepared and distributed to the director general (DG) of each center. The reaction of the CIP's DG was that the study was being based on an inappropriate, conventional production economics framework, which would inevitably focus on yield improvements with rice and wheat in Asia. The proposed approach— couched in terms of supply shifts and the econometric estimation of producer and consumer surplus—could not possibly document progress made in many areas with many crops because of the lack of statistical data. Moreover, it ignored the impact of international centers on the capacities and programs of the national centers. Sawyer decided that CIP should quickly carry out its own impact study to ensure that our story was adequately told.

The center's guiding values and strategies place a strong emphasis on institutional development in the Third World. For this reason, in CIP's impact study, we found it useful to distinguish between two broad types of technology—production technology and R & D technology—and the two corresponding types of impact—production impact and institutional impact (Horton, 1986).

*Production technology* refers broadly to all methods that farmers, market agents, and consumers use to cultivate, harvest, store, process, handle, and utilize crops and their derived products. *R & D technology,* in contrast, refers to the organizational strategies, approaches, and methods that researchers and development workers use in their work. Examples of R & D technology are methods for genetic engineering, strategic planning, and on-farm research.

*Production impact* refers to the physical, social, and economic effects produced by farmers' use of new cultural methods. *Institutional impact,* in contrast, refers to the effects of new R & D technology on the capacity of research and development programs to generate and disseminate new production technology. Whereas previous impact studies focused on production impact, the assessment of an international center's programs needed to pay close attention to institutional impact. This was the course taken at CIP.

Responsibility for preparing the study was given to an interdisciplinary team rather than a team of economists. Scientists and policymakers from developing countries were actively involved in the study. Rather than focusing on econometric estimation of the production impact of new varieties, the CIP study describes and illustrates various types of impact as well as the institutional strategies used to achieve them. Recognizing the significance of collaboration and multiple causation, the study made no attempt to attribute specific, farm-level impacts to CIP. The study describes the strategies employed in program planning and review, interdisciplinary team research, institutional linkages, and training. It then reviews the center's research program and its results to date. Seven case studies illustrate how problems of potato production and use have been solved and how diverse types of institutional and production impacts have been achieved.

While I, as head of the Social Science Department, coordinated the study, taxonomists, breeders, pathologists, entomologists, nematologists, physiologists, seed specialists, research managers, policymakers, communication experts, economists, sociologists, and anthropologists were all actively involved. Major sections of the final report were drafted by biological scientists. Three of the seven illustrative cases were prepared by biologists, two of whom were national program scientists. Two other cases were prepared by an anthropologist, and two were written by economists.

Involvement of scientists and policymakers from developing countries helped focus the study on those problems and accomplishments that CIP's clients considered to be the most important. Individuals from Africa, Asia, and Latin America, as well as Europe and North America, provided frank and critical appraisals of the center's programs, accomplishments, and shortcomings. A selection of their comments is presented in the study report.

Assessments of institutional impacts required information on CIP's interaction with national programs and the resulting effect on national R & D capacities. Three distinct approaches were used to obtain and synthesize the needed information. Initially, country-level information was recorded by CIP's regional scientists in a brief questionnaire requiring simple yes/no answers. The information obtained covered such topics as frequency of CIP contacts (correspondence and visits) with each national program, participation in various types of training and seminars, distribution of research reports, collaborative research projects and/or research contracts in each country, and use of CIP-related technologies in national R & D programs and on farms.

This country-level information was complemented with more precise, quantitative data gleaned from the center's files on training and collaborative research efforts and their impacts on production and institutional capacity.

The third approach involved preparation of seven case studies that illustrated both strategies and impacts. The cases emphasize the reciprocal nature and mutual benefits of CIP's relations with country programs. A case drawn from Vietnam illustrates how CIP has learned from a national program's innovations and has incorporated this knowledge into its own research and training programs to the benefit of other countries. Two cases present economic analyses of the costs and benefits of potato improvement programs.

CIP's impact study met its initial objectives and served some additional purposes as well. In the December 1984 meeting of CGIAR, the study report (CIP, 1984) was frequently referred to as a model for impact assessment. The distinction between production impact and institutional impact is now common in CGIAR, and greater efforts are being made to assess institutional impact (Anderson et al., 1988).

After completion of the initial study, a research project on impact assessment was formalized in CIP's food systems unit with a twofold purpose: to assess CIP's impact on a continuing basis and to improve impact assessment methodologies. A survey conducted in 1986 and 1988 documented the views of national potato program leaders on CIP's impact. A few additional case studies were also done. However, with the "institutional pressure" off, little progress was made either in development of new impact assessment methods or in making impact assessment an ongoing process at CIP.

## The 1989 Study

The second concerted effort to assess CIP's impact occurred in 1989. Again, the stimulus came from outside the center. CGIAR organizes periodic external reviews of centers to assure its members that the centers they support carry out their operations effectively and in line with declared policies. Every five years, a center's programs and management are reviewed by external panels specially contracted by CGIAR.

For an external review, a center is requested to provide an analysis of its main achievements, impacts, and constraints during the previous five years.

In preparation for CIP's most recent external review, in 1989, the Social Science Department coordinated preparation of an impact study. Due to the short time available to prepare the report, systematic polling of national program leaders and in-depth case studies were out of the question. We had no alternative but to base our analysis on information already at hand or that could be quickly generated in house.

We reviewed CIP's programmatic units—each thrust, regional program, training, and information unit—based on five sources of information:

- a questionnaire survey on impact that had been filled out by National Potato Program leaders in 1986
- the 1984 questionnaire survey on impact that had been filled out by CIP regional staff members
- quantitative indicators of achievements and impact that could be gleaned from files at headquarters, primarily on training and on germplasm distribution
- results of a new questionnaire survey on impact to be developed and distributed to CIP's regional staff
- responses to a list of five open-ended questions on achievements, impact, and constraints

The five open-ended questions were deceptively simple: What have been your program's principal achievements with potatoes over the last five years? What have been your principal achievements with sweet potatoes? What have been the main impacts or practical benefits of your work with potatoes? What have been the main impacts with sweet potatoes? What have been the principal constraints to your program's achievements and impact?

To allow the responses to be analyzed with an "idea processing" program ("MaxThink"), people were asked to answer each question with a list of no more than ten achievements, impacts, or constraints. Each response was coded, depending upon its contents. For example, achievements fell into three groups: research, training, and dissemination of information. Constraints were either "internal" or "external." The coded responses were then sorted with MaxThink, following the report outline, and printed out. This material—the opinions of CIP staff concerning the center's achievements, impacts, and constraints, organized by theme—was invaluable in drafting the study report.

An "impact study team" was set up to analyze the information generated through the various questionnaires and that compiled from the files and to write the study report. The team consisted of an entomologist, a tissue culture specialist, a geneticist, two economists, the head of training, an editor, a management specialist, and a secretary. Team members were selected to ensure representation of CIP's major program units. Experience, personal integrity, analytical skills, and writing abilities were also criteria.

Whereas I was formally the team leader, I often served as facilitator. Team members decided that the only way to meet our deadline was to work out of CIP for a week. So, on a Friday in September, we moved to a hotel in Lima.

The team's first task was to review and finalize the outline for the report. In this regard, an important decision was taken: to abandon the mechanical approach of reviewing the achievements, impacts, and constraints of each of CIP's operational units. Instead, we decided to prepare a story with a central theme that would illustrate the integration of CIP's work, its global reach, its collaborative aspects, and its contributions to institution building as well as to potato production in developing countries.

We decided to write about the spread of potatoes to the tropics. Following the logic of science, we began with germplasm collection and screening, continued with the breeding, pest management, seed production and agronomy, and finished up with a chapter on CIP's contributions to institutional development. The team assigned individual responsibilities for writing sections of the report. (This change in outline made it necessary to resort the responses to the five open-ended questions with MaxThink.)

On Sunday afternoon, we met to exchange comments and to discuss our progress. At this time, two more important decisions were made. At the suggestion of the editor, we reversed the planned sequence of chapters and put the "impact punch line" first. Hence the final version of the report begins with institutional development and works backward to the more basic scientific topics like breeding and germplasm collection and maintenance. The second decision was to illustrate the global and collaborative aspects of CIP's work with color maps. To accomplish this, we enlisted the support of a computer graphics specialist.

On Monday and Tuesday, team members revised and documented their sections and prepared statistical material needed for the report. On Wednesday, a draft was presented to CIP's directors. The reaction was unexpectedly positive. Not only did they like the direction the report was taking, they wanted the team to include a section on how impact assessment could be incorporated into CIP's routine management processes.

On Thursday, team members revised their sections once again, and, that night, the entire report was retyped and duplicated so that it could be reviewed by all team members on the eighth, and final, day they met. We expected to meet only briefly on Friday to make a few editorial changes, but we found that many sections still needed much work. The text and figures needed to be checked, and the entire report needed to be edited to ensure readability and internal consistency. That evening I left Lima for a month-long trip (that had been delayed several times), and another team member assumed the leadership role to ensure that the needed writing, editing, graphics, and printing were completed.

The impact study team produced an informative and readable report (CIP, 1989) in a remarkably short period of time. It served CIP well during the external reviews as a source of information and insight on center programs and accomplishments. The report served as a focal point for many discussions with members of the review panels as well as among CIP staff. It is now being produced as a center publication. (The questionnaire results and staff members' responses to the five open-ended questions on achievements, impacts, and constraints, organized by theme and type of response, were also given to the review panels and were greatly appreciated by them.)

Perhaps the most important effect of the impact study was to raise the awareness of study team members, of management, and of others at CIP that a continuous impact assessment process is needed. Before the study, each of us had some information and ideas about the value of CIP's work, but there was no consensus. Moreover, impact information seemed to have little relevance for our work. The impact study began to change this.

As one study team member—a microbiologist—stated

> Before this week, I considered everything beyond the molecule to be pure bureaucracy, and I wanted no part of it. But now I see the light! I've learned more about CIP this week than in the last five years, and I'm glad I did. If everybody had a chance to do this, CIP would be a better place for it.

The assessment process led to a decision that a more systematic mechanism for measuring impact must be developed and implemented. An international planning conference on impact assessment was planned for 1990. It is to involve CIP's clients as well as experts in impact assessment in creating mechanisms for CIP to collect impact information more systematically, on a routine, cost-effective basis, and to ensure that results will be used in priority setting, monitoring, and evaluation. Additionally, results should serve to motivate staff by allowing them to clearly see where their work is producing results.

## Conclusions

The two examples of PAR drawn from CIP experience might appear at the outset to have little in common. But they have many similarities that have important implications for applied research programs. In both examples, the PAR process began as a result of an external stimulus. In the Mantaro Valley, the external stimulus came from young social scientists who brought a different point of view to CIP—a skepticism of the inherent superiority of improved technology. They also had external support: IDRC, the Rockefeller Foundation, and the Inter-American Development Bank. In the impact assessment, the external stimulus was provided by CGIAR-wide efforts to improve monitoring, evaluating, and assessing impact.

In each case, CIP management responded creatively and supported experimentation with PAR. CIP was the first international agricultural research center to embrace anthropology as a "legitimate" scientific discipline and to involve farmers systematically in the R & D process. It was also the first international center to invite representatives of national programs—CIP's direct clients—to participate in program planning and review.

Researchers from different disciplines made unique contributions to PAR. In the on-farm research, biological scientists served as specialists on the potato plant, and their interests focused on learning *about* plant-environment relationships. Economists brought a concern, and methods, for learning *about* farmer management. Anthropologists, in contrast, brought a special concern for learning *from* farmers and methods for doing so. In CIP's work on impact assessment, biological scientists contributed essential knowledge related to their specialties, economists contributed an evaluation framework, and anthropologists once again introduced "the users' perspective," asking, "What have we learned from farmers and from national programs?" Communicators and management specialists also played important roles by focusing the review process on important management issues and by facilitating teamwork.

Whereas in each case the initial goal was to tackle a specific problem—to facilitate "technology transfer" or to prepare for an external review—the results had broad implications for CIP's operations and contributed to the broader understanding of the agricultural R & D process. Experiences with on-farm research resulted in a new paradigm for agricultural R & D. Carrying out the impact study led to new concepts and approaches and also generated commitment from management and staff to make impact assessment a permanent feature of CIP's ongoing activities.

## References

ANDERSON, J. R., R. W. HERDT, and G. M. SCOBIE (1988) Science and Food: The CGIAR and Its Partners. Washington, DC: World Bank.

BAUM, W. C. (1986) Partners Against Hunger. Washington, DC: World Bank.

CHAMBERS, R. and B. P. GHILDYAL (1985) "Agricultural research for resource-poor farmers: the farmer-first-and-last model." Agricultural Administration 20.

CIP (1984) Potatoes for the Developing World. Lima: Author.

CIP (1988) The Social Sciences at CIP. Lima: Author.

CIP (1989) An Assessment of CIP's Programs: Achievements, Impact, and Constraints (Working paper). Lima: Author.

HORTON, D. E. (1984) Social Scientists in Agricultural Research: Lessons from the Mantaro Valley Project, Peru. Ottawa: IDRC.

HORTON, D. (1986) "Assessing the impact of international agricultural research and development programs." World Development 14.

IDRC (International Development Research Centre) (1986) With Our Own Hands. Ottawa: Author.

LIONBERGER, H. P. (1986) "FSR/E in the world systems context." In Farming Systems Research and Extension: Food and Feed (1986 Farming Systems Research Symposium, October 1986). Manhattan: Kansas State University.

RHOADES, R. E. (1984) Breaking New Ground: Agricultural Anthropology. Lima: CIP.

RHOADES, R. E. and R. H. BOOTH (1982) "Farmer-back-to-farmer: a model for generating acceptable agricultural technology." Agricultural Administration 11.

RHOADES, R., D. HORTON and R. BOOTH (1986) "Anthropologist, economist and biological scientist: the three stooges or three musketeers of farmer system research." In J. Jones and B. Wallace (eds.) Applying Science in Farming Systems Research. Boulder, CO: Westview.

RUTTAN, V. (1987) "Toward a global agricultural research system." In V. Ruttan and C. E. Pray, Policy for Agricultural Research. Boulder, CO: Westview.

# 17

# *Conclusions*

## WILLIAM FOOTE WHYTE

Reflecting on the implications of the cases and analyses presented in this book, let us see what we can learn that may help us to improve both research and practice.

Researchers should abandon the fruitless quest for sustainable generalizations on the global relationship between participation and productivity. It does not make sense to assume that any form of participation under any conditions and in any situation, skillfully or clumsily practiced, will lead to gains in productivity. Whatever global correlations researchers find or fail to find will not influence the rapidly growing number of practitioners who are convinced that participation "works" when it is developed skillfully. If we researchers want to help practitioners in this field, we should focus on systematic observation and analysis of projects intended to be participatory, under various conditions, and with favorable or unfavorable results. With that strategy, we may be able to identify the factors, in various types of situations and with varying structures and processes of participation, that are conducive to the development of participatory projects that are not only satisfying to participants but also lead to improved task performance.

For both researchers and practitioners, it is important to recognize the distinction between project success and diffusion of similar projects. We often encounter projects that are successful by any standard of measurement and yet do not lead to diffusion within the organization where they occur— nor do they diffuse to other organizations. We need to discover not only what works in a given situation but also what processes of organizational learning enable people to apply the lessons derived from one situation to other cases.

Researchers can contribute to this organizational learning through studying the diffusion process and comparing cases of rapid diffusion with cases of slow or blocked diffusion. For example, in *Strategies for Learning* (Cole, 1989), Robert Cole shows that the continuing popularity of quality circles in Japan has been powerfully supported by major industrial companies, whose managements take turns in conducting high-visibility meetings in which teams of workers report their successes in improving quality and productivity, along with explaining how they achieved such results. In contrast, in the United States, top management people have not actively supported worker participation in their own organizations and have made no efforts to diffuse worker participation beyond their own firms. As Cole has pointed out in his chapter, in the United States, consultants have taken control of the diffusion process, competing with each other as they try to sell their individual approaches.

In general, in both industry and agriculture, the record suggests that practitioners learn more from each other than from researchers. However, even here researchers can support the organizational learning processes by helping to organize human networks that stimulate and facilitate this learning process. For example, the Work in America Institute continues to support such networks through identifying companies and unions that have been successfully carrying out major sociotechnical systems changes. The institute then arranges for site visits, including some observation of operations and considerable and wide-ranging discussion with the key management and union people involved in the change programs. In Cornell's Programs for Employment and Workplace Systems, the network we have organized particularly for New York firms and unions has yielded such a strong interest as to encourage us to further develop this means of communication among practitioners and between practitioners and researchers. Many other universities are developing programs along similar lines.

In the last half century, an extraordinary human and interinstitutional network has developed in international agriculture to stimulate organizational learning through the flow of information and ideas. The system of internationally funded agricultural research centers originated in 1941 with the creation of CIMMYT, supported by the Rockefeller Foundation and the Mexican government. In 1959, the Rockefeller and Ford Foundations joined with the government of the Philippines to establish the International Rice Research Institute. The spectacular success of these first centers in breeding new high-yielding varieties of wheat and rice spurred intense interest around the world in the creation of new international centers for other crops and for other problems of agricultural research and development.

Because international interest in agricultural research had expanded far beyond the ability of the two foundations to meet the perceived needs, a much broader base of financial support was clearly required. In 1971, CGIAR (Consultative Group on International Agricultural Research) was established under the joint sponsorship of the World Bank, the U.N. Development Programme (UNDP), and the U.N. Food and Agriculture Organization (FAO). World Bank provides the CGIAR chairman and secretariat. FAO provides a separate Technical Secretariat, composed of eminent agricultural and social scientists to advise CGIAR and international centers on research needs, opportunities, and priorities. Although CGIAR is influential in coordinating and stimulating financial support within the system, it does not grant funds to individual centers. Each center seeks its own support from foundations and governments engaged in supporting foreign aid programs. At this writing, this international network includes 13 research centers.

Within this system, there is a very active flow of information and ideas among international centers and between those centers and national agricultural research agencies. The system has not only expanded over the years, it has also proven its ability to generate its own organizational learning, in reshaping structures and programs to meet changing perceptions of needs. For example, the system was originally established in terms of a top-down design: The international center would develop new crop varieties and new farming methods and pass on materials and information to national programs, which would accept what the experts had determined was good for them. As research and experience demonstrated the weakness of this strategy, the system developed new approaches and a new center, ISNAR (International Service for National Agricultural Research) to help national programs adapt and implement some of the fruits of international research and to improve their own research and development capacities. Since its founding in 1980, ISNAR has concentrated particularly on stimulating and guiding national programs whose leaders are seeking to develop more participatory strategies of research and development. The focus of its most recent publications is on what ISNAR calls OFCOR (on-farm client-oriented research), which appears to be participatory action research under another label.

The networks provided by this still-evolving international system support and guide an extraordinary flow of information and ideas through conferences, workshops, training courses, and publications. What is being learned in one part of the world tends to spread rapidly through this network all over the world.

Applied social research in industry or agriculture is necessarily interdisciplinary. In industry, it should involve the integration of information and ideas from the social sciences with information and ideas from engineering, accounting, and management sciences. In agriculture, it should involve integration of social science information and ideas with information and ideas from the plant, soil, and animal sciences and agricultural engineering. Social scientists are generally the ones who take the initiative in attempting to achieve such integration, and yet we begin as strangers on turf controlled by technical specialists.

How can we overcome this handicap and gain the technical information and ideas required for project success? The conventional answer to that question involves using the technical specialists as passive informants. We try to be nice to them to gain their goodwill so that we can pump them for the technical information and ideas we need.

One lesson of this book is that the conventional answer is a poor answer. Treating technical specialists as passive informants exposes us to the risks of misunderstanding or oversimplifying what they are telling us and deprives us of the ideas that they could contribute if they shared ownership in the project.

This book suggests that participatory action research offers a more effective strategy for the interdisciplinary applied research projects. Our authors tell us that the social scientist should not seek to establish such a partnership the moment he or she enters the field. In industry or agriculture, the technical specialists will generally have little understanding of what the social scientist might contribute, and they will react against the newcomer who claims powers they lack. Those social scientists most successful in establishing such interdisciplinary partnerships view themselves initially as participant observers, showing respect for the work of practitioners and technical specialists, and seeking to learn from them. As the social scientist gains an understanding of the organizational culture and work systems, he or she will find ways of contributing that are appreciated by the technical specialists. This will pave the way for establishing the full partnerships represented by PAR. The Ruano chapter develops this theme, and the Horton chapter guides us through a case in which social scientists began work as outsiders and, in the course of years, gained the position of full partnership with technical specialists.

Effective participatory systems depend upon commitment rather than coercion. To be sure, approval and encouragement from the top are essential, but systems that most fully utilize the information and ideas of the members cannot be preprogrammed or tightly controlled. They depend upon voluntary cooperation among members striving to contribute to the organization's mission. For those in superior power positions, the best way to gain the commitment of other members involves taking an interest in their information and ideas and trying to utilize those contributions in problem solving.

For building effective participatory systems, whether in industry, agriculture, or research projects, the requirements for leadership are quite different from those traditionally expected of a leader in a hierarchically designed organization. The leader should be able to project a vision of the organization's mission, with broad potential appeal to members, and then guide and facilitate the changes necessary to advance toward that vision.

In participatory action research, this means that the researcher must be willing to relinquish the unilateral control that the professional researcher has traditionally maintained over the research process. That does not mean that the professional researcher must accept every idea put forward by key practitioner collaborators. It does mean that the researcher must rely upon rational discourse and powers of persuasion in planning and implementing PAR projects that meet the needs and interests of both research professionals and our collaborating practitioners.

## *Reference*

COLE, R. E. (1989) Strategies for Learning. Berkeley: University of California Press.

# About the Authors

**Dominick R. Argona** is Manager of Employee Involvement in Xerox Business Products and Systems Group, Webster, New York. In his 17-year career with Xerox, his most recent position was Manager of Employee Involvement and Recognition for the corporation, working worldwide to enhance involvement of Xerox people in business. In 1984, he received the coveted Xerox President's Award for his pioneering role in employee involvement. A frequent speaker at management and engineering conferences, he also serves as Xerox liaison to community organizations and colleges. He holds an M.S. degree from SUNY.

**Chris Argyris** is James Bryant Conant Professor at the schools of Business and Education at Harvard University. He has earned honorary doctorates from six universities, both in the United States and abroad. His most recent books are *Strategy Change and Defensive Routines* and *Action Science,* with Robert Putnam and Diana Smith.

**Michael Bassey** is Senior Programme Officer in the International Development Research Centre (IDRC), specializing in the support of agricultural postproduction systems research and the application of rapid rural appraisal techniques in West Africa. He holds a Ph.D. in mechanical engineering from

Queen's University and has taught in the areas of engineering and energy use at the University of Sierra Leone from 1975 until he joined IDRC in 1982. He was chairman of the Sub-Commission on Energy for the Economic Commission of West African States (ECOWAS) from 1980 to 1982 and is a founding member of the African Association of Post Harvest Technology.

**Robert E. Cole** is Professor of Sociology and Business Administration at the University of California at Berkeley. In recent years, he has concentrated on comparative research on participatory systems in industry in Japan, Sweden, and the United States, which culminated in the book *Strategies for Learning*. He has been Professor of Sociology and Business Administration and Director of the Center for Japanese Studies at the University of Michigan. He has a Ph.D. in sociology from the University of Illinois.

**Anthony J. Costanza** is Manager of the Rochester, New York, Joint Board of the Amalgamated Clothing and Textile Workers Union. He is also an International Vice President of ACTWU, a member of the board of directors of the Amalgamated Bank, and Director of the Sidney Hillman Health Center in Rochester. He has held leadership positions in the Rochester-area United Way and the American Red Cross. In 1951, he went to work with the company that became Xerox. From 1974 to 1988, he was General Shop Chairman for the Xerox local. In 1984, he received Xerox's highest recognition, the President's Award, for his role in guiding the Quality of Work Life and Employee Involvement process, the first time that an hourly or union employee had ever received that award.

**Max Elden** is an American who has become a major contributor to Norwegian action research in industrial democracy. Following his doctorate in political science at the University of California, Los Angeles, he won a postdoctoral fellowship from the Royal Norwegian Center for Scientific and Technical Research. He began his work in Norway with Einar Thorsrud and has continued in research and teaching in Norway to this day. He has served as Director of the Institute for Social Research in Industry (IFIM) and is currently Professor of Organization and Quality of Work Life at the University of Trondheim. He is now also Professor in the School of Business of the University of Houston.

**Michael E. Gaffney** is Director of Programs for Employment and Workplace Systems (PEWS) in Cornell University's School of Industrial and Labor

Relations. He concentrates on action research to preserve jobs in New York State. His Ph.D. is in cultural anthropology, and his introduction to the field of work redesign (and action research) came while conducting ethnographic research on the occupation of merchant seaman. (He is also a licensed deck officer and Great Lakes pilot.) He has consulted with several shipping companies and seafaring unions and with three National Research Council committees. He has published extensively on organizational change in shipping.

**Davydd J. Greenwood**, John S. Knight Professor and Director of the Center for International Studies and Professor of Anthropology at Cornell University, specializes in the study of political economy, ethnic conflict, and industrial development. Two of his four books are on the Basques.

**Douglas E. Horton** is Senior Research Officer with ISNAR (International Service for National Agricultural Research) in the Hague, the Netherlands. From 1975 to 1989, he served in CIP, the International Potato Center, in Lima, Peru. As head of CIP's social sciences department, he introduced a blend of social science activities involving economics, anthropology, and sociology. Born on a farm, he earned B.S. and M.S. degrees in agricultural economics from the University of Illinois and a Ph.D. in economics from Cornell University. His doctoral thesis was a study of land reform in Peru.

**Jan Irgens Karlsen** has a graduate degree in psychology from the University of Oslo, Norway. Beginning in 1972, he worked with Einar Thorsrud in the Norwegian Work Democracy Program, assuming responsibility for diffusing new forms of work organization to the service sector. From 1978 to 1980, he was Associate Professor at the Regional University of More and Romsdal. Since 1983, he has been Director of the Institute for Social Research in Industry (IFIM) at the University of Trondheim.

**Peter Lazes** is Senior Extension Associate in Cornell University's School of Industrial and Labor Relations (ILR). He was previously Co-Director and Co-Founder for Employment and Workplace Systems (PEWS), a research and consulting institute within the ILR. He is currently developing a new program for applied research with national labor unions. He has established participation in the private and public sectors, from industry to health centers. He has written articles and produced videotapes on work restructuring and organizational change. His Ph.D. is in clinical and industrial psychology.

**Morten Levin** received an undergraduate degree in mechanical engineering, a master's in operations research, and a graduate degree in sociology. He is Associate Professor in Organization and Work Science at the Norwegian Institute of Technology, where he is in charge of the Ph.D. degree program for training action researchers. His principal research interests are the participative design of new technology, local indigenous development, and transfer of technology to small and medium-sized companies.

**Richard Maclure** is Assistant Professor in the Faculty of Education of the University of Ottawa. He specializes in comparative and international education. He holds a Ph.D. from Stanford University, and, in 1989, he received an Outstanding Doctoral Dissertation Award from the American Educational Research Association. He has worked extensively in West Africa: as a secondary school teacher in Nigeria (1974-1976), as a field director for Foster Parents Plan International in Burkina Faso (1980-1983), and as an International Development Research Centre (IDRC) programme officer responsible for supporting West African educational research (1987-1989).

**Ramiro Ortiz** has been a consultant to DIGESA, the Guatemalan agricultural extension agency, in a new program to develop participatory systems integrating research and extension. From its creation in 1973, he has worked with ICTA, the innovative Guatemalan agricultural research agency, serving first on on-farm research, then as Regional Director, and finally as national Technical Director. He has an undergraduate degree in autonomy from the San Carlos University in Guatemala, has an M.S. in soils productivity from the Colegio de Post-Graduados in Mexico, and is completing the Ph.D. program at the University of Florida in agronomy and farming systems.

**Larry A. Pace** is Associate Professor of Management at the University of Louisiana in Shreveport. In his years with Xerox Corporation, he helped to establish the Employee Involvement Process. He has a Ph.D. in industrial psychology. He writes, speaks, and consults on organizational effectiveness and applied resource management issues.

**Sergio Ruano** began his career with the Guatemalan land reform program and was with the socioeconomic unit in ICTA, the Guatemalan agricultural research agency, from 1974 to 1982. From 1983 to 1986, he led a socioeconomic team on research and development of potato farming in 10 Central American countries, in collaboration with CIP, the International Potato

Center, in Peru. From 1987 to 1989, he served as coordinator of a project on management of research and extension for CATIE, the International Center for Research and Education in Tropical Agriculture in Costa Rica. For CATIE, in 1990, he is serving as Guatemalan coordinator of a project on integration of agriculture, forestry, and animal husbandry. He has an undergraduate degree in anthropology from San Carlos University and M.S. and Ph.D. degrees from Cornell University in rural sociology.

**José Luis González Santos** is General Manager of the URKIDE cooperative group located in Azpeitia. At the time of the FAGOR project, he was Director of Personnel for the FAGOR group of the Mondragóon cooperatives, Chairman of the Governing Council of FAGOR Electrotécnica, and a member of the General Governing Council of FAGOR. After receiving baccalauerate degrees in philosophy and commerce and working for two private firms, he joined the cooperatives in 1966. He has served in both elective and staff positions in FAGOR and two of its constituent cooperatives.

**Donald A. Schön,** as an industrial consultant, a government administrator, and a president of a nonprofit social research consulting organization, has worked as a researcher and practitioner on problems of technological innovation, organizational learning, and professional effectiveness. He was invited, in 1970, to deliver the Reith Lectures on the BBC. His books include *Invention and Evolution of Ideas* (formerly *The Displacement of Concepts*), 1963; *Technology and Change*, 1967; *Beyond the Stable State*, 1971; *Theory in Practice: Increasing Professional Effectiveness*, 1974, and *Organizational Learning: A Theory of Action Perspective*, 1978, both of the latter with Chris Argyris; *The Reflective Practitioner*, 1983; and *Educating the Reflective Practitioner*, 1987. He is currently Ford Professor in the Department of Urban Studies and Planning at MIT.

**Richard E. Walton** is the Jesse Isidor Straus Professor of Business Administration, Harvard University. He has contributed to theories of social action and has facilitated social change. He has served on the editorial boards of several social science journals, on the boards of several American corporations, and on two national committees established to address problems in American industry. His most recent book, *Innovating to Compete,* presents a theory of the innovative capability of social systems that grew out of one of his assignments to help develop policy recommendations.

**William Foote Whyte** has been President of the Industrial Relations Research Association, the American Sociological Association, and the Society of Applied Anthropology. *Street Corner Society* is his best-known book, and his most recent is *Making Mondragón: The Growth and Dynamics of the Worker Cooperative Complex* (with Kathleen King Whyte). He is now Professor Emeritus and Research Director of Programs for Employment and Workplace Systems in Cornell University's School of Industrial and Labor Relations. He has a Ph.D. in sociology from the University of Chicago.

A - work w/ "Peter Lazes" type
of consultant.

788-0096
Marion

Work up/train CST groups in
industry as part of work toward
flattening org. hierarchies/
leveling class differences.
  └ improve working quality of life
  └ increase respect of workers
        wn org.
  └ secure jobs
  └ provide paths of development;
        opportunities for growth

= genesis

problem solving as a social process

_____

Justice in an Unjust World
      Karen Lebacqz
Foundations for a Christian Approach
to Justice